THE **TANK** MUSEUM

TANKS

THE HISTORY OF ARMOURED WARFARE

ROBIN CROSS & DAVID WILLEY

FOREWORD BY
DAN SNOW

ANDRE
DEUTSCH

CONTENTS

FOREWORD

In 1916 a new weapon system was born. This would change warfare to such an extent that its unmistakable outline became a symbol of warfare itself. Armoured fighting vehicles, or tanks, altered the course of twentieth century history. A triumph of innovation in the face of the appalling slaughter of the First World War, the tank was rushed from the drawing board to the battlefield in under two years. As this beautifully illustrated book shows, it was embraced by all combatants who all realised its potential, some more effectively than others. Nearly all the tanks featured are preserved at the fantastic Tank Museum in Dorset which gives us an unprecedented picture of the life cycle of these monsters.

Tanks were a major step on the path to the mechanization of war. Scientists managed to replace human flesh, blood and bone with steel and petroleum. It accelerated the process by which war became not just a clash of men on the battlefield but of industries and entire societies.

When the tank went into battle during the Somme Campaign in September 1916 the results were mixed but the British commander, Douglas Haig, was sufficiently impressed to place a massive order of vehicles for use the following year. The tank would disappoint those who hoped it might break the deadlock of the trenches by itself, but it played a key part in the rout of the German army in summer and autumn of 1918.

Since then, armoured vehicles have played a leading part on battlefields from northern France in 1940 to the Korean peninsula. Tanks spearheaded the brilliant German thrust through the Ardennes, they drove Rommel from North Africa, clashed at Kursk, swam ashore at D-day, slowly edged towards Berlin from East and West, fought each other to a standstill on the Golan Heights and the Sinai Desert, crushed dissent in Prague and Budapest, swept away the South Vietnamese regime and toppled Saddam Hussein.

The word "tank" is almost synonymous with military strength, the outline has become its symbol. Few weapon systems have had as big an impact as the tank in the first 100 years of its life.

DAN SNOW

TITLE PAGE A Matilda II tank undergoes servicing in the desert. The camouflage screen helped hide the tank from aerial reconnaissance and probably provided shade to the crew.

ABOVE A British Second Lieutenant uses his radio to control the actions of his troop of Chieftains. The Chieftain was the British Army's main battle tank between the mid-1960s and the mid-1980s.

OPPOSITE M26 Pershings of the U.S. 2nd Armoured Division move through the ruins of the German city of Magdeburg after its capture in April 1945.

CHAPTER 1

THE ORIGINS OF THE TANK

THE TANK, THE MOST REVOLUTIONARY DEVELOPMENT IN LAND WARFARE TO COME OUT OF THE FIRST WORLD WAR, EMERGED AS A SOLUTION TO A PRESSING STRATEGIC PROBLEM THAT BECAME APPARENT WITHIN MONTHS OF THE WAR'S START. THE LATE SUMMER AND EARLY AUTUMN OF 1914 SEEMED TO HERALD A WAR OF MOVEMENT, AS THE BELGIANS AND THE BRITISH EMPLOYED ARMOURED CARS DURING THE SO-CALLED "RACE TO THE SEA", IN WHICH ATTEMPTS BY THE GERMANS TO ENVELOP THE FLANKS OF THEIR ADVANCE PROGRESSIVELY PUSHED THE TWO SIDES TOWARD THE NORTH SEA COAST.

Yet before long, trenches brought deadlock to the Western Front. The first – initially just scrapes in the ground – appeared in September 1914. Within weeks, the stalemate they had produced on the Aisne sector spread down the congealing battleground from the North Sea to the Alps. The pattern was set for the next three-and-a-half years as the war assumed the aspect of a gigantic siege dominated by artillery and the machine gun.

The Landships Committee

Both sides cast around for a new weapon to break the grinding defensive deadlock. The Germans began experimenting with chemical warfare and first employed chlorine gas on 22 April 1915 against the Allies at Ypres. Yet despite localized successes – at Ypres the Germans punched a 6.5-kilometre (4-mile) gap in the French front line – it did not prove to be a decisive weapon.

The Allies cast around for another solution. Their troops on the Western Front needed a weapon capable of crushing barbed wire and crossing the broken ground between the opposing trench systems to bring directly aimed fire on the enemy while remaining protected from hostile machine guns and artillery. In February 1915 the Landships Committee was established by Winston Churchill, First Lord of The Admiralty, to devise such a weapon.

At first the project retained a naval flavour, hence the term "landship". The Committee initially had three members: Sir Eustace Tennyson d'Eyncourt, the Admiralty's Director of Naval Construction; Colonel Wilfred Dumble, formerly the manager of the London Omnibus Company and now serving with the Naval Brigade; and Flight Commander Thomas Hetherington of the RNAS (Royal Naval Air Service). Their deliberations were kept secret from the Board of the Admiralty, the Treasury and Lord Kitchener, all of whom were expected to block the project.

The birth of the tank

The tank had many begetters. The naval men in the original Landships Committee never came up with a viable design (see overleaf) and in the end development of an effective tracked armoured fighting vehicle fell to the Army. It owed much to the vision of a scientifically trained Royal Engineer and veteran of

LEFT A German defensive position with machine guns and wire. The early hope and expectation that men alone would be able to capture such positions with the support of some artillery was soon dashed.

BELOW LEFT The Tsar tank showed the "big wheel" idea was not just confined to Britain. Designed by a Russian team, it was initially shown to the Tsar as a model and he ordered its full scale construction. With a tricycle arrangement, it proved unbalanced. It failed at its trial in August 1915 and in 1923 was broken up for scrap.

OPPOSITE ABOVE A Minerva Armoured Car of the Belgian Army in 1914. The use of armoured cars had been trialled by a number of countries prior to the First World War. As trench warfare developed and stifled the use of road bound armoured cars, the Belgian Army sent its armoured car force to assist the Russians on the Eastern front.

OPPOSITE BELOW A Holt 75 tractor in use in British service towing artillery on the Western Front. The American Holt company had agents selling their tractors to the British, French, Austrian and German armies in the first years of the war.

the Boer War, Colonel Ernest Swinton. In his autobiography, *Eyewitness* (1932), Swinton recalled how he hit upon the idea of the tank in the autumn of 1914.

In July of that year, when Europe was still at peace, Swinton had received a letter from an acquaintance, Hugh F. Marriott, a mining engineer, who alerted him to the military possibilities of the American-manufactured Holt Caterpillar Tractor as a transport vehicle in time of war. Swinton passed the information on and then forgot about it until October 1914, by which time he had been sent by Lord Kitchener to the Western Front as the official British war correspondent. While there, Swinton remembered the possibilities of using the caterpillar track in a fighting vehicle.

The British War Office had already launched trials of the Holt tractor at Aldershot but only in an artillery-towing role. In October 1914, Swinton suggested to Sir Maurice Hankey, Secretary of the Committee of Imperial Defence, the adoption of the Holt track, to carry a steel box armed with cannon and machine guns across no man's land, through the enemy trenches and on to the enemy artillery, suppressing his machine gunners and infantry on the way. This new weapon would enable its infantry support to reach their objectives without suffering crippling casualties.

"Little Willie"

Swinton's scheme eventually found a backer in Winston Churchill and his proposal went forward to the Landships Committee, which gave the order to build an experimental vehicle on 29 July 1915. The two men responsible for building and designing the first tank were William Tritton, managing director of the Foster's agricultural machinery factory in Lincoln, and Lieutenant Walter Wilson of the Royal Naval Reserve.

Both men were experienced engineers. Tritton had built a giant wheeled trench-crossing vehicle; in peacetime Wilson had been a gearing expert and the designer of aero-engines, automobiles and lorries. His Hallford lorry was widely used in the First World War. On 26 August, a wooden mock-up, initially dubbed the "Tritton Machine", was unveiled.

Trials of the machine itself began near Lincoln early in September 1915. The "Tritton Machine" was a rectangular boiler-plate box carried on "Creeping Grip" tracks from the Bullock Tractor Company of Chicago. It was topped by a dummy turret intended to house a 2pdr gun and several machine guns. It was powered by a 195hp Daimler engine while steering, stability and trench-crossing capability were provided by a pair of trailing wheels.

The "Tritton Machine" looked like a modern tank but proved a great disappointment. The War Office required it to cross a trench 1.5 metres (5 feet) wide but, it could manage only 1.2 metres (4 feet). In the winter of 1915 it underwent a makeover, was rebuilt with new track frames and tracks, was fitted with a real turret and acquired a new name, "Little Willie". However, it failed to meet fresh War Office trench-crossing requirements and was superseded by the prototype of all British heavy tanks of the First World War.

"Big Willie"

By the winter of 1915 the War Office required a landship to cross a trench 2.4 metres (8 feet) wide and climb a parapet 1.4 metres (4ft 6in) high. To meet these requirements, Walter Wilson designed "Little Willie's" successor, the rhomboidal-shaped "Big Willie", with tracks running round the top of the hull. Wilson dispensed with a turret on top of the hull and ensured a low centre of gravity by installing two naval 6pdr guns in half turrets (sponsons) projecting from each side of the hull. The power unit, track and tail wheels were the same as those for

THE NAVAL LANDSHIPS

The Landships Committee's quest for the breakthrough weapon followed two lines – big-wheeled and tracked vehicles. A mock-up vehicle with huge wheels was built, but it was vulnerable to artillery fire.

Engineer Colonel R.E.B. Crompton and Bramah Joseph Diplock of the Pedrail Transport Company developed a single wide track, with fixed wheels running on a moving belt and giving low friction and low ground pressure. Building on a request from the Director of the Air Department of the Admiralty, for a two-tracked vehicle with a 12pdr gun housed in a turret, Crompton came up with a 30-ton vehicle. He presented it to the Landships Committee in March 1915 and was given the go-ahead to build 12 machines to equip the putative Landships Squadrons 20 and 21 of the RNAS.

His design envisaged that the landships would be unarmed and used to carry trench-raiding parties in direct assaults on the enemy lines. However, the design did not survive an inspection he made of conditions on the Western Front 1915. He decided to split the landship into two half-hulls connected by an articulated coupling, which he hoped would improve its manoeuvrability. In addition he installed four gun turrets reminiscent of a warship.

These changes delayed the construction of the 12 RNAS landships and they were quickly overtaken by other designs. A single unarmoured half-hull machine weighing 32 tons was completed by Stothert and Pitt of Bath and underwent trials as reaching a maximum speed of 24 km/h (15 mph). The vehicle was never used in action.

LEFT Looking more like a runaway tram, the Pedrail machine is tested at the Trench Warfare establishment at Porton Down. It was not a success.

BELOW LEFT: Little Willie's greatest success as a test bed vehicle centred on the track. Early experiments with available track failed; only a new design, with inner flanges to secure the track to corresponding grooves on the hull succeeded and this design was used on all the British First World War tanks.

BELOW RIGHT: The first guns fitted to "Mother" and the subsequent Mark I male tanks were ex-naval six pounder guns. These guns could fire high-explosive rounds and solid shot ideal for smashing concrete pillboxes.

"Little Willie", against which "Big Willie" competed in trials at Hatfield Park in Hertfordshire at the beginning of 1916.

At the Hatfield trials "Big Willie" succeeded in crossing a three-metre (10-foot) trench and riding over a vertical obstacle 1.4 metres (4ft 6in high). Some in the British high command remained sceptical about the new weapon. Lord Kitchener dismissed "Big Willie" as a "pretty mechanical toy", but Sir Douglas Haig, commander of the BEF from December 1915, was keen for the speediest possible use for the new machines, which were codenamed "tanks" because without their guns they looked like vehicles for carrying water. Appropriately renamed "Mother", the tank was soon to make its debut on the battlefield.

"Mother" going through a trial at Burton Park outside Lincoln. The new shape of Mother enabled it to cross a German trench whereas Little Willie would have failed.

CHAPTER 2

INTO BATTLE

THE FIRST TANKS ARRIVED ON THE WESTERN FRONT IN AUGUST 1916 IN THE MIDST OF THE SOMME CAMPAIGN, BRITAIN'S FIRST REALLY BIG OFFENSIVE, WHICH LASTED FROM JULY TO NOVEMBER. BY THEN IT HAD ALREADY BECOME ENMIRED IN A SERIES OF SMALLER ACTIONS AND WOULD ULTIMATELY RESULT IN THE GAIN OF JUST 10 KILOMETRES (6 MILES) AT THE APPALLING COST OF AROUND 600,000 ALLIED CASUALTIES.

Haig had ordered some 150 of the new tanks to try to break the deadlock, encouraged by the favourable report of his observer at the Hatfield trials, Major Hugh Elles, a Royal Engineers officer at General Headquarters. The tanks and their crews became an element in the Heavy Section of the Machine Gun Corps (MGC), which Elles was to go on to command (and later the Tank Corps).

The tanks to be employed in the battle were 28-ton Mark Is. Essentially the same as the "Mother" prototype, they were basically metal boxes with lozenge-shaped sides on top of which the tracks ran. They came in two versions – male and female. Males were emplacement destroyers armed with 6pdr guns

mounted in sponsons which projected on either side of the hull. Female Mark Is carried only machine guns to deal with enemy troops. Both versions were uncomfortable and exhausting for the eight-man crews to operate inside an undivided hull. Their maximum speed over broken ground was 6.5 km/h (4 mph), slower than the accompanying infantry, and their bulk made them conspicuous targets. They could easily be disabled by shellfire and were by no means bullet-proof.

Baptism of fire

In February 1916, Colonel Swinton had submitted a memorandum to the War Committee of the Cabinet urging

OPPOSITE TOP LEFT Tanks were divided into Male and Female. Here a female tank shows her two Vickers machine guns in the sponson – the protruding bay addition shaped like a bay window on each side.

BELOW A Mark I male tank on the Somme. The framework above the tank was covered in chicken wire and was put on C Company tanks to stop German stick grenades landing on the flat roof.

that the tanks should not be used in "driblets" but in one great "combined operation" on an 8-kilometre (5-mile) front accompanied by infantry, gas and smoke. Their routes of approach should be carefully prepared well in advance and some of the tanks should be equipped with wireless sets.

However, when they first went into action on 15 September 1916, two-and-a-half months into the Somme offensive, Swinton's recommendations were for the most part ignored. The action chosen for the tank's debut was at Flers-Courcelette, a large-scale offensive designed to punch a line into the German defences and restore mobility to the Somme sector. Mechanical fragility, as much as any shortcomings in their tactical deployment, marred the effectiveness of the 32 Mark I tanks of C and D Companies, Heavy Section Machine Gun Corps, that made it to the start line. Nine broke down, five ditched and 10 were damaged by enemy fire.

Inside the machine the temperature was broiling – reaching 50°C (122°F) – and the atmosphere was rank with petrol fumes and carbon monoxide. Lack of suspension meant that the crew were tossed around as the tank moved over broken ground on unsprung tracks, risking serious injury. If the tank was hit, slivers of hot steel flew about, exposing the crew to splash similar to that experienced in steel mills. They wore leather and mail face-masks and a leather helmet to cushion heads against collisions.

Steering was immensely difficult. It was controlled by varying the speed of the vehicle's two tracks and demanded the attentions of four of the crew – two drivers and two "gearsmen". One driver (the tank's commander) worked the brakes, while the second operated the primary gearbox. The commander could also effect modest turns by pulling a steel cable to block one of the two large wheels trailing the tank and so make it slide in the required direction.

Communication inside the inferno of the hull was rudimentary. The driver, after setting the primary gearbox, communicated with the "gearsmen" by hand signal after getting their attention

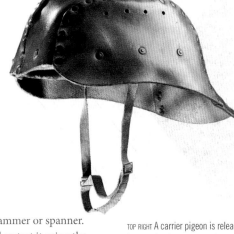

by hitting the engine block with a heavy hammer or spanner. If the engine stalled, the "gearsmen" would restart it using the starting handle – a large crank between the engine and the gearbox. The deafening din inside the hull made communication with command posts by wireless all but impossible. Carrier pigeons, released from a hatch in the sponsons, provided an alternative, as did flags, semaphore and coloured discs. One of the tanks damaged by enemy fire was commanded by Lieutenant Basil L.Q. Henriques of C Company. He later recalled moving up to the line on the night of 13 September:

We moved off from our camp behind the lines at 5 p.m. on the 13th. We went in a long procession and progress was slow as corners take some time in manipulating. Troops rushed to the side of our route and stood, open-eyed; thousands swarmed round us and we seemed to cheer people up as we went.

The reception Henriques and his comrades received from the enemy on the 15th was less friendly: *As we approached the Germans they let fire at us with might and main. Then a smash*

TOP RIGHT A carrier pigeon is released from a pistol port on a tank sponson. Communications were rudimentary – flags and semaphore were used and early wireless sets experimented with, but they were vulnerable to the jarring of a tank.

ABOVE RIGHT The leather helmet was designed without a brim to allow a crewman to look out of a vision port without knocking the helmet backwards. They proved unpopular because dismounted crews could be mistaken from a distance for German soldiers wearing a spike-less Pickelhaube.

ABOVE LEFT Bullet "splash" – pieces of molten lead that found their way through crevasses in the hull or paint flakes flung from the inside of the tank on the impact of bullets outside – could blind a crewman. This device was issued to crews as a safety measure.

against my flap at the front caused splinters to come in and the blood to pour down my face. Another minute and my driver got the same. Then our prism glass broke to pieces, then another smash, I think it must have been a bomb, right in my face. The next one wounded my driver so badly we had to stop. By this time I could see nothing at all, my prisms were all broken, and one periscope, while it was impossible to see through the other. On turning round I saw my gunners on the floor. I could not make out why. As the infantry were now approaching and it was impossible to guide the car [tank], and as I now discovered that the sides weren't bullet proof I decided that to save the car from being captured I had better withdraw.

Despite all the hazards and mechanical breakdowns, nine tanks did manage to forge ahead of their supporting infantry, straddle trench lines and engage the enemy's infantry and machine guns, driving the Germans from the village of Flers. These tanks played a significant role in the British advance on 15 September of about 1,800 metres (2,000 yards) on an 8-kilometre (5-mile) front between Flers and Courcelette.

This initial success raised fleeting hopes of a breakthrough, but bad weather intervened, mud hampered operations and the battle became mired in the tactics of attrition. Nevertheless, the tanks exerted a powerful psychological effect on the German defenders, who at first felt utterly powerless against the "monsters" crawling along the top of their trenches, enfilading them with bursts of machine-gun fire.

In the final phase of the Battle of the Somme, a small number of tanks performed well at Beaumont-Hamel, and some 60 Mark Is and IIs took part in the Battle of Arras in April 1917. The

ABOVE LEFT The first ever note sent by infantry to a tank in action at 09.15, 15 September 1916. Rifleman J.W. Dobson, from New Zealand, carried the first message to a tank in action, and guided it to its target. He was company runner in the 2nd Battalion, New Zealand Rifle Brigade.

TOP AND ABOVE RIGHT Basil Henriques took part in the first tank attack at Flers. Enemy fire caused the prism that he was looking through to smash and glass splattered his face. When the glass was removed, he had a piece mounted on a ring and gave it to his wife Rose.

Mark IIs were mechanically identical to the Mark Is, but had been used solely for training and were insufficiently armoured.

Arras

The great battles at Verdun and the Somme in 1916 had failed to overcome the strategic deadlock on the Western Front, and in spring 1917 the Allies planned new offensives to break the impasse. Yet as British finalized their preparations for their attack at Arras, the Germans completed their withdrawal to the heavily fortified Hindenburg Line, a retreat during which they systematically destroyed all roads, railway bridges and buildings along their way. This left the Allies with a rain-sodden and snow-covered wasteland to cross before confronting a purpose-built defensive position of formidable strength.

After a five-day bombardment, the offensive began promisingly. On 9 April, the first day of the battle, the Canadian Corps secured most of Vimy Ridge, the German-held high ground at the northern end of the British line. Such was the speed of the Canadian infantry's advance toward the ridge that they parted company with the eight Mark IIs of No. 12 Company, D Battalion, which found the going very hard.

… the company was fated not to catch up with the infantry. On passing Litchfield, Pulpit, and Zivy Craters we reached Hunland and the shelled area, which the night's rain had turned into a sponge, quite unable to bear 30 tons or so. Before the Boche second line was reached every commander was outside picking a way for his tank, but even that method was of no use and halfway to the Lens road every tank had bellied and remained so despite two or three hours' spade work by the crews. In those days there were no unditching beams and the spars and spuds [wider track plates]

BELOW The C Company tank, Crème De Menthe, rumbles forward on 15 September 1916. One of the rear wheels has already been lost. The tank was photographed by official photographers and when this image appeared in the British press it was copied by souvenir manufacturers.

with which tanks were fitted were useless and only served to catch up and wind all loose wire around the tank. There was nothing to do but stand by for orders, which Major Watson brought personally during the afternoon when the crews were withdrawn to camp. Luckily there was no stopping the Canadians that day and they took all their objectives.

Heavy rain produced seas of mud in which tanks stuck fast. Then snow carpeted the battlefield, making them highly visible targets for German gunners. Few if any of the 60 tanks committed to Arras escaped the potentially fatal consequences of ditching, breakdown or damage from enemy shells. All 10 tanks of No. 8 Company, C Battalion, were disabled, but not before they had knocked out a number of German machine guns and sniper positions.

In No. 9 Company only five machines went into action. Second Lieutenant Williams' tank (C50) took a hit from a "whizz-bang [77mm shell] through the conning tower" before his tank ditched. Williams then conducted running repairs on his right track, where two guide rails were broken. The repairs took four hours, only for the tank to ditch a second time. The redoubtable

ABOVE Female factory workers paint the inside of a tank. White paint was used to try and reflect light around the interior of the vehicle.

RIGHT One of the German responses to the appearance of the tank was to create 50 batteries of 7.7cm guns. These could be kept hidden close to the front line.

Williams was running again after another one-and-a-half hours, but darkness prevented him coming to the aid of infantry held up by a strongpoint. He returned the next morning to knock out the strongpoint, but while pursuing the retreating enemy his tank was hit by a heavy shell, which killed Williams and three of his men and wounded two more.

Although tanks were beginning to prove their worth, Arras once again demonstrated their proneness to mechanical defects and their terrible vulnerability to well-placed obstacles and enemy counter-fire.

A view from the other side of the hill provided by 27th German Division's war diary of April 1917 provides the enemy's assessment of an Allied weapon with which they were becoming familiar:

Ordinary wire entanglements are easily overcome by the tanks. Where there are high, dense and broad entanglements, such as those in front of the Hindenburg Line, the wire is apt to get entangled with the tracks of the tanks. On 11 April one tank was hopelessly stuck in our wire entanglements. Deep trenches, even 2.5 metres (eight feet) wide, seem to a serious obstacle to tanks.

At long ranges by day tanks will be engaged by all batteries that can deliver fire with observation and that are not occupied with other more important tasks. All kinds of batteries put tanks out of action on 11 April. Battery commanders must be permitted to act on their own initiative to the fullest possible extent. By night fire at short ranges only promises good results. The 11 April proved that rifle and machine-gun fire with armour-piercing ammunition can put the tanks out of action. Fire directed at the sides of tanks is more effective than fire at the fore end. The greatest danger for the tanks is the ready inflammability of the petrol and oil tanks. Machine-gun fire is capable of igniting them. The garrison of the trench will take cover behind the traverse and will direct their fire at the hostile infantry following the tanks; firing on tanks with ordinary small arms ammunition is useless.

LEFT A Mark II male tank, Iron Duke, at Arras. Already the rear wheels have been removed because they were virtually useless. "Spuds" or wider track plates, have been added at intervals to assist spreading the weight over softer ground.

CHAPTER 3

THE BATTLES OF PASSCHENDAELE AND CAMBRAI

THE FIRST NINE MONTHS OF TANK OPERATIONS FROM THE SOMME TO ARRAS HAD PRODUCED MIXED RESULTS, BUT FAR FROM BEING DISCOURAGED, HAIG REACTED BY ORDERING 1,000 MORE MACHINES. IN NOVEMBER 1916 HE EXPANDED THE SIX TANK COMPANIES OF THE HEAVY BRANCH OF THE MACHINE GUN CORPS INTO THE BATTALIONS OF WHAT WAS TO BECOME, ON 28 JULY 1917, THE TANK CORPS COMMANDED BY HUGH ELLES.

Two months before the creation of the Tank Corps, Haig had reported to the War Office: "… events have proved the utility of Tanks … both as a means of overcoming hostile resistance … and as a means of reducing casualties in the attacking troops and I consider that sufficient experience has now been gained to warrant the adoption of the Tank as a recognised addition to existing means of conducting offensive operations".

Haig's overriding preoccupation in the summer of 1917 was the launching of a British offensive in the Ypres salient (which became the Battle of Third Ypres, also known as Passchendaele). The aim was to drive to Ostend to capture the enemy's submarine bases and sever the Belgian railways on which German communications depended. His intelligence staff voiced their misgivings about the waterlogged ground over which he was to fight, but on 25 July 1917 he informed the War Cabinet that he was ready.

The Germans had ample warning of the offensive. By the time the attack went in, nearly two million combatants were crammed into the Ypres salient. Haig's preliminary bombardment destroyed the area's fragile drainage system and his 13 infantry divisions advanced on 31 July into a morass further exacerbated by heavy rain.

On the Somme, tanks had been thrown forward in uncoordinated fashion. At Passchendaele, they stuck fast in the mud. Colonel J. F.C. Fuller, who was to become a pioneer of armoured warfare in the interwar years, recalled the dismal scene at Poelcapelle on the approach to Passchendaele in October 1917:

I waded up the road which was swimming a foot or two in slush … the road was a complete shambles and strewn with debris, broken vehicles, dead and dying horses and men; I must have passed hundreds of them as well as bits of men and animals littered everywhere. As I neared Poelcapelle our guns started to fire … the nearest approach to a picture I can give is that it was like standing in a gigantic Primus stove. As I neared the derelict tanks the scene became truly appalling; wounded men lay drowned in the mud … The nearest tank was a female. Her left sponson doors were open. Out of those protruded four pairs of legs; exhausted and wounded men had sought refuge in the machine, and the dead and dying lay in a jumbled heap inside.

Although the battlefield at Third Ypres was manifestly unsuitable for the deployment of the new Mark IV tank, Haig

BELOW LEFT This Mark IV tank sports a large tactical number (102) for easy recognition. Training tanks were given three-digit numbers – the first digit corresponding to the company or, later, battalion to which the tank belonged.

BELOW RIGHT The Sponson of a Mark IV Male tank showing the shortened 6-pounder gun – the longer guns of the earlier models sometimes caught on obstacles. The Hotchkiss machine guns have been replaced by Lewis guns in the ball mounting.

RIGHT Not all tanks made it across the fascines. In the centre of the Cambrai attack, Hyacinth has come to grief. She is surrounded by soldiers of the 1st Battalion Leicestershire Regiment.

TOP AND MIDDLE In July 1917 the Tank Corps was formed and a new cap badge issued along with the distinctive, and still worn, arm badge.

BOTTOM The first tank crews were formed as a section of the Machine Gun Corps called the Heavy Branch and they wore the crossed Vickers machine guns of the Machine Gun Corps as their badge.

THE MARK IV

SPECIFICATION

CREW: 8

WEIGHT: 28 tons

ARMOUR: 12mm (0.47in)

ARMAMENT: 2 x 6pdr, 4 x Lewis machine guns (Male), 6 x Lewis machine guns (Female)

TOP SPEED: 6km/h (3.7mph)

OPERATING RANGE: 56km (35 miles)

ENGINE: Daimler 105hp, petrol

The Mark IVs had been introduced in June 1917 at Messines Ridge, where they outpaced infantry over dry ground. While similar to the Mark I, II and III, the new model incorporated a number of changes prompted by battle experience. It was fitted with an improved radiator, silencer and pressed-steel track with greater grip, although the last was still only good for about 32km (20 miles). The disposition of the 12mm (0.5in) armour plating proved effective against armour-piercing bullets, although the Mark IV remained vulnerable to German artillery.

The male Mark IV's main armament was changed from long 40-calibre six-pounders to the short 23-calibre versions, minimizing damage when the tank ditched; and the sponsons were modified (in both male and female versions) so that they could be swung inwards on rail transport.

The Mark IV's crew were provided with improved safety hatches, and the fuel supply for the engine was now by means of a vacuum feed system, more reliable than the Mark I's gravity feed. Petrol was carried in an armoured container outside the tank's hull at the rear, where it was less of a fire risk. The Mark IV's 105hp Daimler engine was retained from the Mark I, although it was recognized that the tank remained underpowered.

On its nose the Mark IV carried a fascine, a wood-and-chain bundle some 3 metres (10 feet) long and 1.4 metres (4.5 feet) in diameter, which was dropped into trenches to ease the tank's crossing. Trench-crossing was also improved by the fitting of a "tadpole tail", a mild-steel extension which increased the span that could be traversed from 3 metres (10 feet) to 4.3 metres (14 feet).

HULL DETAILS — INTERIOR.   SCALE 1½ INCH TO THE FOOT.

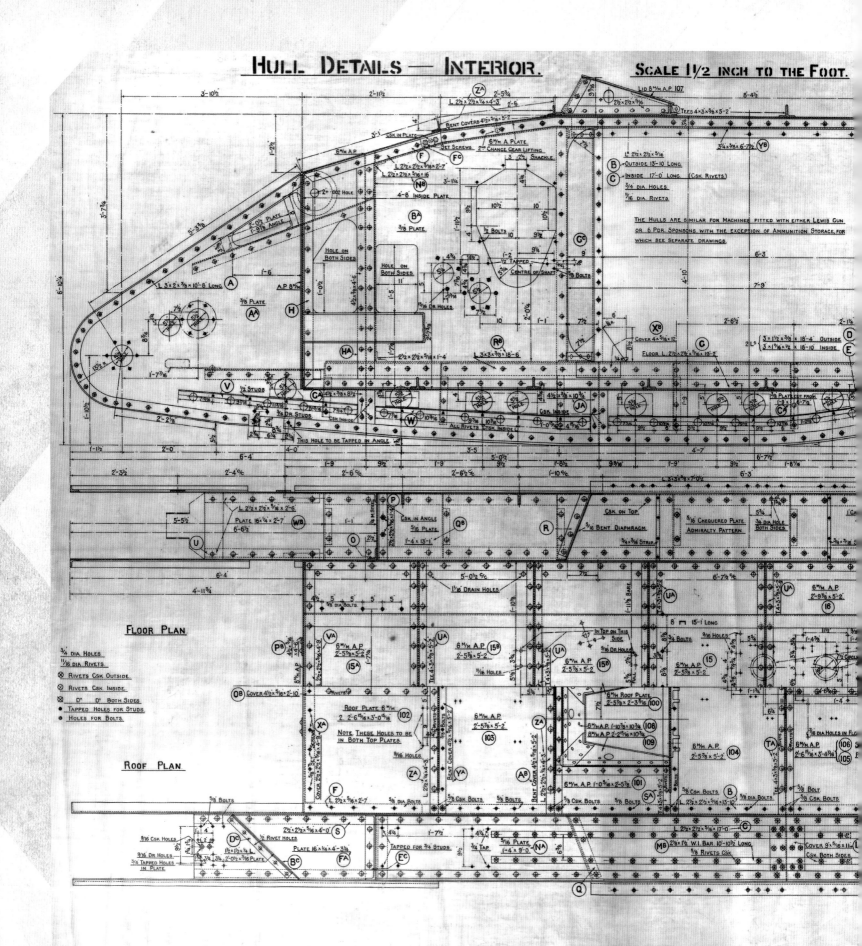

Floor Plan

Roof Plan

THE HULLS ARE SIMILAR FOR MACHINES FITTED WITH EITHER LEWIS GUN OR 6 PDR SPONSONS, WITH THE EXCEPTION OF AMMUNITION STORAGE FOR WHICH SEE SEPARATE DRAWINGS.

¾ DIA HOLES
11/16 DIA RIVETS
⊗ RIVETS CSK OUTSIDE
⊗ RIVETS CSK INSIDE
⊗ D° D° BOTH SIDES
● TAPPED HOLES FOR STUDS
○ HOLES FOR BOLTS.

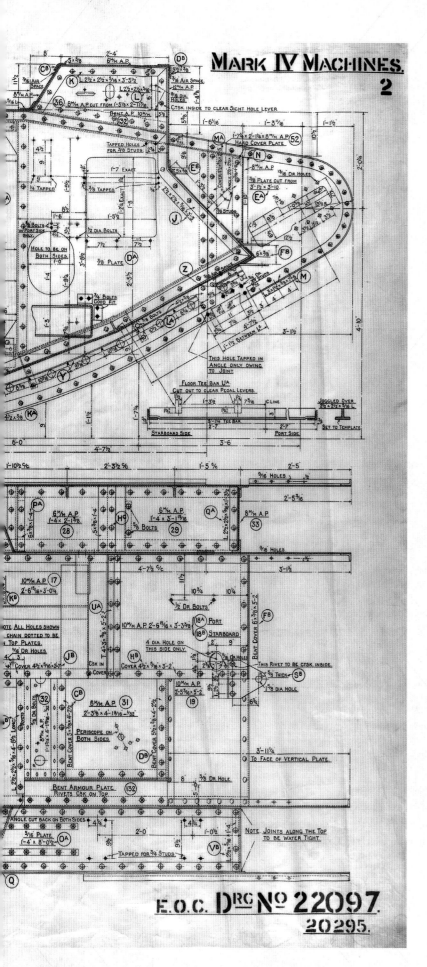

brushed aside a request by Sir Eustace Tennyson D'Eyncourt, the naval architect who had chaired the Landships Committee, that they be withdrawn from the battle and reserved for use on more appropriate terrain. "Even under such conditions," Haig replied, "they have done valuable service more than sufficient to justify this decision."

The Battle of Cambrai

The seeds of the Battle of Cambrai had been sown in August 1917, before the disaster at Passchendaele became manifest. Originally conceived as a raid by tanks and infantry south of Cambrai, a quiet, albeit well-fortified sector which was held in no great strength by German Second Army, it was supposed to last for a matter of hours before the attacking force withdrew. Yet by the late autumn of 1917, Haig was desperate for a success of any kind to offset the Passchendaele debacle. The modest plan for a tank raid was expanded into a penetration to Cambrai and beyond. The opportunity presented itself when Brigadier-General Elles, now commanding the newly formed Tank Corps, suggested a plan to breach the Hindenburg Line – the defensive system to which the German had withdrawn in February–March 1917 – with a surprise attack launched over firm, unbroken ground toward Cambrai.

The man behind the plan to use tanks for the first time en masse, a staff officer with the Tank Corps, Colonel J.F.C. Fuller, proposed a revolutionary attack by 476 tanks and infantry, launched without a preparatory artillery bombardment. The terrain – mostly rolling downland – was good for tank operations. Surprise was the key.

The attacking forces of General Julian Byng's Third Army would concentrate secretly while artillery registered silently without firing ranging shots, a precaution made possible by the

LEFT One of the original blueprint drawings used in the manufacture of the British Mark IV tank. It came to light only when the Vickers Defence Company had a clear-out of old drawings in 2004.

FASCINE

Commander of the Mark IV Harrier, recalled: "We were given enormous fascines, consisting of 75 bundles of brushwood bound together with chains into a cylindrical mass ... They were hoisted back onto the top of the tank, and when the tank was nosed up to the trench, a quick release gear allowed the fascine to drop straight into it, thus allowing the machine to be lowered gently down onto it, and the nose to grip the other side ... When Harrier came to the second Hindenburg Line trench, my Sergeant, Callaghan, stopped the tank to adjust its position, I released the dropping gear and our fascine fell to the bottom. But it had fallen askew. Callaghan gently lowered us on to it; but the tracks would not grip it and went round uselessly ... With patience and skill Callaghan put the engine in neutral gear, raced the engine to maximum speed and jerked in the clutch again and again ... we finally got the tracks in a firm position where they got a bite and we crawled out of the trench."

Special Order No 6.

1. To-morrow the Tank Corps will have the chance for which it has been waiting for many months, — to operate on good going in the van of the battle.

2. All that hard work & ingenuity can achieve has been done in the way of preparation

3. It remains for unit commanders and for tank crews to complete the work by judgment & pluck in the battle itself.

4. In the light of past experience I leave the good name of the Corps with great confidence in their hands

5. I propose leading the attack of the centre division

Hugh Elles
B.G.

19th Nov. 1917.   Commanding. Tank Corps.

Distribution to Tank Commanders .

advances in artillery technology during the war. Bombardment would be withheld until dawn on the day of the attack, when the first wave of tanks left their start lines. The first task to be undertaken by the tanks was the crushing of the barbed wire entanglements in front of the Hindenburg Line. This had previously been the responsibility of the artillery and had produced disappointing results on the Somme.

The tanks, working in sections of three, were to cross three lines of German trenches, dropping their fascines in succession at each obstacle. In each section, one tank was to move some 90 metres (100 yards) ahead of its two companions, suppressing enemy fire while it led the infantry forward. The infantry, advancing in flexible file formations, were to follow immediately behind the escorting tanks. After the tanks had cleared a way for them through the deep belts of German wire and suppressed the enemy's machine guns, the infantry would mop up remaining resistance and provide the tanks with close-quarter protection from German guns.

Smoke shells would smother the German observation positions while aircraft of the Royal Flying Corps (RFC) bombed and machine-gunned communication centres, gun pits and entrenchments. The clearing and securing of the German trench lines was to be the preliminary to the release of the cavalry to exploit the breach in the German line.

There were two major flaws in this bold plan. There was no provision for reserves and the tank advance was to be made on too wide a front, rather than against carefully chosen tactical points. Moreover, the axis of the advance would channel the tanks between two canals, the Canal du Nord and the St Quentin-L'Escaut. These waterways would have provided protection in a swift raid, but in the more ambitious operation now envisaged would leave the tanks vulnerable to determined counter-attack.

A series of feints to the north and south of the intended sector of attack were launched to mislead the enemy, but on 19 November an intercepted British telephone message, "Tuesday Flanders", raised the suspicions of the commander of German

OPPOSITE Special Order No 6 from the Commander, Maj Gen. Hugh Elles to the men of the Tank Corps, issued on 19 November 1917 before the Cambrai attack. The order is still read by the Royal Tank Regiment as part of their Cambrai Day commemorations.

BELOW Mark IV tanks fitted with their fascines are brought up by train ready for the Cambrai attack. The logistic planning involved in the preparation for the attack was enormous and remarkably successful.

Second Army, General von der Marwitz, and he inserted another division into his defences.

At 6.20 a.m. on 20 November, some 380 fighting tanks, concentrated in nine battalions, rumbled off their start line. They were supported by 54 supply tanks fitted with sledges, 32 equipped with grapnels for dragging wire to create gaps for the cavalry, two tanks carrying bridging equipment and five wireless tanks (which could send messages in Morse code back from the front, albeit slowly and with limited reliability).

Simultaneously, Third Army's artillery opened up, driving the German defenders into their dug-outs, where they remained, confident that the bombardment, like so many others, would last for days. This assumption was shared by the German High Command, which made no countermoves. As a result, by the end of the first day Third Army had advanced some 8 kilometres (5 miles), opening up a 10-kilometre (6-mile) gap in the Hindenburg Line. It had destroyed the equivalent of two German divisions, capturing 120 guns and 7,500 prisoners.

Tanks and infantry had won a tactical victory, but strategic gain proved elusive. On 20 November, the tanks outran the infantry and were over an hour ahead of them when they reached the vital bridges across the St Quentin-l'Escaut canal at Masnières and Marcoing. One of the bridges, already weakened by a demolition charge, collapsed under the weight of a tank, and the battle in this sector developed into a duel between German artillery and the tanks. The British infantry and cavalry, when they finally arrived were reduced to the role of spectators.

There was a similar delay on the centre-left of the British advance at Flesquières Ridge. The commander of 51st Division, Harper, had chosen to adopt different tactics to those devised by the Tank Corps, and in this sector the tanks were allowed to forge too far ahead of the infantry, who missed the gaps in the wire and were cut up by German machine-gun fire.

A window of opportunity slammed shut. The few German guns that remained firing were able to pick off tank after tank at point-blank range as, unsupported by infantry, who would have made short work of the gunners, they shouldered the crest.

The Germans abandoned Flesquières in the small hours of the 21st, but they had slowed the momentum of the advance. The British, their infantry exhausted and their tank force depleted, could make no headway. The Germans had also found a formidable counter to the tanks in the 77mm (3in) field gun, previously used as a truck-mounted anti-aircraft gun. By the end of the battle at Cambrai, these had taken a heavy toll on British tanks.

Although it was not clear at the time, the fighting at Cambrai – which continued for five days, at the end of which a German counter-attack had retaken most of the British gains – was a harbinger of most of the elements of major land battles in the Second World War. These included the employment of armoured vehicles; unregistered artillery fire; the use of smoke and machine-gun barrages; the achievement of air superiority and the contribution of air support; and the use of infantry as "moppers-up" of resistance rather than the principal offensive spearhead. These lessons also gave Colonel Fuller much food for thought.

BELOW LEFT Commanded by 2nd Lt Walter Farrer, Flying Fox II edged across the bridge at Masnières only to have it collapse. The crew managed to escape, but the chance of a breakout across the canal was gone.

BELOW The German counter attack at Cambrai meant many tanks that might have been recovered by the Tank Corps were lost. The German Army would put a number of these back into service as part of their own Tank Force.

OPPOSITE In late 1917 tanks began tours of towns and cities in Britain to help raise money for the war effort. The appearance of a tank caused a flurry of press activity and the campaign was hugely successful in raising money and promoting the tank as a British success.

Tank Week

JULY 22 to 27.

TANK EGBERT II

WILL VISIT

SCUNTHORPE, July 26=27,

And will be Opened on the first day by

Capt. WYNDHAM P. THOMAS

Managing Director of The Redbourn Hill Iron & Coal Co., Ltd.

Nº73   Printed by HILL, SIFFKEN & CO. Ltd. (L.P.A. Ltd.), Grafton Works, Holloway, N.7

CHAPTER 4

THE FIRST FRENCH TANKS

THE COMBAT DEBUT OF THE MARK I DURING THE BATTLE OF THE SOMME HAD CONCENTRATED THE MINDS OF THE BRITISH AND FRENCH HIGH COMMANDS ON THE POSSIBILITIES OFFERED BY ARMOURED FIGHTING VEHICLES AND PROMPTED AN EXCHANGE OF INFORMATION AND A DEGREE OF COLLABORATION.

Prominent in these discussions was a French artillery officer, Jean-Baptiste Eugène Estienne, who is often referred to by his fellow countrymen as "the father of the Tank".

In the summer of 1915, Estienne learnt that a barbed-wire cutter on a tracked Holt-type chassis was being developed by the auto-engineer Eugène Brillié, of the Schneider Company, and the chemist and inventor Jules Louis Breton, who in the First World War served as France's Undersecretary of State for Inventions and National Defence. Estienne bombarded the headquarters of the French Army's commander-in-chief, General Joseph Joffre, with letters proposing offensive uses for such a vehicle, which he dubbed a "Land Battleship", but Joffre's staff did not forward them to the general.

Unlike the British, whose Landships Committee exercised an overall, determining role in the development of the tank, the French approach to a problem which Estienne had identified at the beginning of the war was characterized by a patchwork of competing interests ignorant of each other's efforts. On 9 December 1915, Estienne accompanied General Pétain, commander of the French Second Army, to a demonstration of the chassis of the Schneider tank, which was to be built in both armed and armoured versions (tracteur armé et blindé). The project, of which Estienne had only the vaguest knowledge, reignited his enthusiasm for the Land Battleship.

On 1 December 1915, a week before he attended the demonstration, Estienne had written a personal letter to Joffre, a fellow artilleryman, urging the creation of an all-terrain breakthrough force of armoured vehicles and infantry. This resulted in a meeting on 12 December with Joffre's chief-of-staff, General Jules Janin, three days before the Schneider tank was given the official go-ahead and an initial order for 10 machines placed. On the same day, Estienne approached Louis Renault, pioneer of the French auto industry and wartime manufacturer of 75mm (2.95in) shells, with a project to build tanks. Renault rebuffed the approach, but on 18 January Estienne convinced Joffre of the soundness of his plan.

The Schneider and Saint-Chamond Tanks

Out of the competing projects for a French armoured combat vehicle, two heavy tanks emerged. The Schneider was essentially an assault gun, the ancestor of all self-propelled artillery.

Although he had not been involved in its conception, Estienne was put in touch with Brillié's design team at Schneider and was able to influence the production version.

The first batch of machines called "tracteurs Estienne" were delivered in September 1916, the month in which the British Mark I made its combat debut on the Somme. Subsequently the machines became known as "chars d'assault" or simply "chars".

The Schneider was a large armoured box sitting on a lengthened Holt caterpillar chassis and powered by a 70hp engine. The tank's frontal nose piece and tail skid at the back were both features of Brillié's original design for the wire-cutter. Its 75mm (2.95in) howitzer was fitted in a sponson on the right-hand side of the hull and it also carried two Hotchkiss machine guns, one on each side of the hull.

Design flaws in the Schneider quickly became evident. Its overhang at the front and rear meant cross-country performance and trench-crossing capability were poor; the traverse of its main armament was limited; both vision and ventilation were inadequate; the internal fuel tanks posed a potential fire risk in action; there was no exit on the left-hand side; and its armour provided insufficient protection, particularly from the German anti-tank "K" bullets, which sprayed shrapnel and molten lead over the crew when they penetrated the hull. A programme of modifications was launched, but proceeded at a snail's pace.

The Schneider was meant to be the French Army's heavy tank, but it had a rival, the Saint-Chamond, which had not been ordered by the Army but emerged from a political-industrial fix made behind the backs of Joffre, Estiennne and the directors of Schneider. The man behind the subterfuge was Jules Louis Breton, who authorized Forges et Aciéries de La Marine et d'Homécourt, an engineering firm based at Saint-Chamond, near Lyon, to design an improved version of the Schneider.

The prototype, completed in September 1916, was more heavily armed than the Schneider, with a 75mm (2.95in) field gun mounted on the front plate – the most powerful gun mounted on any tank before 1941 – and four Hotchkiss machine guns (one on each side, one at the front and one at the back). But the Saint-Chamond had many of the design drawbacks of its predecessor. Like the Schneider, it was an assault gun with a big overhang at front and rear, poor cross-country performance, problematic handling, inadequate vision, and difficult exit

ABOVE General Jean-Baptiste Estienne was a leading proponent of the use of armoured vehicles.

OPPOSITE TOP A Schneider tank is loaded on a truck to leave the factory. The 75mm (2.95in) howitzer is clearly visible along with the Hotchkiss machine gun mount.

OPPOSITE Three knocked-out Schneider tanks show the sad reality of combat for many of the early French tanks.

arrangements. It boasted electric transmission, which eliminated the gear-changing difficulties inherent in all the early tanks and simplified steering, handled by controls at the front and rear of the machine. However, the transmission proved unreliable and led to a large number of breakdowns.

The Nivelle Offensive

In the autumn of 1916, as the fighting at Verdun was winding down, General Robert Nivelle, who had succeeded Pétain as the commander of forces in the sector, launched a series of lightning counterstrokes that regained the ground lost since February with relatively few casualties. After his success at Verdun, Nivelle succeeded Joffre as the French commander-in-chief, promising to end the war with one swift blow of "violence, brutality and rapidity".

The Allied plans for joint offensive in the spring of 1917, with the British high command reluctantly placing itself under French orders, was dislocated by the German withdrawal to the heavily fortified Hindenburg Line, that began on 16 March. Brimming with a self-confidence which bordered on the pathological, Nivelle ignored the changed circumstances. His plans remained unmodified when the offensive began on 16 April on a 40-kilometre (25-mile) front east of Soissons.

Before the battle began, Nivelle had predicted 10,000 casualties as the price of victory. In the first four days alone, French Fifth and Sixth Armies suffered 120,000 casualties. Nivelle's tanks, which made their combat debut on 16 April, also took heavy losses. One hundred and thirty-two Schneiders were committed on the first day of the offensive, but many broke down or ditched when they tried to cross German trenches and were pounded to pieces by enemy artillery. Fifty-seven were destroyed and many others damaged beyond repair.

The Saint-Chamonds followed the Schneiders into action on 5 May at Laffaux Mill. Of the 16 deployed, several ditched in trenches but only three were destroyed in combat. Subsequently, 12 tank groups fielding Saint-Chamonds were formed, and the tank found useful employment as an assault gun in the summer of 1918, when movement was restored to the battlefield, and they were able to stand off and batter German field guns at a safe distance. By then, however, the French had turned their attention to a new, lighter design of tank.

SAINT-CHAMOND

SPECIFICATION

CREW: 9

WEIGHT: 23 tons

ARMOUR: 11mm (0.43in)

ARMAMENT: 75mm gun, 4 x Hotchkiss machine guns

TOP SPEED: 12km/h (7.5mph)

ENGINE: Panhard-Levassor 90hp, petrol

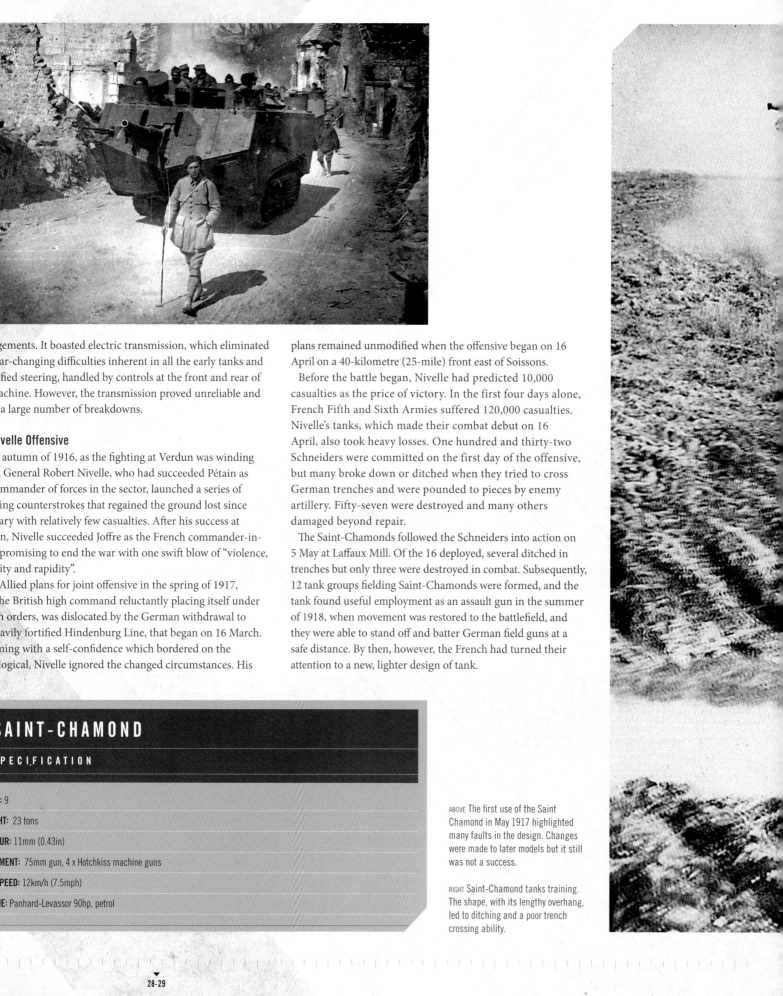

ABOVE The first use of the Saint Chamond in May 1917 highlighted many faults in the design. Changes were made to later models but it still was not a success.

RIGHT Saint-Chamond tanks training. The shape, with its lengthy overhang, led to ditching and a poor trench crossing ability.

CHAPTER 5

THE TANK COMES OF AGE

1918 SAW THE RETURN OF MOBILITY TO THE WESTERN FRONT AND WITH IT A NEW CHANCE FOR THE TANK TO SHOW ITS WORTH. THE GERMANS' SPRING OFFENSIVE, WHICH OPENED IN MARCH, LED TO RAPID ADVANCES AND BY 3 JUNE THEY WERE ONCE AGAIN ON THE MARNE ONLY, 90 KILOMETRES (56 MILES) FROM PARIS.

An Allied counter-thrust was imperative and on 24 July, the commander-in-chief, Marshal Ferdinand Foch, announced: "The moment has come to abandon the general defensive attitude forced on us until now by numerical inferiority and pass to the offensive."

France's Light tank: the Renault FT
The tank would play a significant role in the Allied riposte. And it was to assume new forms. The early British and French models, which favoured armour over mobility, were heavy, slow-moving weapons with limited range and prone to breakdown.

BELOW A British delegation came to see the new Renault tank at Champlieu, the specialized artillery test ground. The Tank Corps used a number of Renault tanks — mainly for liaison duties.

Warfare always contains lengthy periods of waiting around. Here in the summer of 1918, Canadian troops rest by the roadside as some stretcher bearers talk to the crew of a Renault on liaison duties.

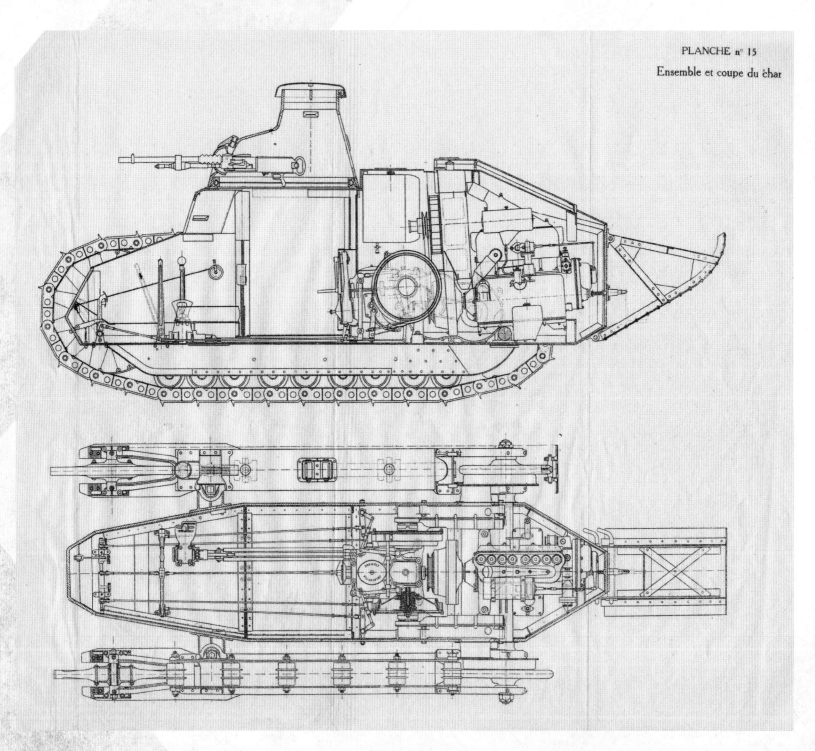

In November 1916, the French pioneer Jean-Baptiste Estienne proposed that tank development should move in a radically different direction.

Estienne took as his starting point lightness and mobility, rather than protection. When he had previously approached the auto engineer Louis Renault in 1915 in relation to the development of a heavy tank, Estienne had been turned down. A year later Renault, who had been previously too preoccupied with other war work, quickly took up his proposal for a more mobile tank and the project moved forward with surprising speed.

The Renault FT tank was to be a light type tasked with infantry support. Because Renault was sceptical that the production engines then available would give a heavy tank a sufficient power-to-weight ratio, he commissioned his leading designer, Rodolphe Ernst-Metzmaier, to come up with a vehicle that would weigh no more than seven tons. Renault himself drove the prototype on its trials in February 1917.

An initial order was made for 150 tanks to be used as command vehicles with the heavy battalions. Initial criticism that the tank was too lightly armed, with its circular, cast-steel turret carrying a Hotchkiss 8mm (0.3in) machine gun, was met in April 1917

ABOVE Drawings of the First World War Renault Char D'Assaut 18 Chevaux from the original tank manual, issued to crews to explain the basic maintenance tasks required and the key features and statistics of the vehicle. The back of the manual contains fifteen drawings showing sectioned parts of the tank and annotated system diagrams.

when Estienne insisted that some vehicles should mount a small cannon. The weapon chosen was a 37mm (1.45in) Puteaux gun housed in a Berliet polygonal turret of riveted plate. This turret, later fitted to many production models, was in turn superseded toward the end of the war by a circular turret designed by the Girod company.

The Renault FT made its combat debut on 31 May during the second Battle of the Marne, the final German offensive of 1918 before the tide turned against them. Some 30 FTs broke up a German attack but, lacking infantry support, were forced to withdraw. Captain Aubert, a section commander with 304th Company, Second Light Tank Battalion, 501st Special Artillery Regiment, took part in the French attack of 31 May:

Again the signal, "Advance". This time we advanced amongst arms and trophies flung down by the enemy in his retreat. We fired a few rounds against the features from which automatic fire appeared to come. Our infantry did not seem to be following up. They merely watched us draw away from them. At the head of a ravine at what appeared to be about 600 yards [550 metres] range, an anti-tank gun unmasked. We saw the flash of discharge. It was evidently firing at us. The first rounds fell in quick succession in front of us. They appeared to be duds. They rolled over and over in clouds of dust but did not burst. Without halting the crew commander opened fire against the gun which replied vigorously. In the course of this duel a shell pitched just in front of the tank, powdering with a hot and dusty

BELOW LEFT The Renault makers plate on the Renault FT tank.

BELOW RIGHT The Renault tank was produced with a Hotchkiss 8mm (0.3in) machine gun (shown here) or a 37mm (1.46in) Puteaux gun. This example is a training tank; 150 were made with un-hardened steel and had plaques placed on them to warn of this fact.

smoke the faces of the crew at the portholes. But the mobile gun was a match for the stationary. With a quick tack the tank quickly silenced the enemy's fire. We advanced again, zig-zagging towards the cannon, which did not reply.

The Battle of Hamel

By the summer of 1918, the British Mark IV heavy tank had been superseded by the Mark V, which from the outside looked similar to its predecessor, but incorporated some significant internal changes. The new tank made its combat debut on 4 July 1918 at the Battle of Hamel, in northern France, 3 kilometres (1.9 miles) north-west of Villers-Bretonneux. This was an engagement designed to deny the Germans control of a village that acted as a salient into the Allied rear and allowed them to continue to threaten Amiens. The principal Allied component in the battle was the Australian Corps, commanded by Lieutenant-General John Monash, an insightful commander who employed a number of innovatory tactics at Hamel: the parachute dropping of cases containing medical supplies and rifle ammunition; the use of supply tanks in the same role; and the employment by

battalion headquarters of signalling rockets to convey urgent messages to the rear.

Sixty fighting and four supply tanks of the British 5th Tank Brigade were employed in the assault, and coloured diagrams emblazoned on their hulls enabled supporting infantry units to identify and follow them. The infantry was to advance behind a creeping barrage. The tanks of 5th Brigade, though, failed to arrive at the start line before the infantry had jumped off and was quickly engaged in heavy fighting. As the sun came up, the Mark Vs finally arrived on the field of battle and rapidly mopped up lingering areas of resistance.

In the build-up to the battle, Monash had calculated that his objectives could be secured in some 90 minutes. He was only three minutes out – it took 93. The tanks were withdrawn at 1730, taking many wounded men with them, leaving the infantry to beat off a German counter-attack during the night. Although Hamel was a small-scale engagement in the broad sweep of the war – no tanks were lost and casualties among their crews were 13 wounded – it foreshadowed the end of trench warfare. An all-arms attack had quickly overwhelmed an entrenched enemy.

BELOW This Mark V (H41) is shown in the markings of 8th (H) Battalion Tank Corps at the time of the Battle of Amiens – 8 August 1918. Commanded by a young officer named Harold Whittenbury, this tank took part in the battle. Its young commander was awarded the Military Cross.

OPPOSITE Mark V tanks advance in the August 1918 campaign carrying cribs. Cribs were a re-usable form of fascine, made up of large pieces of timber with a metal framework.

THE MARK V

SPECIFICATION

CREW: 8

WEIGHT: 28 tons

ARMOUR: 14mm (0.55in)

ARMAMENT: 2 x 6pdr, 4 x Hotchkiss machine guns (Male), 6 x Hotchkiss machine guns (Female)

TOP SPEED: 7.4 km/h (4.6mph)

ENGINE: Ricardo 150hp, petrol

The biggest drawback to the Mk IV had been its inefficient driving system, which demanded the attention of four of its crew. It had long been recognized that an improved transmission system operated by one man was vital to the further development of the tank. After trials held at Oldbury in March 1917, a gearbox designed by Major Watlter G. Wilson was chosen. Wilson also worked on the tank's more powerful engine, the 150hp Ricardo. On the roof toward the rear of the tank was a raised cabin, with hinged sides, which enabled the crew to attach the unditching beam without having to leave the vehicle. An additional machine-gun mount was fitted at the rear of the hull.

The first Mark Vs arrived in France in May 1918. Four hundred were built. Its main armament was the naval 6-pounder. A number were converted into so-called Hermaphrodites (also known as the Mark V Composite) with the fitting of one male and one female sponson, a measure intended to ensure that it was not outgunned when confronted by male Mark IVs captured by the Germans or the German A7V.

CHAPTER 6

TANK AGAINST TANK // THE GERMAN A7V

THE GERMANS WERE RELUCTANT CONVERTS TO THE EMPLOYMENT OF ARMOUR ON THE FIRST WORLD WAR BATTLEFIELD. IT WAS NOT UNTIL BRITISH MARK Is WERE USED AT FLERS IN 1916 THAT THE GERMAN HIGH COMMAND SAT UP AND TOOK NOTICE OF THE NEW WEAPON OF WAR.

In September 1916 a body was finally established to examine the problem, the Allgemeines Kriegsdepartement, 7 Abteilung, Verkehrwesen, or General War Department 7, Traffic Section (the nomenclature was a security device). Its tasks included the collation of information on Allied tanks, the development of anti-tank measures and an indigenous tank design. Its first effort, the revival of a pre-war plan for a 550-ton "armoured land cruiser", conjures images of H.G. Wells, and the concept was rapidly shelved

The man responsible for designing the first German tank was Joseph Vollmer, an engineer and captain in the reserve. Vollmer followed the path taken by his British contemporaries Tritton and Wilson. His starting point was an early form of tracked haulage truck, the Bremer Marien Wagen, which he fitted with a steel body. However, this proved unsuccessful in trials, and only one prototype was built.

Vollmer then turned to Holt tracks built under license in Hungary. These were lengthened and sprung to accommodate the longer chassis of a 30-ton vehicle able to cross trenches 1.5 metres (5 feet) wide, reach a speed of at least 12 km/h (5 mph) and be armed with machine guns and cannon. The first, unarmoured, prototype built by Daimler-Benz and powered by two coupled-together 100hp engines, underwent trials in Berlin at the end of April 1917. Subsequent modifications included the addition of more machine guns and an improved observation post, before production began in October 1917 with an initial order of 100 vehicles. By now the tank had acquired the designation A7V, after General War Department 7, and was classed as a Sturmpanzer Kraftwagen or assault armoured motor vehicle.

The A7V in action

German instructions issued in January 1918, shortly before the first use of the A7V, were essentially similar to those given to the British Tank Corps. The Regulations for the Employment of Assault Tank Detachments state that the task of the tank was to provide infantry support and demolish obstacles, particularly strongpoints and machine-gun posts. Close contact with the

LEFT More than 50 of the A7V Uberlandwagen vehicles were made. As a tracked transport vehicle it had limited success because, like the tank, the ground clearance was poor and in 1918 fuel supplies to power the thirsty twin engines were limited. The swastika was used as a unit identification sign for one of the units.

infantry was deemed to be "of the highest importance". Where necessary, sections of engineers were to be attached to help the tanks across difficult terrain. Smoke, the cover of darkness and other forms of concealment were to be used to hide the German tanks, which would return immediately to cover after the accomplishment of a mission.

Toward the end of March 1918, the Germans launched the so-called Ludendorff Offensive, aimed at providing a knock-out blow in the West by driving a wedge between the French and British lines. The attacks, spearheaded by stormtroops, began in thick fog on 21 March. By now, the A7Vs were ready to make their combat debut and during the first day of the offensive, five tanks of Abteilung (combat group) 1, under the command of Captain Greiff, were deployed north of the Saint-Quentin Canal. Three tanks broke down before they entered combat while the remaining pair halted a British counter-attack. This minor engagement was the prelude to an historic encounter, just over a month later, the first tank-against-tank combat in military history.

On 24 April, in early morning mist, thickened by smoke and gas, three Abteilungen of A7Vs – comprising 13 tanks – led infantry toward the wooded Bois d'Aquenne and the villages of Villers-Bretonneux and Cachy. They were spotted by British infantry, who warned the crew of a male Mark IV commanded by Lieutenant Frank Mitchell, that there were "Jerry tanks about!". Mitchell's was one of three British tanks in the vicinity. The other two were "females", armed only with machine guns.

The appearance of the A7Vs caused panic as they rolled forward, rapidly outdistancing the German infantry. Mitchell's crew were in a bad way. They had been caught by the gas, which puffed their smarting eyes and burned patches of skin. As Mitchell peered through a loophole, he saw " … a round squat-looking monster was advancing; behind it came waves of infantry, and further away to the left and right crawled two more of these armed tortoises." The A7Vs were about 275 metres (300 yards) away.

The action which now unfolded was 30 minutes of slow motion manoeuvering during which the faster A7Vs gained the upper hand. Machine-gun bullets rattled on the sides of Mitchell's Mark IV as the tanks fired ranging shots. Then both the females were hit, forcing them to withdraw. Mitchell's rear gunner had also been wounded by an armour-piercing bullet that had penetrated his tank's plate and his gunner's eyes were inflamed by the lingering gas.

Then, seven Whippet light tanks, which had been despatched to deal with the German infantry, blundered into the battle.

GERMAN ANTI-TANK WEAPONRY

The Germans were forced to devise anti-tank weaponry to respond to the new threat. Early in 1917, the 3.7cm TAK from Rheinmetall had been rushed to the front as a dedicated anti-tank gun firing armour-piercing shells and it proved relatively effective. Alternatively, enemy tanks could be lured beyond the German trench line to be engaged by the 7.7cm field guns of an infantry division's artillery regiment firing ordinary high-explosive (HE) and later armour-piercing (AP) rounds.

Infantry from pioneer battalions were formed into anti-tank detachments and equipped with bundled charges of grenades to disable tank tracks. This method of attack was dependent on machine-gunners dispersing the Allied infantry following the tanks. Flamethrowers and mortars could be used as a direct hit on the tank's top surface often started a fire. Initially, anti-tank rifles used the same cartridges and bullets as the regular rifle round, with the bullet reversed and given an increased propelling charge. The armour-piercing K bullet could be fired from an infantry rifle and, provided it struck at the right angle, gave about a 30 per cent chance of penetrating 8mm (0.3in) of armour.

Three were hit before the rest beat a hasty retreat, believing that they had been fired on by artillery. Mitchell, despairing of hitting a moving target, decided to stop his tank and succeeded in scoring a hit on the A7V's turret, bringing it to a standstill: "Another roar and yet another puff at the front of the tank denoted a second hit! Peering with swollen eyes through his narrow slit the gunner shouted words of triumph that were drowned by the noise of the engine. Then once more he aimed … and hit a third time".

Accounts of the engagement differ. Mitchell was convinced that had had disabled the A7V and had fired on its crew as they baled out of their tank. The Germans believed that the A7V was able to withdraw under its own power. Whatever the truth, the encounter was an historic one.

THE A7V

SPECIFICATION // A7V

CREW: 18

WEIGHT: 30 tons

ARMOUR: 30mm (1.2in)

ARMAMENT: 5.7cm Maxim-Nordenfelt, 6x 7.92mm Maxim machine guns

TOP SPEED: 12km/h (7.5mph)

ENGINE: 2 x Daimler 101hp, petrol

The 30-ton A7V was a classic armoured box armed with a front-fitted 5.7cm Maxim-Nordenfelt gun (which had a lower rate of fire than the British tanks' 6 pounders) or a Sokol, a captured Russian Nordenfelt variant, and six water-cooled machine guns, two on each side and two at the rear. It had a massive crew of 18.

The A7V carried up to 60 cartridge belts (each of 250 bullets) for its machine guns and 180 rounds for the gun, a figure which rose to 300 on operations. The 500 litres of fuel were stored internally to feed the coupled engines, giving the A7V an off-road speed of about 3 mph (5 km/h) and a range on roads of 60 kilometres (37 miles). Off-road the range dropped to 32 kilometres (20 miles). In comparison with British tanks, the A7V had thicker, although unhardened armour, and a higher power-to-weight ratio, but its high centre of gravity and overhang at front and rear made it a poor cross-country performer and trench-crosser. The driver's view of the ground directly in front of the tank was obscured by the A7V's hull, resulting in a blind spot of some 10 metres (33 feet).

LEFT This colour scheme was recreated on a full scale replica of the A7V built in 2009. Only one A7V remains – taken to Australia as a trophy at the end of the war.

BELOW A7V Hagen, tank number 528 from Abteilung 2, near Villers Bretonneux in April 1918. Despite its bulky appearance and 30 ton weight it could travel at twice the speed of a British Mark IV tank on firm ground.

CHAPTER 7

THE LAST TANKS OF THE FIRST WORLD WAR

THE GERMAN OFFENSIVES ON THE WESTERN FRONT HAD PETERED OUT BY JULY 1918, TO BE SUCCEEDED BY THE ALLIED HUNDRED DAYS COUNTER-OFFENSIVE WHICH BROUGHT THE WAR TO A CLOSE. INCREASING NUMBERS OF TANKS PLAYED A ROLE IN THESE FINAL BATTLES.

During the Battle of Amiens on 8 August 1918, 288 Mark Vs, along with 96 Whippet medium tanks, 72 Mk Vs* (a variant lengthened by 2 metres (6 feet) for crossing wider German trenches), 12 Austin armoured cars and 90 French FTs were employed on a 40-kilometre (25-mile) front in a single day in an anticipation of modern armoured warfare.

It was a day characterized by Quartermaster-General Erich Ludendorff, as the "black day of the German Army", during which the British and French delivered a double blow on the Western Front. The British again attacked on the Somme, but learning the lessons of Cambrai they avoided a preliminary bombardment and supported their offensive with 462 tanks. Fog masked the initial thrust, which within 24 hours had driven 16 kilometres (10 miles) into the German positions. After suffering over 100,000 casualties, the Germans fell back on the Hindenburg Line.

The Ulster artilleryman Aubrey Wade saw the tanks moving up in the small hours at Amiens:

Lumbering grey shapes loomed up. The caterpillar flanges bit deep into the road as they advanced. They were the biggest of all their tribe, with machine-guns fore and aft, tractor belts propelling them like ships with squat conning towers. One by one they rolled past towards the trenches, tank succeeding tank as I stood and marvelled at their number."

Wade watched as the attack went in: *... never before had such a barrage been fired in the Amiens sector. It was colossal. North and south the line was aflame with gunfire. Under cover of a travelling wall of shell bursts [a creeping barrage] the Fifth Australian Division, whom we are to follow, stormed the line. The army of tanks arose slowly from its hiding places behind the front-line trenches and heaved itself over, to the terror and confusion of the enemy front*

Not everything went the Allies' way on 8 August. A Mark V, Tank No. 9003 "Barrhead", 2nd Battalion, Tank Corps, operating with the 2nd Australian Division, had been in action for 16 hours when it joined an attack with infantry south of Harbonnières:

The attack commenced at 1.30 pm. Strong opposition was met with from machine guns, anti-tank guns, artillery and bombing aeroplanes. The machine guns were soon silenced. Barrhead's six-pounder guns opened fire on some splendid targets and her machine

THE WHIPPETS AT CACHY

Whippets were first used to stiffen regular tank battalions in additional "X-Companies". While serving in this role, they were involved in the first tank-versus-tank encounter at Villers-Bretonneux on 24 April 1918. On the same day, and in the nearby hamlet of Cachy, Whippets scored a singular success against a large body of German infantry.

A reconnaissance aircraft of the newly formed Royal Air Force (R.A.F.) had spotted two battalions of enemy infantry just east of a trench feature known as the Cachy Switch Line, where they were hidden from British infantry. The pilot dropped a message over X Company, 3rd Battalion, Tank Corps, equipped with Whippets, reporting the enemy's exposed position. The Company commander steered his seven Whippets toward the point of the sighting and discovered the Germans resting with their weapons laid aside.

The Whippets attacked. In the carnage that followed, the Whippets accounted for about 400 of the enemy, some of them crushed under the tanks' tracks. Three Whippets were damaged by fire from an A7V which they had not seen and another was destroyed. The enraged German infantry, whose mission it had been to take the village of Cachy, made short work of the dismounted crews of the damaged Whippets. Denied their objective, they later rallied around the A7V some distance to the east of the village.

BELOW An amazing machine, this is Arnold's tank Musical Box with wounded sheltering beside the vehicle after the famous action on 8 August. As Arnold and his crew were captured at the end of the action, the full story of the day's events did not emerge until after the war.

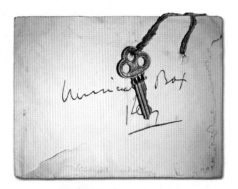

guns poured forth a leaden hail of bullets on the Germans who were seen running in all directions. Pushing ahead and getting near the objective, the artillery fire became very heavy; shells kept bursting around Barrhead so the driver steered a zig-zag course to avoid them and meanwhile the gunmen kept up a heavy fire. At this time one of the crew was wounded, and while the NCO (non-commissioned officer) was examining his wounds, the tank was hit by a shell. The concussion from this shell threw the crew all over the tank and filled it with suffocating fumes. I got four of the crew outside and placed them at the rear of the tank as they were all wounded. On re-entering the tank to ascertain what had happened to the other two members of my crew I found them both dead. The shell, which must have been a large high-explosive, had hit the tank in front of the right-hand sponson and burst inside, wrecking the cylinders of the engine.

The tank commander dressed the wounded men and despatched three of them to the nearest dressing station before going in search of a stretcher for the other man, who was immobilized by his wounds. As he returned, Barrhead was hit again and burst into flames. The badly wounded man subsequently died.

The Black Day of the German Army

At Amiens, Whippet light tanks had driven deep into the German rear and one of them, nicknamed "Musical Box" advanced so far that it became cut off behind the German lines. Whippet No. 344 of the 6th Battalion, Tank Corps, commanded by Lieutenant C.B. Arnold, had moved off at zero hour on 8 August, and after crossing the railway line at Villers-Bretonneux became detached from its unit. Undismayed, Arnold went to the aid of Australian infantry who had come under heavy artillery fire. Musical Box raced 550 metres (600 yards) across the face of the German battery before silencing it from the rear with its machine guns. For the next nine hours, Arnold went on a rampage in the German rear, dispersing a battalion of infantry, shooting up observation balloons and harassing lines of communication before the Germans recovered their balance German fire eventually punctured the cans of petrol stored on the Whippet's hull, flooding the fighting compartment with fumes and forcing the crew to breathe through the mouthpieces of their box respirators. At 1530, Musical Box was set on fire. As the crew bailed out, the driver was shot and killed and the rest of the crew taken prisoner. For his pains, Arnold received a rough interrogation and spent five days in solitary confinement sustained by a single bowl of soup a day.

The Whippet stemmed from a 1916 proposal by William Tritton for a fast, manoeuvrable and, above all, cheap tank. The prototype, the first British tank with a revolving turret, taken from an Austin armoured car, took part in the tank trials at the beginning of March 1917. Field Marshal Haig immediately ordered 200, of which the first two arrived on the Western Front with the Tank Corps's F Battalion on 14 December 1917. The Whippets were unsprung, giving a track life of about 30 kilometres (20 miles), similar to the Mark IV, and the fighting compartment was a fixed polygonal turret at the rear of the vehicle. The Whippet's two 45hp Tyler engines were of the type used in contemporary double-decker buses and were housed in a forward compartment, each driving one track.

Designed to exploit tactical opportunities following breakthroughs made by heavy tanks, the Whippet first went into action in March 1918, and won its spurs covering infantry divisions reeling from the German spring offensives. By the end of the war, 3rd Tank Brigade fielded Whippets, with 48 vehicles in each of its two battalions.

LEFT The key from Musical Box — saved by Arnold throughout his captivity — was later presented to The Tank Museum.

BELOW Whippet tanks move up with infantry in the August advances. The Whippet, when not in action, was driven with the rear door open to try and dissipate the tremendous heat that could build up in the cab.

CHAPTER 8

BETWEEN THE WARS // BRITISH TANKS AND TACTICS

THE FIRST WORLD WAR HAD SEEN AN ACCEPTANCE THAT TECHNOLOGY COULD BE APPLIED TO THE SOLUTION OF PRESSING MILITARY PROBLEMS. THE WAR IN THE AIR EMPHASIZED THE IMPORTANCE OF RECONNAISSANCE, WHICH IN TURN ACCELERATED THE DEVELOPMENT OF FIGHTER AIRCRAFT, AND ULTIMATELY THE BOMBER.

Yet on the land battlefield, Colonel J.F.C. Fuller's proposal to direct mechanized forces against the enemy's concentrations of command, control and logistics in deep penetration advances was yet to reach a wide audience.

Fuller's doctrine met with much resistance, and for a variety of reasons. The first was that after the war ended in November 1918, there was a shortage of funds to direct into the development of new armaments, and an understandable reluctance to do so after the conclusion of "the war to end all wars". The British Army disbanded most of its tank formations and was left with five battalions equipped with Mark Vs and the Mark C medium tank, a rhomboidal machine designed by William Rigby, with a four-man crew and main armament of five .303 machine guns. An initial order was placed for 6,000 Mark Cs, but the order was cancelled at the end of the war and only 50 were delivered. The Mark C participated in the Victory Parade of 1919, but the only action it saw was the suppression of rioting trade unionists in Glasgow in 1919. From the mid-1920s it was replaced by the Medium Mark I and Medium Mark II.

The pace and innovation in tank design inevitably slackened, as the budget for developing successors to the Mark C was squandered on the Medium Mark D, and the government's Tank Design Department was axed in 1923, leaving tank development in private hands. This meant in practice the Vickers-Armstrong company, which in 1920 had competed against the Tank Design Department for a new Light Infantry Tank, putting forward a lozenge-shaped design reminiscent of First World War types. The Vickers design incorporated a number of improvements, including sprung suspension and fully revolving turret and was also much smaller and lighter than the Mark C, but its advanced transmission was unreliable and the design was abandoned. Vickers persisted and developed the Light Tank Mark I, prototypes of which underwent trials at Bovington in 1923.

The tank, which was renamed the Medium Tank Mark I in 1924, was powered by a 90hp Armstrong Siddeley aero-engine. A cylindrical bevelled turret on top of the hull carried a quick-firing three-pounder (47mm/1.8in) gun and four ball mountings for Hotchkiss machine guns. The three-man turret

BELOW A cross section of a Vickers Medium showing the engine – an Armstrong Siddeley V8. This was the first turreted tank to enter British service and though built in relatively small numbers was very influential.

OPPOSITE On the right two Mark I Vickers Medium tanks and on the left a Mark II.

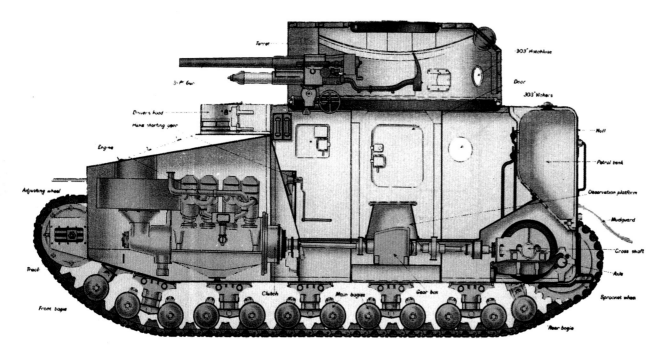

represented a major innovation, as the tank commander was no longer distracted by having to perform the tasks of the loader or gunner. Now better able to appreciate what was going on around him, this would theoretically give him a considerable edge in combat, but the advantage was not widely recognized and the feature was not replicated until the introduction of the PzKpfw III in 1937.

Nevertheless, the Medium Mark I's design had a number of defects. Its internal layout, with the petrol tanks inside the main compartment, increased the tank's vulnerability. In spite of its four mountings, the turret could provide room for only one machine gun at a time. There were two more machine guns inside the hull, but the gunner who fired these was also the tank's mechanic. The tank's 6.25mm (0.25in) plating could be penetrated by light machine-guns, and its high profile presented many shot traps for anti-tank rifles.

In the interwar years the Medium Mark I became a familiar image used to show a modernized British Army and it served until 1938 alongside its improved successor, the Mark II, in the Royal Tank Corps (which had been established in 1923). Supporters of the armoured idea had to wait until the late 1920s before the development of medium-weight tanks with cross-country speeds approaching 32 km/h (20 mph), reliable suspension and tracks, as well as a radius of action of more than 200 kilometres (120 miles). These brought a new dimension to mechanized warfare and allowed the testing of J.F.C. Fuller's concept of long-range penetration relatively free from the role of infantry support. Sceptics, however, contended that the new tanks' armour was inadequate and not offset by speed. Nevertheless, priority was given to their production because they could be used to police colonial possessions and they were cheap. Heavy tanks weighing in excess of 20 tons were ruled out simply on the grounds of expense.

In the late 1920s, mechanized manoeuvres had been conducted by the short-lived Experimental Mechanised Force (later renamed the Armoured Force), but this formation had been dissolved by the end of the decade. Yet prejudice against anything resembling full-scale mechanization of the British Army ran deep. Many in the military establishment wholeheartedly agreed with Rudyard Kipling when he described the 1930 mechanized manoeuvres on Salisbury Plain as "smelling like a garage and looking like a circus", while as late as 1936 Alfred Duff Cooper, the Secretary of State for War, told the eight cavalry regiments which were about to be mechanized,

BASIL LIDDELL HART

(1895-1970)

An influential theorist and advocate of armoured warfare, Basil Liddell Hart served in the First World War with the King's Own Yorkshire Light Infantry, seeing action at Ypres and on the Somme in July 1916. Between 16 and 18 July he went missing in Mametz Wood and emerged suffering from the effects of phosgene gas.

He remained in the Army until 1924, when he left to become assistant military correspondent of the *Morning Post* (later the *Daily Telegraph*). By the time he stepped down, in 1935, Liddell Hart was the most influential military commentator in Britain and a fervent supporter of the armoured idea.

In November 1920, in a lecture at the Royal United Services Institute (RUSI), he outlined his "Strategy of the Expanding Torrent", an anticipation of Blitzkrieg by which an army "would ensure that the momentum of the attack was maintained right through the whole of the enemy's system of defence, which might be miles deep". He had reached this conclusion with the help of J.F.C. Fuller, with whom in later years he enjoyed a prickly love-hate relationship.

Liddell Hart returned to this theme in his 1927 work *The Remaking of Modern Armies*, in which he argued: "The development of mechanical firepower has negated the hitting power of cavalry against a properly equipped enemy. But on land the armoured caterpillar car or light tank appears the natural heir of the Mongol horseman, for the 'caterpillars' are essentially mechanical cavalry. Reflection suggests that we may well regain the Mongol mobility and offensive power by reverting to the simplicity of a highly mobile army."

In the early 1920s, Liddell Hart's writings were absorbed by Heinz Guderian, who was to become the foremost German proponent of Blitzkrieg. Guderian wrote in his memoirs, *Panzer Leader* (1952), "It was Liddell Hart who emphasized the use of armoured forces for long-range strokes, operations against the opposing army's communications, and also proposed a type of armoured division combining panzer and panzer-infantry units". Liddell Hart, in a foreword to the English edition, paid Guderian the compliment of being both the "exponent and executant" of a new idea in the art of waging war.

"It is like asking a great musical performer to throw away his violin and devote himself in future to the gramophone."

Nevertheless, in 1931 a tank brigade was formed on a provisional basis, and demonstrated effective ways of mass manoeuvre controlled by radio. In 1934, it was put on a permanent footing and until 1938 was the only mechanized formation in the British Army, fielding most of its tanks.

RIGHT Tanks had the privilege of leading the Victory Parade in 1919. Ironically the tanks that were used saw no action in the war – they were the new type, the medium Mark C.

CHAPTER 9

GERMANY REARMS

THERE IS AN APOCRYPHAL STORY THAT ADOLF HITLER, WHILE WATCHING AN EXERCISE INVOLVING MARK I TANKS AT KUMMERSDORF, DECLARED, "THAT'S WHAT I NEED. THAT'S WHAT I WANT TO HAVE!". IT IS APTLY SYMBOLIC OF THE FÜHRER'S ACHIEVEMENTS AFTER HE GAINED POWER IN 1933, WHICH CAME AT THE EXPENSE OF EXACERBATING A DEEP RIFT WITHIN THE GERMAN ARMY.

This divided the proponents of the armoured idea, most notably Heinz Guderian, from traditionalist officers such as General Ludwig Beck, German Chief of Staff from 1933 to 1938, when he resigned in protest against Hitler's war plans.

In January 1934, Hitler had secretly given orders for the Army to treble its strength from the 100,000 limit established by the 1919 Treaty of Versailles, an increase to be achieved within nine months. Hitler's first year as Chancellor also saw a near quadrupling of the nation's defence budget, and in March 1935 he announced the existence of a German airforce, the Luftwaffe.

Von Seeckt's legacy

Hitler's ambitious programme of military expansion owed much to the groundwork laid by General Hans von Seeckt, from 1919 to 1926 Commander-in-Chief of the Reichsheer, or National

Army, retained by Germany after the Treaty of Versailles. In the post-war purge of officers, only the best were retained. Von Seeckt also expected that every subaltern could command a battalion and every field officer a division. As a result the Reichsheer emerged as a close-knit, exceptionally professional and efficient force.

Stern and austere, Seeckt was nicknamed "the Sphinx". He was imaginative in circumventing the Versailles restrictions on the Germany army's possession of heavy equipment which meant that up until 1932 soldiers on manoeuvre trundled dummy "tanks" mounted on bicycle wheels. After a long series of negotiations with the Allies, the Germany Army was allowed to build a small armoured vehicle with a revolving turret which, though it had no weapon, was extremely useful in teaching officers the elements of armoured warfare. He

LEFT AND ABOVE Prior to the Second World War, the German military ordered that armoured vehicles should have a two-tone camouflage scheme. The colours painted were Dunkelbraun Nr. 45 (dark brown) and Dunkelgrau Nr. 46 (dark gray), colours that are tonally hard to distinguish on black and white images.

also encouraged the development of 8 and 10-wheeled reconnaissance vehicles (Sonderkraftfahrzeug) to get around the prohibition on tracked vehicles.

Von Seeckt had fought on the Eastern Front in the First World War, being closely involved with the planning of the Gorlice-Tarnow offensive of 1915. There, he experienced a war of movement, very different from the obsession with static warfare that so infected the French high command's mentality in the interwar years. His 1921 book *Leadership and Battle with Combined Arms* outlined the critical tactical and operational ideas which were to inform the Germany army in the first three years of the Second World War.

Despite his highly conservative political views, Seeckt was quite prepared to strike a secret deal with the communist-controlled Soviet Union in 1922 for the training of German army and air force personnel in Russia. In spring 1927, after Seeckt had stepped down, two experimental tanks, mounting a 75mm (0.3in) gun, codenamed "Army Vehicle 20" and built secretly in Germany, were sent to the Soviet Union for trials at Kazan. They were followed by smaller types, one of which only carried machine guns, the forerunner of the Panzerkampfwagen I.

Perhaps Seeckt's most important legacy was to encourage a mode of thinking which looked to the future rather than dwelling morbidly on the experiences of 1914–18. He saw the next war as a series of highly mobile operations of artillery, infantry, armour and air power working together to concentrate superior firepower and overwhelm the enemy at crucial points, an anticipation of Blitzkrieg.

Panzerkampfwagen I (PzKpfw I)

By 1933, the secrecy which had shrouded German re-armament was dissipating, but because the development of a stable of armoured vehicles would take a number of years, the decision was taken initially to build light vehicles which the new armoured formations could use for training and acclimatization.

Krupps began production of the PanzerKampfwagen I (PzKpfw I) in 1934. The Model A, of which only 300 were manufactured, was underpowered and was replaced by the longer and more powerful Model B, of which over 2,000 were built. The PzKpfw I was a small, two-man tank which, even by the modest standards of the day, left a lot to be desired. Its hull was lightly armoured and its many crevices and joints made it vulnerable to attack. The M305 60hp four-cylinder engine was

ABOVE General Hans von Seekt.

BELOW The propaganda value of the tank was eagerly seized on by the Nazi Party and its symbol of strength can be seen here at a rally at Kamenz in Saxony.

Kraftfahrtruppen-Motorisierung

121

Aufklärungsabteilung. Motorisierte Aufklärungsabteilungen dienen in erster Linie der Ausspähung des Gegners. Ihr Kern sind schnelle Panzerfahrzeuge auf Rädern mit einem Aktionsradius von 200–300 km.

122

Panzerkampfwagen im Gelände. Der Raupenkettenantrieb ermöglicht dem Panzerkampfwagen das Fahren in fast jedem Gelände, das Nehmen starker Steigungen und das Durchbrechen selbst starker Hindernisse.

123

Panzerspähwagen. Es gibt leichte und schwere Wagen. Erstere tragen MG., letztere auch panzerbrechende Waffen. Beide sind geländegängig. Die Geschwindigkeit beträgt 70–100 km.

124

Verlastete Truppe. Häufig werden Truppen aller Waffengattungen, die sonst zu Fuß marschieren, zu schnellem und überraschendem Einsatz bei großer Entfernung auf Lastwagen verladen.

125

Motorisierte Artillerie. Vor allem die schweren Batterien werden in steigendem Maße motorisiert. Die Räder der Zugmaschinen laufen teilweise auf Ketten, wodurch hohe Geländegängigkeit erzielt wird.

126

Kradschützen. Kraftradschützenverbände mit allen Waffen der Infanterie bilden eine wichtige Ergänzung der Kampfkraft der Panzerdivisionen und Aufklärungsabteilungen.

Kraftfahrtruppen-Motorisierung

127

Funkwagen. Nur durch eine reiche Ausstattung mit Funkgerät ist es bei Panzerverbänden möglich, die Gefechtsleitung sowie die Verbindung nach rückwärts und zum Nachbarn aufrechtzuerhalten.

128

Panzerkampfwagen. Der Panzerkampfwagen hat zwei Mann Besatzung. Der eine führt den Wagen und ist gleichzeitig Schütze am Doppelmaschinengewehr, der andere bedient den Motor.

129

Panzerwagen im Verband. Panzer auf Raupen (Tanks) sollen zusammen mit den übrigen Kampfmitteln der „Panzerdivisionen" in überraschendem und geschlossenem Angriff die Schlacht entscheiden.

130

Mannschaftstransportwagen. Die Panzerdivisionen haben außer Panzerkampfwagen (Tanks) und Kradschützen auch motorisierte Infanterie, Artillerie, Pioniere, Aufklärungs-, Nachrichten- und Panzerabwehrverbände.

131

Personenkraftwagen. Höhere Stäbe und die motorisierten Truppen verfügen heute über zahlreiche Personenkraftwagen. Am meisten sieht man den einfachen, aber sehr leistungsfähigen Kübelwagen.

132

Durch dick und dünn! Der „PKW." soll Führer und Meldung überall hinbringen können. Daher werden an Motor, Festigkeit und Geländegängigkeit des Wagens und an den Fahrer hohe Forderungen gestellt.

barely adequate and little or no consideration was given to crew comfort. The tank's suspension was plagiarized from the British Carden Lloyd light tanks of the 1920s.

The vision of the PzKpfw I's commander was restricted when the hull was closed down and as a result he spent much of his time standing up with the upper half of his body exposed. The turret was traversed by hand, and the commander also had to fire the tank's two machine guns. The PzKpfw I saw active service with the Nationalists in the Spanish Civil War (1936–39), during which some were fitted with 20mm (0.8in) cannon to improve their limited fire power.

The PzKpfw I next saw action in March 1938, when the 2nd Panzer Division took part in the Anschluss, the German annexation of Austria. The operation was mounted as a political demonstration rather than a military exercise, and the tanks were decorated rather than camouflaged. Their progress was frequently halted by celebrating citizens decking them with flowers, and many broke down on their way to Vienna. Lieutenant Helmut Ridge, one of the PzKpfw I crew members during the Anschluss, recalled that most of the tanks, *often coughed and spluttered to a halt when rattling along the road. This meant dismounting, opening the access hatches, and trying to start them up again. Changing the spark plugs or operating the fuel pumps by hand – at the cost of blackened, burnt and bruised fingers and faces – sometimes got the "beast" started again with a loud bang; otherwise it was ignominiously taken away by the recovery team.*

The Anschluss and the subsequent dismemberment of Czechoslovakia in March 1939 were dubbed the "flower wars" by the Wehrmacht (as the Reichsheer had become in 1935). Sterner tests lay ahead for the Panzerwaffe, Germany's armoured force, and during the Second World War the PzKpfw I and its successor the PzKpfw II were to serve in the campaigns in Poland, Norway, France and the Low Countries, the Balkans, North Africa and the invasion of the Soviet Union. By the outbreak of war the standard bearer of the armoured idea was Heinz Guderian, who had led the German armoured units during the Anschluss, and a whole new family of German

PZKPFW II AUSF F

SPECIFICATION

CREW: 3

WEIGHT: 9.35 tons

ARMOUR: 30 mm (1.2in)

ARMAMENT: 1x 2cm KwK 30 or 38 gun, 1x 7.92mm MG 34 machine-gun co-axial with main armament

SPEED: 40 km/h (25 mph)

ENGINE: Maybach HL62 140hp petrol

The PzKpfw II was ordered in July 1934 as a stopgap in the development of the PzKpfw III and was designed by Maschinenfabrik Augsburg-Nürnberg (MAN) with a layout similar to the PzKpfw I. The first three variants of the PzKpfw II – the Ausf A, B and C – were very similar, but the Ausf B carried a more powerful engine, new gears and tracks and was heavier than the Ausf A. The Ausf C, which appeared in 1937, had thicker armour, further increasing its weight. By 1939 1,226 PzKpfw IIs were deployed in the Polish campaign (alongside 1,445 PzKpfw Is). Faster variants, the Ausf D and E, could reach speeds of 55 km/h (34 mph), but their cross-country performance was disappointing. The PzKpfw II's 20mm (0.8in) gun had a maximum range of 600 metres (660 yards) and fired only armour-piercing (AP) ammunition. The final variant, the Ausf F of 1940, was given thicker armour and a higher-velocity – although still 20mm (0.8in) – gun. However, the added weight placed a strain on the tank's engine. The PzKpfw II formed the backbone of the Panzerwaffe in 1939. Production continued until early 1944, when some 2,000 PzKpfw IIs and variants had been made. The tank's chassis was used in a number of special-purpose vehicles; an amphibious version (Schwimmpanzer II) was prepared for Operation Seelöwe (Sealion) the aborted cross-Channel invasion of England; a reconnaissance vehicle, the Luchs (Lynx), entered service in 1943; a flamethrower conversion known as Flammpanzer II, the Wespe (Wasp) self-propelled 105mm howitzer; and the Marder (Marten) tank destroyer.

PREVIOUS PAGES Two pages from a 1936 German cigarette card album. Smokers were encouraged to collect the cards – all showing coloured images of the German Army – and stick them in the album. Similar albums can be found from most European countries of the time, featuring sportsmen, film stars, wildlife and transport.

ABOVE The development of the PzKpfw I and II tanks was partly to gain experience in tank construction for German industry and partly to train the German army in the use of tanks. Here PzKpfw I tanks advance as part of a training exercise.

RIGHT Tanks practise a river crossing in 1939. Within a year the tactics being practised here would be used for real when the Meuse river was crossed at Sedan.

CHAPTER 10

GUDERIAN

IN THE AFTERMATH OF WORLD WAR I, MILITARY THEORISTS GRAPPLED WITH THE DEVELOPING DOCTRINE
OF MECHANIZED WARFARE. THEIR AIM WAS TO AVOID THE DEADLOCK OF TRENCH WARFARE AND RESTORE
MOVEMENT AND MANOEUVRE TO THE BATTLEFIELD.

Progress was initially slow, partly due to the mechanical
unreliability of armoured fighting vehicles of the 1920s, and
also because of the continued esteem accorded by military
establishments to horse-mounted cavalry.

A new approach to mechanized warfare evolved in Germany
following Adolf Hitler's repudiation of the Treaty of Versailles
and adoption of a policy of rearmament – initially secret and
subsequently announced to the world in March 1935. The
doctrine is generally referred to as Blitzkrieg ("lightning war").
It had many begetters but the man most closely associated with
its application was Colonel (later General) Heinz Guderian, a
signals and motor specialist who had fought at Verdun in 1916
and had seen at first hand the senseless carnage of modern
static warfare.

Guderian's enthusiasm for tanks was kindled in 1922
when he held a post in the Inspektion der Krafttruppen
(Inspectorate of Motorized Troops). In 1928, he began
teaching tank tactics to classes composed of officers of all
arms assembled at the Kraftfahr-Lehrstab (Motor Instruction
Staff) in Berlin. In the late 1920s, he refined his ideas about
the employment of armour, rejecting the current French
doctrine that tanks must be subordinated to the infantry
and instead arguing that tanks should form a separate,
independently operating arm to reclaim the decisive role
played by cavalry in previous centuries.

Guderian's commitment to the armoured idea was to find
eloquent expression in his 1937 book, *Achtung Panzer!*,
which argued for an "indirect approach". This ignored
the frontal engagement of the enemy and his destruction
by sheer weight of fire and focused instead on the rapid
dismantling of his command and control system. The critical
point on the battlefield, the Schwerpunkt, was to be smashed
open by independent and fast-moving armoured formations
co-ordinated by radio. These would penetrate the enemy's
defences, drive deep into the rear and then, using the follow-
up infantry and artillery, slice up the isolated survivors in a
series of pockets. The process would be hastened by the use
of bombers.

In 1930, Guderian became commander of the 3rd Kraftfahr
Abteilung, a motorized battalion equipped with dummy tanks
and anti-tank guns based near Berlin. Great emphasis was

placed by Guderian on tank-to-tank radio communication,
which was. regarded with great suspicion by his seniors. When
informed that Guderian intended to "lead from the front by
wireless", General Ludwig Beck replied, "Nonsense! A divisional
commander sits back with maps and a telephone. Anything else
is utopian."

In October 1931, Guderian was appointed Chief of Staff of the
Inspectorate of Motorized Troops, headed by General Oswald
Lutz, a keen supporter. In June 1934, he followed Lutz to the
newly formed Kraftfahr-Kampftruppen (Motorized Fighting

ABOVE General Guderian, Hitler and Field
Marshal Keitel, the Chief of the German
Defence staff, in 1943.

OPPOSITE Prior to the Second World War,
Guderian battled with traditionalists
in the German Army who saw the
tank only as a support weapon for
the infantry. Here his publication is
titled "*The panzer troops and their
cooperation with other arms*".

Troops), which performed its first divisional manoeuvres in July 1935. That autumn, in the flush of openly declared German rearmament, three panzer divisions, based in Weimar, Würzburg and Berlin were established. Although he was only a colonel, Guderian was given command of the Würzburg formation, a posting that for the next two years effectively kept him at arm's length from any armoured policy making.

Guderian's rapid rise as the champion of the armoured idea did not meet with universal approval, as he later admitted in his post-war autobiographical work, *Panzer Leader*:

… when it was a matter of setting up an independent, operational air force, or of developing the newly conceived armoured force within the Army, the Army General Staff opposed these innovations. The importance of these two technical achievements insofar as they affected the operations of the combined Armed Forces was neither sufficiently studied nor appreciated, because it was feared that they might result, in the one case, in a decrease in the importance of the Army as a whole and, in the other, in a lessening of the prestige of the older arms of the service.

In the mid-1930s, the military conservatives might have had a point. Although technical advances had sharpened the weapons of offence, they could argue that they had also improved those of defence, making it possible for the latter to hold up attacks with comparatively small forces. Moreover, it was clear that Germany did not possess the resources to fund the creation of a mass conscript army while simultaneously breathing life into the armoured idea. A panzer division cost about 15 times as much to equip and maintain as an infantry division. Before 1939, there was little evidence to suggest the wisdom of such a heavy expenditure.

In autumn 1938, Guderian was made Chief of the Mobile Forces, including both armoured and motorized troops, and their Inspector General – in part a ploy by the more senior artillerymen in the Reichswehr, Generals von Brauchitsch and Beck, to ensure that he remained on the sidelines. During the occupations of Austria (March 1938) and Czechoslovakia (March 1939) he commanded armoured columns, and when war broke out in September 1939, he led XIX Panzer Corps in the invasion of Poland.

The unresolved tension between the traditionalists – the infantry and artillery – in the German Army and the proponents of the armoured idea meant that on the eve of war only about one in 20 of its divisions was armoured and 90 per cent of its tanks, PzKpfw Is and IIs, were obsolescent. The Army's two main fighting tanks, the PzKpfw III and IV, were both undergunned and few in number: of 3,195 tanks in total, just 309 were PzKpfw IIIs and IVs. Germany's mechanized force, like its French equivalent, was effectively subordinated to the traditional strategy of decisive manoeuvre by a mass army and the proponents of the indirect approach, whether or not they knew it, had lost the argument.

ACHTUNG PANZER!

Guderian's ground-breaking book opens with a insightful analysis of Allied tank operations in the First World War, criticizing British and French failures to attack in sufficient depth and to provide strong, mobile reserves to exploit success. The Allies succeeded in breaking into the enemy front but never through it. Moreover, the tanks were held back by the slow pace of infantry and horse-drawn artillery.

Guderian's solution was the fully mechanized panzer (armoured) division built around a fast, heavily armed medium "breakthrough" tank, not the heavy infantry support tanks favoured by the French. The commanders of these tanks would be trained to fight in large formations, providing the maximum concentration of firepower. Following close behind would be fully motorized infantry, whose role was to mop up and exploit the breakthrough and protect the vulnerable flanks of the salient created by the panzers from counter-attack by the enemy's armoured forces.

Guderian considered that the enemy's tanks presented the principal threat. A tactical air force, collaborating closely with panzers, was essential. Guderian concluded, "We thus sum up our demands for a decision-seeking panzer attack in these terms; suitable terrain, surprise and mass deployment in the necessary width and depth."

CHAPTER 11

SOVIET ARMOUR // 1930-42

DURING THE 1930S, THE SOVIET UNION HAD BEEN A LEADER IN THE DEVELOPMENT OF LARGE ARMOURED FORMATIONS AND SEVERAL MECHANIZED CORPS HAD BEEN FORMED. THESE OWED MUCH TO THE STRATEGIC RADICALISM OF MARSHAL MIKHAIL NIKOLAYEVICH TUKHACHEVSKY, STALIN'S CHIEF OF STAFF, A FORMER TSARIST OFFICER WHO BECAME ONE OF THE MOST SUCCESSFUL BOLSHEVIK COMMANDERS OF THE RUSSIAN CIVIL WAR.

Tukhachevsky was greatly influenced by the writings of Fuller and Liddell Hart and was the driving force behind the creation of the Soviet Union's mechanized corps, which he saw as the perfect instrument to deliver his own theory of "deep operations", in which infantry-support heavy tanks and fast cavalry tanks would cut through the enemy's frontal defences to penetrate to the rear. In common with like-minded German proponents of armour, notably Guderian, Tukhachevsky encountered fierce resistance from the Soviet military establishment, but nevertheless his recommendations were broadly accepted by the Red Army and incorporated into its Provisional Field Regulations of 1936.

Tukhachevsky did not survive Stalin's purge of the military and was shot, along with seven other generals, on 11 June 1937. By the autumn of 1938, the firing squads had accounted for three of the Red Army's five marshals, 13 of its 15 army commanders and 186 of its 406 brigadiers. The result was the consolidation of the power of military reactionaries like Marshal Klimenti Voroshilov, an old crony of Stalin and Commissar for Defence, who slammed Tukhachevsky's reforms into reverse. After the lessons of the Spanish Civil War and the dismal performance of the Red Army in the Finnish campaign of 1939–40 were misunderstood, the mechanized corps were broken up.

Khalkin Gol

However, a different conclusion about the employment of armour was reached in 1939 by General Georgi Zhukov. He was the commander of the First Soviet Mongolian Group during the Soviet Union's brutal jostling with Japan's Kwantung Army in 1939 on the border between Mongolia and the Japanese-controlled state of Manchukuo. Japanese attempts to extend their border by pushing across the Nomonhan River escalated from a minor incursion into a major battle – Khalkin Gol – in which Zhukov's 500 BT-5 and BT-7 tanks enveloped the Japanese Sixth Army and broke into its rear area in a demonstration of Tukhachevsky's deep penetration tactics and an anticipation of Germany's Blitzkrieg triumphs of 1940.

As a result, Stavka, the Soviet high command, reversed policy and ordered an urgent recreation of the Red Army's armoured divisions. However, the launching of Operation Barbarossa, the Axis invasion of the Soviet Union, on 22 June 1941, caught the Red Army in the

middle of this hasty reorganization. By the end of 1941, all large Soviet armoured units had been destroyed or disbanded because of crippling losses and replaced by smaller brigades, regiments and battalions used in an infantry-support role.

Thus, in the battles around Moscow which followed the Soviet counter-offensive of December 1941, the Red Army was unable to encircle large German groupings because it lacked the necessary tank formations. Stavka concluded that there was little chance of achieving operational success without the addition of larger tank and mechanized corps and tank armies.

The Long Road Back

New formations appeared in the summer of 1942, only to be chewed up in fierce battles in the Donets corridor and the Caucasus. Control by infantry officers unused to armour, tactical rigidity and superior German battlefield reflexes once again put the future of the Soviet tank arm in doubt, but now there was a sufficient number of able and experienced corps commanders to convince Marshal Fedorenko, Chief of the Main Administration for Armoured Forces and a hesitant convert to the armoured idea, that there could be no turning back. Crucially, the Red Army also now had a new weapon, the T-34/76.

ABOVE The May Day Parade in Red Square 1940. At this time the pact between Hitler and Stalin was still strong, the Soviet Union supplying raw materials to Hitler's arms industry.

OPPOSITE The BT-7 tank was an improvement on the earlier BT-5 with a more powerful engine and an all-welded construction of thicker frontal armour.

ABOVE The T40A had internal floatation tanks and a trim vane to stop water flooding across the front of the tank.

RIGHT The relatively fast speed of the BT7 helped make up for the thin armour.

GENERAL PAVEL ROTMISTROV

(1901—82)

Rotmistrov was a passionate advocate of tank armies and an outstanding tactical and operational commander. In the spring of 1942, Stavka had activated 12 tank corps and two tank armies. In April, Rotmistrov became commander of 7th Tank Corps (from July part of Fifth Tank Army). In the battles around Voronezh, Stalingrad and Rostov, he began to formulate a method of operations based on a high degree of agility and powerful, direct and active manoeuvre. At the time, however, Fifth Tank Army remained no more than an infantry army with a strong armoured element with an independent tank brigade. Despite having a theoretically higher complement, in practice the tank brigade usually fielded just under 50 tanks in two tank battalions of about 23 tanks each. In the early stages of the war these units were better suited tactically to commanders who were learning the basics of armoured warfare in the middle of a campaign and needed small units to move quickly into gaps in the defence as they appeared. Rotmistrov was convinced that the mixture of tanks and infantry was a mistaken policy and that the future lay with all-tank armies. His brilliance licensed what, in other circumstances, might have been seen as fatal individualism. Early in 1943, Stalin was persuaded to authorize the creation of five proper tank armies. Rotmistrov was appointed to command Fifth Tank Army, which was to play a vital role at the Battle of Kursk.

CHAPTER 12

MECHANIZED ARMOUR IN THE SPANISH CIVIL WAR

IN THE AUTUMN OF 1939, GERMANY STOOD ON THE BRINK OF A WORLD WAR IN WHICH ITS ARMOURED FORCES WOULD INITIALLY DOMINATE ITS EUROPEAN RIVALS. THE PRINCIPAL GERMAN ASSET WAS A CORE OF SUPERB OFFICERS WHO WERE APOSTLES OF THE ARMOURED IDEA. ONE OF THEM WAS GENERAL RITTER VON THOMA.

As a colonel, von Thoma had commanded the ground element of the German Condor Legion that fought for General Franco's Nationalists against the Soviet-backed Republicans during the Spanish Civil War (1936–39). The Condor Legion's main armoured weapon was the PzKpfw I, which had been ordered as a light training vehicle in 1933. The first prototype was delivered in 1934 and production began in July 1934. The PzKpfw I's lightly armoured hull made it highly vulnerable to attack by the Republicans' Soviet-designed T-26, which was armed with

a 45mm (1.8in) gun. The first consignment of German tanks arrived in September 1936. Von Thoma recalled:

By a carefully organized dilution of the German personnel I was soon able to train a large number of Spanish tank crews. I found the Spanish quick to learn – though also quick to forget. By 1938 I had four tank battalions under my command – each of three companies with fifteen tanks in a company. Four of the companies were equipped with [captured] Russian tanks. I also had 30 anti-

FIASCO AT FUENTES DE EBRO

In October 1937, the Republican Army launched a drive on the city of Zaragoza, spearheaded by the International Tank Regiment, the last Soviet tank unit sent to Spain. Two hours before the attack went in, the regiment was informed that it was to carry infantry on its vehicles. The decision was opposed by advisers and officers, who felt that it would subject the infantry to unnecessary risk. The attack went in shortly after midday on 13 October. The 48 BT tanks of the International Tank Brigade fired off a salvo and then set off "like an express train", with the infantry clinging to the sides. Many fell off, to be crushed by the tanks following behind. As the tanks crossed their own lines, they attracted friendly fire before negotiating a difficult descent to the plains below. There, they became bogged down in a maze of cane fields and ditches, and came under fire from Nationalist field and anti-tank guns. After running out of ammunition and lacking infantry support, the tanks were forced to withdraw. They were ordered to return to extract vehicles which were stranded, a task that resulted in heavy infantry casualties and the loss of tanks.

tank companies." Some 400 German tank personnel gained combat experience in Spain, with up to 200 serving at any one time.

Stalin steps in

The captured Soviet tanks that von Thoma used in Spain (for each of which he paid a 500-peseta bounty) were nine-ton T-26 light tanks supplied by the Soviet Union to the Spanish Republicans. Before the outbreak of war, the Republican government's armoured forces consisted of just two armoured regiments, mostly equipped with Renault tanks of First World War vintage. The first shipment of Soviet tanks arrived in October 1936, and by the end of the Spanish Civil War, 281 of the 331 tanks despatched to the Republicans had been T-26s, the most widely produced Soviet tank of the 1930s. The remainder were Bistrokhodny ("Fast") tanks, or BTs, 11-ton tanks which were derived from an American design by J. Walter Christie, but with a Soviet-built turret and gun and intended for deep manoeuvre operations. Writing in *The Times* on 8 April 1937, J.F.C. Fuller observed,

The three types of tanks I have observed in Spain, Italian [three-ton CV3 tankettes], German and Russian are not the product of tactical study, rather merely cheap mass production.

Tactical timidity

During the Spanish Civil War, both sides remained tactically conservative in their employment of armour. Von Thoma confessed that "General Franco wished to parcel out the tanks among the infantry – in the usual war of generals of the old school. I had to fight this tendency constantly in the endeavour to use to use the tanks in a concentrated way."

The commander of the Republican tank element, General Dmitri Pavlov, was equally reluctant to use his tanks in independent operations. He saw their role as supporting the

OPPOSITE Here PzKfz I tanks await action. While German tank crews did learn lessons in Spain, most of the actual fighting was carried out by Spanish tank crews.

ABOVE This 1935 model Spanish tank crew helmet was copied from the Italian version and used by Franco's tank crews. The badge has the Francoist Eagle and cross.

LEFT Ritter von Thoma led the German armoured force in Spain. He found it hard to reach a conclusion on the best use of tanks. The tank forces were spread into small formations and rarely had an opportunity to display their potential, being used mainly to bolster the infantry of both sides.

infantry, but non-existent radio communications between Republican armour, infantry and artillery undermined any effective co-operation. In addition, Pavlov's tank brigades were wary of combining with the other arms which often launched attacks along wholly predictable axes of advance. Moreover, most Republican infantry units had no training in operating with tanks, were plagued by low morale and many simply refused to accompany the tanks into action.

The Spanish Civil War saw many tank skirmishes, but no pitched tank battles. From mid-October 1937 the number of Soviet tank crews fell away, although some personnel remained as advisers. The last major operation in which Soviet tank crews took part was the bitter battle for Teruel, which lasted from 15 December to 22 February 1938. The 104 tanks which were committed to the fighting, the better part of the Soviet tank force in Spain, were not used en masse; individual battalions were assigned to support different attacks launched in foul weather and mountainous terrain. Both the tanks and their crews earned the praise of the infantry they supported and losses were relatively modest; some 24, of which seven were captured. Sixty-three more required overhaul in the field or factory rebuilding.

General Pavlov returned from Spain to become the head of the Red Army's Directorate of Tank and Armoured Car transport. Based on his advice, the Red Army broke up its large armoured formations and distributed them among the infantry, a decision that was to have dire consequences in summer 1941.

OPPOSITE A propoganda poster from the Spanish Civil War showing a stylised tank that could "smash fascism".

BELOW A Soviet-built T-26 light tank, captured by the Nationalists and placed on display. The tank was by far the best in use in the civil war but it only had an engine life of 150 hours before a major overhaul and 800km (497 miles) of travel before the tracks wore out.

CHAPTER 13

THE EVE OF THE SECOND WORLD WAR

THE THREAT OF WAR WAS THE DRIVING FORCE BEHIND ADOLF HITLER'S FOREIGN POLICY IN THE 1930S. HE PLAYED BRILLIANTLY ON THE POPULAR DESIRE FOR PEACE IN BRITAIN AND FRANCE, THEIR GOVERNMENTS' FEAR OF A BLOODLETTING EVEN MORE TERRIBLE THAN THAT OF 1914–18 AND THEIR EXTREME RELUCTANCE TO FORGE LINKS WITH THE SOVIET UNION.

In France, Hitler's reoccupation of the Rhineland in March 1936 prompted a re-examination of defence priorities, and that September saw the introduction of a mechanization programme and the creation of three Divisions Légères Méchaniques (DLMs, light mechanized divisions) and two Divisions Cuirassées (DCRs, armoured divisions). Progress, however, proceeded at a snail's pace.

Nevertheless, new tanks were introduced. In 1936, the Char B-1 heavy tank entered service, as did the fast, hard-hitting Somua S-35 medium tank. However, political infighting and industrial unrest fatally undermined the mechanization programme. In 1936, 120 tanks a month had been produced, but a year later the numbers had fallen to just 19. The French arms budget rose fourfold, but much of it was frittered away.

Warnings ignored

At the beginning of 1935, the French intelligence agency, the Deuxième Bureau, noted the appearance of Germany's first panzer division and its intended role, but the warning fell on deaf ears. Like many of their British counterparts, French cavalry officers were wedded to the belief that "oil is dirty, dung is not". To them, tanks, and aircraft were unlikely to rewrite the rules of warfare.

There were a few notable dissenters, among them the politician Paul Reynaud and the soldier Major Charles de Gaulle. As early as 1924, Reynaud had been urging the establishment of a mobile, offensive army. Later, he found a willing ally in de Gaulle, who argued in a series of articles for the creation of two armoured divisions. In 1934, de Gaulle published a book, *Vers L'Armée de Métier* (*The Army of the Future*), expanding his ideas, which resulted in his removal from the 1936 promotion list.

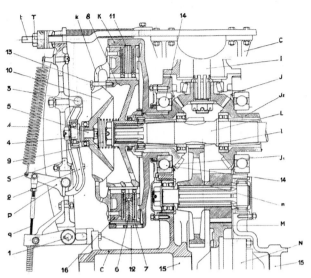

Comme dans l'embrayage principal, les disques à cannelures extérieures sont en deux pièces, avec conduits de ventilation. L'appareil comporte 3 surfaces de friction (la cale 16 remplace une paire de disques qui ont été supprimés sans inconvénients).

Fig. 30. — **Coupe de l'embrayage de direction côté gauche.**

Par un plan suivant l'axe du fléau S (le couple conique supposé rabattu dans le plan de coupe).

Les repères "lettres" se réfèrent aux figures 28 et 29.

I - Arbre auxiliaire commandé par le moteur.	S - Fléau des leviers.
j - Pignon sur l'arbre I.	T - Écrou de réglage.
J, J₁ - Roues dentées commandées par J.	t - Tige de l'écrou T fixé sur le bâti C.
K - Tambour d'embrayage secondaire.	I - Articulation du fléau S.
k - Plateau compresseur d'embrayage.	2 - Levier poussoir actionné par Q, est calé en 3.
L - Arbre conduit des embrayages.	4, 5 - Gaine de butée sur billes.
l - Pignon sur l'arbre L.	6 - Disques à cannelures extérieures.
P - Levier de commande d'embrayage.	7 - Disques à cannelures intérieures.
q - Câble sous gaine.	8 - Moyeu cannelé sur l'arbre L.

9 - Ressort de rappel du plateau K.
10, 11, 12 - Passage d'air de refroidissement.
13 - Vis de retenue de plateau K.
14 - Roulement de butée des embrayages.
M - Roue dentée sur le différentiel N.
N - Boîtier du différentiel auxiliaire.
15 - Logement des roulements du différentiel N.
m - Train réducteur.
16 - Cale d'épaisseur.

sont du type à disques multiples; ils comportent un plateau compresseur *h*, susceptible de comprimer ces disques sous l'action du levier *Q* actionné par le câble sous gaine *q*. Ce levier *Q* est monté sur le fléau *S*, lequel est articulé à sa partie inférieure (en *I*) et reçoit à la partie supérieure la butée de l'écrou de réglage *T*. Cet écrou porte par denture sur une rondelle dentelée, immobilisée, ce qui assure son indesserrabilité.

Fig. 29. — **Bloc "Mécanisme".**

Les repères C à S se retrouvent sur la figure 28.

C - Boîte de mécanisme.	k - Plateau compresseur d'embrayage.
b - Arbre primaire accouplé avec l'embrayage.	Q - Levier de poussoir d'embrayage.
h - Accouplement avec l'arbre auxiliaire du moteur.	q - Câble sous gaine.
I - Arbre auxiliaire de mécanisme.	s - Ressort de rappel.
e - Arbre transversal de différentiel principal.	S - Fléau des leviers articulé à sa base.
g - Poulie de frein.	T - Écrou de réglage d'embrayage.
K - Tambour d'embrayage de direction côté gauche.	t - Tige filetée fixée au carter.
	U - Logement de la pompe à huile.
	u - Remplissage d'huile.

V - Jauge d'huile.
v₁, v₂, v₃ - Tuyauteries de graissage.
X - Couronne ou stator.
x - Turbine de ventilateur.
v - Raccord du tachymètre.
Z - Leviers de commande des baladeurs.
w - Pattes d'attache avec le carter d'embrayage.
Y - Boîte de verrouillage.
z - Leviers des baladeurs.

TOP RIGHT French re-armament after German reoccupation of the Rhineland led to the creation of three Light Mechanized Divisions, or Divisions Légères Méchaniques (DLMs), made up of cavalry regiments. The Somua S-35 was a tank designed for cavalry use and had the first all cast hull and turret. This tank belonged to the 18th Régiment de Dragons.

OPPOSITE ABOVE The Char 2C tank was designed in the First World War. Only ten of these 70-ton monsters were built and they were obsolete by 1940 but used for propaganda purposes. .

OPPOSITE The markings of the 4th Cuirassiers of 1st DLM. They adopted a badge showing Joan of Arc.

ABOVE AND RIGHT Pages from the SOMUA S35 tank. This edition of the 78-page manual was published in 1938 and shows images of the vehicle and the main automotive systems. Vehicle manuals usually came in three types: the user manual for the crew; a workshop manual for guidance on major servicing or replacement of larger parts or systems; and a parts list for ease of recognition and identification of specific components. A tank is made of many thousands of individual parts, many of which could be unique to that model of vehicle.

CHAR B-1 HEAVY TANK

SPECIFICATION

CREW: 4

WEIGHT: 32 tons

ARMOUR: 60mm (2.36in)

ARMAMENT: 1x 75mm, 1x 47mm, 2x machine-guns

TOP SPEED: 28 km/h (17 mph)

ENGINE: Renault, 6-cylinder

The origins of the Char B-1 lay in the 1921 competition initiated by the Section Technique des Chars de Combat, headed by General Estienne, for the design of a 15-ton tank armed with a hull-mounted 47mm (1.8in) or 75mm (3in) gun. The result was the Char B, which weighed 32 tons and was armed with a hull-mounted 75mm (3in) gun, two fixed machine guns in the front of the hull and two turret-mounted machine guns. Only 35 of these tanks were made before an improved model was introduced – the Char B-1 bis. Some 365 of these were buillt. The B-1 bis suffered from the disadvantage of a one-man turret. The commander in the turret acted as gunner and loader, supervised the other members of the crew and directed a platoon or squadron of other tanks. The driver had to pass ammunition to the gunner and aimed and fired the hull-mounted 75mm (3in) gun. This could only fire ahead and had to be elevated by the driver with a hand wheel. The radio operator and loader seated in the centre of the tank could see nothing. Because the B-1 was conceived as an infantry-support weapon, it had a limited road range of 140 kilometres (87 miles) in high gear, and was reliant on lorried tankers with fuel hoses for refuelling. The B-1 proved a doughty opponent against under-gunned German armour and often seemed impervious to fire.

Although *The Army of the Future* lacks the incisive analysis which distinguished Guderian's *Achtung, Panzer!*, de Gaulle was rightly scornful of the passive military mentality whose greatest folly was the Maginot Line, the concrete and steel fixed defensive positions along France's eastern frontier which were the embodiment of defeatism. He believed that mobility and manoeuvre were the keys to the defence of France and urged the formation of a wholly professional army at whose heart would be six armoured divisions supported by air power.

"Fit for the scrap heap"

De Gaulle's message was politely ignored. Even worse, the lessons of the Spanish Civil War were misread in France. The poor performance of tanks in the field, a combination of inadequate technology and military mulishness, merely served to confirm the overall mistrust of armour. While talking to the British Chief of the Imperial General Staff, General Sir Cyril Deverell in 1936, General Maurice Gamelin, his French equivalent, dismissed the German armour used in Spain as "fit only for the scrap heap".

In 1937 a new French Army Instruction on Tactical Employment of Major Units stated: "... technical progress has not appreciably modified, in the tactical sphere, the essential rules laid down by its predecessors". The infantry was to be "entrusted with the principal duty in battle. Protected and accompanied by its own guns and by the guns of the artillery, and occasionally preceded by combat tanks and aviation, etc., it conquers the ground, occupies it, organizes and holds it." These overriding priorities stifled the intermittent attempts by the French Army to bolt aspects of the armoured idea on to its infantry-artillery-based superstructure. It was too little too late.

In May 1940, some 800 French tanks were placed in the cavalry divisions (DLMs) and approximately 800 more were dispersed in independent battalions under the infantry. The remainder equipped the three new armoured divisions (DCRs) which had only been formed that year. Each of the armoured divisions fielded only half the number of tanks that made up the German panzer divisions. The 4th Armoured Division, which was barely half-formed, was commanded by General Charles de Gaulle.

ABOVE The trumpet banner of the 507th Tank Regiment, commanded by Charles de Gaulle.

ABOVE LEFT The Renault Char B-1 – the most significant tank in French service (and prior to the Second World War judged by many to be the best in the world). It had a 75mm (2.3in) howitzer in the hull that could fire high-explosive rounds and a high velocity 47mm (1.8in) gun for anti-tank use in the turret.

OPPOSITE TOP RIGHT This Char B-1 was captured by the Germans. Liberated by the British in 1945, it spent some time at the School of Tank Technology before coming to the Tank Museum.

OPPOSITE BELOW RIGHT The bulk of the Char B-1 echoed the design of the British tanks of the First World War.

CHAPTER 14

CASE WHITE // THE GERMAN INVASION OF POLAND

BEFORE DAWN ON 1 SEPTEMBER 1939, THE LUFTWAFFE BEGAN A BOMBARDMENT OF STRATEGIC POINTS INSIDE POLAND. IT WAS THE PRELUDE TO A DEMONSTRATION OF THE SPEED AND STRIKING POWER WHICH THE WEHRMACHT HAD BEEN DEVELOPING DURING THE 1930S.

The Polish Army was dispersed along its borders, with little or no reserve, inviting swift envelopment by two German Army Groups: Army Group North, under General von Bock, attacking from Pomerania and East Prussia on both sides of the Polish Corridor (the strip of Polish-controlled land separating the main part of Germany from East Prussia); and Army Group South, commanded by General von Rundstedt, driving from Silesia and Slovakia. The two Army Groups' 58 divisions included seven armoured, four light armoured and four motorized infantry divisions. They deployed some 3,200 tanks and armoured vehicles, supported by about 2,000 aircraft, including 900 bombers and 230 dive-bombers.

Poland had 32 infantry brigades, 11 cavalry brigades and two mechanized brigades. The Polish armour consisted of some 220 modern light tanks mounting 37mm (1.5in) guns, around 800 obsolete tankettes and 90 armoured cars. The Poles had signed treaties with Britain and France, under which they were expected to hold out against the Germans for two weeks before their allies mobilized and attacked Germany in the west. The attack by Poland's allies never came.

Debacle

Within two days, the Luftwaffe had gained total air superiority and the Polish cordon defences had been splintered into uncoordinated groups. The German plan involved a double pincer movement: the inner of these was to close on the Vistula near Warsaw; while the outer pincer was to meet on the Bug River at Brest Litovsk, 160 kilometres (100 miles) east of the Polish capital.

The German armoured and motorized divisions, which formed just under 30 per cent of the invasion force, were not concentrated to operate independently of the infantry as advocated by Guderian, but were distributed among the armies in corps-sized groupings. Guderian himself, leading XIX Panzer Corps, which had been ordered to operate in close co-ordination with the left flank of General Küchler's Third Army as it advanced from East Prussia to the east of Warsaw, was champing at the bit for his armour to be allowed to slip the leash. On one memorable day, XIX Corps's one motorized and two panzer divisions advanced 80 kilometres (50 miles) in 12 hours.

Nevertheless, from beginning to end in the three-week

POLISH TANKS OF 1939

On the eve of the German invasion, the Poles fielded some 1,020 tanks, of which 220 were modern Renault R35s, Vickers Es, and 7TPs, the last of Polish design. The remainder consisted of older models, including tankettes and French FTs. The Polish armour was no match for German. The TK3 and TKS tankettes were Polish-built and based on the Vickers chassis. The TK3s were armed with a Hotchkiss machine gun while some upgraded TKS carried a 20mm (0.8in) anti-tank rifle capable of penetrating any German armour, but very few were available in September 1939. In 1936, the Poles ordered the Renault R35 light tank to replace its obsolescent FTs. Fifty were delivered in 1939, but they were of limited use. They traded protection for speed; their engines overheated, and their main armament, the short-barrelled Puteaux 37mm (1.46in) gun was suitable only against casemates and machine-gun nests. Against German tanks they were useless. The single-turret 7TP tank was the most successful development of the Vickers E by a foreign company.

campaign against Poland, the movement of German armoured forces was closely co-ordinated with those of the infantry armies they were supporting. The panzer forces were tasked with spearheading the general advance by the whole army and their orders were not to mount any independent action. They were not to make any deep penetrations into the enemy's rear; rather they were given the traditional task of protecting the infantry's flanks, which was the principal concern of the German high command.

Poland's fate was sealed on 17 September, when the Red Army invaded from the east, fulfilling the terms of the Nazi–Soviet Non-Aggression pact of August 1939. Five days later, 3rd Panzer Division joined a joint victory parade with the Soviets in Brest-Litovsk. The Soviets did not make a good impression. A German soldier described their equipment as "a collection of oily junk". For 3rd Panzer, the fighting was over, the division withdrew to East Prussia and XIX Motorized Panzer Corps was dispersed, leaving Guderian with just his headquarters staff.

In the Polish campaign the Panzerwaffe had lost 236 tanks written off as wrecks. However, the arm's crews and their commanders had gained invaluable experience and

OPPOSITE The use of reconnaissance and liaison by air with planes, such as this Fiesler Fi156 Storch, meant front line units could be kept informed of developments even if radio communications failed.

ABOVE Poland's agony was compounded when Soviet forces entered from the East. Here German and Soviet troops converse beside a Russian BA 1 armoured car.

FOLLOWING PAGES Polish 7TP Light Tanks fitted with the Swedish-made 37mm (1.5in) Bofors gun. The earlier version of the 7TP had twin turrets. The hull was based on the Vickers 6 Ton Tank which had been widely exported or licence-built by many countries during the 1930s.

POLISH CAVALRY OF 1939

SPECIFICATION: 7TP

CREW: 3

WEIGHT: 9.5 tons

ARMOUR: 17mm (0.67in)

ARMAMENT: 1x 37mm, 1x 8mm machine gun

TOP SPEED: 32 km/h (20 mph)

ENGINE: Saurer diesel 6-cylinder

The Polish Army possessed some 1,020 tanks in 1939, they also fielded around 70,000 cavalrymen in 11 Brigades. Polish cavalry were trained to operate as a fast-moving mobile reserve and generally dismounted from their horses and fought on foot using infantry tactics. They were armed with modern weapons such as machine guns, wz.35 anti-tank rifles, TKS tankettes and 37mm (1.5in) Bofors anti-tank guns. Within hours of the invasion Polish cavalry units used these weapons and tactics to inflict a defeat on the German Panzers, but it soon became clear that cavalry no longer had a decisive place on the battlefield.

had been tested in battle, something which their French and British counterparts had yet to experience. Guderian had been able to handle panzer and light divisions as a single entity, a significant step toward the triumphs of 1940. The advocates and opponents of armoured warfare had been given much food for thought. German armour had moved fast and maintained its momentum throughout the campaign, confounding those who had maintained that lack of logistic support would ensure that it would grind to a halt.

OPPOSITE ABOVE The realities of modern warfare would soon show cavalry as a vulnerable force on a modern battlefield.

OPPOSITE BELOW Three hundred TK 3 tankettes were built with a trailer that could be towed by the tank across country. On roads the trailer carried the tankette and was powered along by the tank engine, saving precious track mileage.

BELOW After the campaign the white crosses were repainted, as they created too clear an aiming mark for enemy gunners.

CHAPTER 15

BLITZKRIEG

ON 10 MAY 1940, GERMANY BEGAN ITS OFFENSIVE IN THE WEST, CODENAMED SICKLE STROKE (SICHELSCHNITT), BY ATTACKING HOLLAND AND BELGIUM. THE ORIGINS OF THE OPERATIONAL PLAN FOR THE INVASION LAY IN DISCUSSIONS BETWEEN ARMY GROUP A'S CHIEF OF STAFF, ERICH VON MANSTEIN, AND GENERAL HEINZ GUDERIAN, COMMANDER OF XIX PANZER CORPS. A MEETING BETWEEN MANSTEIN AND ADOLF HITLER IN FEBRUARY 1940 FIRED THE FÜHRER'S ENTHUSIASM, AND DETAILED PLANNING BEGAN.

The invasion of Holland and Belgium was designed to draw the British Expeditionary Force (BEF) and much of the French strength north. The bulk of the German armour would then break through the weakly held Ardennes sector in the south, cross the River Meuse and cut a swathe across northern France to the Channel, trapping the Allied forces inside a huge pocket. The attack on Holland and Belgium was to be delivered by Army Group B, with two panzer corps in its order of battle. The Sichelschnitt blow was to be executed by General Gerd von Rundstedt's Army Group A, spearheaded by three panzer corps. In the south, Army Group C was to mount holding attacks on the Maginot Line and along the Upper Rhine.

The Allied high command played a willing albeit unwitting part in Sichelschnitt. The French General Maurice Gamelin, the Allied commander-in-chief, was convinced that the

ABOVE The French defensive system relied on a massive series of defensive structures – the Maginot line – and a mobile force to meet any German aggression through Belgium should it appear. Here a French anti-tank gun is sited in a pillbox on the border.

RIGHT The close co-operation with the Luftwaffe was vital in the success of the German advance. Luftwaffe officers travelled with the tanks in radio-equipped half-tracks and armoured cars, ready to call on air support as aerial artillery.

German attack, when it came, would be a mechanized version of the Schlieffen Plan, which had been the operational plan for Germany's initial offensive on the Western Front in 1914. Gamelin expected it would outflank the Maginot Line, the fortified defensive system on the French border, with an attack through Holland and Belgium. He planned to order the 13 divisions of the BEF and 27 of the best divisions of the French Army to move up to support the 11 Dutch and 22 Belgian divisions along the line of the River Dyle.

Allied and German armour

The opposing armies were fairly evenly matched in terms of armour. The Germans disposed of some 2,500 tanks, the majority of which were PzKpfw Is and IIs. The French fielded about 3,000, of which 2,285 were modern. The BEF had at its disposal 200 light tanks and 100 heavier infantry tanks. It had no dedicated armoured formations – Britain's only tank division, First Armoured, was not yet combat-ready.

What decided the outcome was the very different ways in which the German and Allied high commands intended to use their armour. The French tanks had poor operating ranges and 80 per cent of them were not equipped with radio.

Moreover, the French tanks were distributed haphazardly among Gamelin's army groups, and over half were tied to the slow-moving infantry. In contrast, all 10 of Germany's panzer divisions and all six motorized divisions were deployed in the West.

German armoured doctrine emphasized the offensive and the maximum of initiative at the lower levels of command. The panzer formations – which were essentially self-contained combined-arms units containing armour, motorized infantry and engineer formations – were tasked with attacking on narrow, tactical fronts to achieve, with air co-operation, deep penetrations at the Schwerpunkt (decisive point) and then to unbalance the enemy with rapid exploitation of the breakthrough.

In contrast the French, scarred by the huge losses in the First World War, envisaged a battlefield in which the careful control exercised by senior commanders would minimize casualties. The emphasis was on defence in depth. Mobile forces were to be kept away from enemy fire and artillery was tasked with supporting the infantry and armour. Tank formations were earmarked to support key infantry units. It was a recipe for disaster.

Superior and simplified command arrangements, which ran down from Hitler and his personal headquarters, Oberkommando der Wehrmacht, OKW, to the Army high command, Oberkommando der Heeres, OKH, and then directly to the army groups, also gave the Germans an advantage over

OPPOSITE ABOVE A PzKpfw II crosses the river Semois at Bouillon as part of the advance. The momentum of the advance caused panic in parts of the French Army.

OPPOSITE BELOW Having crossed the Somme River (on the left), vehicles of the 7th Panzer Division dog-leg around the railway line and work their way through a valley in the hillside to continue their advance.

BELOW Tanks break through the wall of the Chateau du Quesnoy. The "fear factor" engendered by tanks on infantry can be well imagined when seeing such images.

FLAVION

15 MAY 1940

After establishing bridgeheads on the west bank of the Meuse, Panzer Group Kleist beat off a succession of French counter-attacks. The French then attempted to land a heavier blow with their three armoured divisions (DCRs), but its failure highlighted the gulf between the French and German approach to armoured warfare. It took 14 hours for the tanks of 1st DCR to crawl the 37 kilometres (23 miles) to the front line. When they reached their harbour area at Flavion, no attempt was made to conceal their Char Bs and Hotchkiss 39s. Lacking a "Jerry can" system to allow crews to replenish their vehicles, the French armour had to await the arrival of lorried tankers with fuel hoses. As they were refuelling, they were surprised by 66th Panzer Battalion whose Czech-built PzKpfw 38(t)s and PzKpfw IIs attacked in a wedge formation. The 38(t)s had to approach to within 200 metres (220 yards) to fire their 37mm (1.5in) into the thinner side armour and ventilation grilles of the Char Bs. PzKpfw IVs attacked the lorries with HE (high-explosive) shells. Only 17 of the 175 tanks of the 1st DCR survived the bruising encounter. Many crews, deprived of fuel, destroyed their own tanks. By the morning of 16 May, a 65-kilometre (40-mile) gap had opened up in the French line, through which 7th Panzer Division poured.

the Allies. Similarly, the air support the Luftwaffe could offer through its Ju87 Stuka dive bombers, which acted as airborne artillery in effect, enabled the Germans to pulverize points of Allied resistance.

Fall of France

The Dutch had capitulated within five days and Belgium's main fortified position at Fort Eben-Emael was rapidly neutralized by the Germans. Following Gamelin's plan, the BEF and French armies wheeled north-east on the Dyle Line, while in the Gembloux Gap the first major tank battle of the Second World War was fought on 12–13 May between German XVI Panzer Corps (3rd and 4th Panzer Divisions) and the French First Cavalry Corps (II and III Light Mechanized Divisions), which was covering the deployment of French First Army along the Dyle Line. Both sides lost more than 100 tanks, but the Germans were able to recover and repair many of their damaged vehicles while the French withdrew, leaving their stricken armour on the battlefield.

However, the real danger for the Allies loomed to the south. Army Group A, spearheaded by Panzer Group Kleist, was pushing through the Ardennes. This was the point of maximum danger for the German southern thrust. A colossal

OPPOSITE Typical of the confused command and waste of resources shown by the French Army at this time was the loss of Char B tanks at Beaumont. Seven tanks retreated toward the town. There out of fuel and cut off by the advancing Germans the tanks were used to block the main street. Here German soldiers inspect the carnage.

ABOVE Bourgueil, a Char B tank of the 1st DCR, sits abandoned near Bergues. Having moved into Belgium, the cream of the French tank force had to retreat back into France when the true location of the German attack became apparent.

LEFT Hitler confers with von Rundstedt as the campaign develops. He was surprised by the suddenness of the breakthrough and victory.

LIGHT, CRUISER AND INFANTRY TANKS

By the late 1930s, the British had developed three distinct types of tank – light, cruiser and infantry. Infantry tanks were designed to operate with infantry and were slow-moving and heavily armoured against anti-tank guns. The cruisers were intended to fulfil the cavalry role of pursuit and exploitation and were faster than the infantry tanks and more lightly armoured. The light tanks were tasked with reconnaissance and policing roles.

The engagements of the Battle of France demonstrated that in a high-intensity battle, infantry tanks were too slow, while the cruisers were under-armoured and liable to break down. Tackling these problems eventually blurred the dividing lines between the two classes of tank.

ABOVE A Hotchkiss H38 light tank heads toward the front. The tank forces of the Allies and Germans were evenly matched in 1940.

LEFT A British tank crewman's fibre helmet. It has the emblem of the 9th Armoured Division. The Panda bear was chosen as this was a training, not a fighting formation.

traffic jam built up as 41,140 vehicles, including 1,222 tanks, crawled through the Ardennes. Army Group A was for the moment terribly exposed, but there was no Allied intervention from the air.

In contrast, the Luftwaffe played a vital role in securing three bridgeheads across the Meuse, between 13 and 15 May. On 13 May, 310 bombers, 200 dive bombers and 30 fighters flew 1,215 sorties in a rolling series of attacks along a 5-kilometre (3-mile) stretch of the Meuse around Sedan. During these operations French Ninth Army was destroyed and Second Army badly mauled. Bursting out of the Meuse bridgeheads, German armoured formations drove through northern France on an 80-kilometre (50-mile) front between 16 and 21 May. Commanding Army Group A's XIX Panzer Corps, Heinz Guderian cut through the French defences at Sedan and forced the crossing of the Meuse and in so doing vindicated all his pre-war advocacy of the armoured idea. For the Allies, the Battle of France was now lost.

CHAPTER 16

A22 CHURCHILL INFANTRY TANK

THE CHURCHILL INFANTRY TANK BEGAN LIFE AS AN ARMOURED THROWBACK. INTENDED AS A
SUCCESSOR TO THE MATILDA II. WORK BEGAN IN SEPTEMBER 1939 ON THE PROTOTYPES, DESIGNATED
A20, AT HARLAND AND WOLFF IN BELFAST. THE NEW HEAVY INFANTRY TANK WAS REQUIRED TO CROSS
WIDE TRENCHES AND NEGOTIATE SHELL-CHURNED GROUND.

Four prototypes were produced, and their rhomboidal shape
and side-mounted sponsons recalled the Mark IVs and Vs of
the First World War. With Britain at war, many senior officers
clung to the belief that fighting on the Western Front would
take the same form as the later battles of 1918, when movement
was restored to the battlefield but at the cost of huge casualties
(which amounted to 240,000 for the British Army between 21
March and the end of April 1918).

The A20 never progressed beyond the prototype stage, but
Vauxhall Motors, who had won the contract for the next
infantry tank, the A22, used it as a starting point for their
design. British fortunes in the war were at a low point, as the

BEF had just been bundled out of France, leaving all its heavy
equipment behind, and a German invasion remained a real
threat. Vauxhall were given only 12 months in which to move
into production. The decision was made to accelerate the
process by using the A20's Bedford Twin Six 350hp engine in
the new tank, which was given the name Churchill, though
whether that of the wartime Prime Minister or his distinguished
ancestor, the Duke of Marlborough, remains unclear.

Pilot models were available within seven months, and the
first 14 production tanks came off the line in June 1941. Such
a breakneck schedule was accompanied by many teething
problems, which took another year to rectify, but the Churchill

ABOVE LEFT There is some debate as to
whether the tank was named after the
Prime Minister or his relation, John
Churchill Duke of Marlborough.

ABOVE RIGHT The No. 1 Demolition bomb
fired from the Petard mortar. This
40lb charge contained a small
amount of propellant in the vertical
shaft to fling the charge out to a
maximum of 100m (328 ft). The blast
effect of this was considerable.

emerged as a more modern design with a low silhouette and thick armour, both essential requirements on the battlefield of the mid-war years.

Less reassuring was the Churchill's 2pdr gun, an anachronism by 1940, which was the main armament of the Churchill Is. This was supplemented by a 3-inch close support howitzer, mounted low down in the front of the hull alongside the driver in an arrangement similar to the French Char B-1 heavy tank. The Churchill II and later marks dropped the hull gun in favour of a BESA machine gun. By March 1942, the 6pdr gun was available and was fitted to the turret of the Churchill III. The Mark VII had a 75mm (3in) gun and the Mark VIII a 95mm (3.7in) close-support howitzer. Some 200 of the Churchills in North Africa were modified to accommodate a 75mm (3in) gun, with a dual HE/AP capability, and a 0.3in Browning machine gun – both taken from American tanks – in the turret. This conversion was known as the NA75 (North African 75mm). From 1943, Vauxhall developed a more heavily armed Churchill based on

ABOVE The Petard mortar demonstrator. A spigot sprung forward on firing and detonated a propellant charge in the round which in turn rested in the barrel, indicated by the tray on the left. The mortar breaks upward to allow the crewman to load a round through a sliding roof hatch. The Petard is then brought down ready for firing.

A22 CHURCHILL INFANTRY TANK

SPECIFICATION

CREW: 5

WEIGHT: Marks I and III 38.5 tons; Marks III to VI 39 tons; Marks VII and VIII 40 tons

ARMOUR: Marks I to VI 102mm (4in); Marks VII and VIII 152mm (6in)

ARMAMENT: Mark I 1x 2pdr in turret and 1x 3in howitzer in front plate, one BESA machine gun; Marks III and IV 1x 6pdr gun, 2x BESA machine guns; Mark IV (NA75) 1x 75mm gun ex-Sherman, 1x .30 Browning machine gun in coaxial mounting, 1x machine gun in hull; Mark V 1x 95mm howitzer, 2x BESA machine guns; Mark VI 1x 75mm gun, 2x BESA machine guns; Mark VII 1x 75mm gun, 2x BESA machine guns; Mark VIII 1x 95mm howitzer, 2x BESA machine guns

TOP SPEED: Marks I to VI 25km/h (15.5 mph); Marks VII and VIII 20 km/h (12.5 mph)

ENGINE: Bedford Twin Six 350hp petrol

the Mark VII. This was the A43 Black Prince, armed with a 17pdr housed in a bigger turret, which in turn required a wider hull. By May 1945, six prototypes had been built, but as the Centurion main battle tank had begun its production run, the project was abandoned.

The Churchill was the first British tank with the Merritt-Brown regenerative steering. This saved a great deal of power and enabled the driver, who steered with a tiller, to make sharper turns, until in neutral he could turn the tank on its axis. The Merritt-Brown system, or variants of it, was to become integral to subsequent tank design.

The Churchill was capable of negotiating the heaviest ground and tackling steep hills which the enemy deemed tank-proof. Moreover, its roomy hull permitted conversion to many other roles, including the Ark (armoured ramp carrier), which could be driven into an anti-tank ditch or against a sea wall, enabling other vehicles to drive over it, and the AVRE (Armoured Vehicle Royal Engineers). Other variants included a gun carrier, of which 24 were built for home defence in 1941; most of these were later converted to carry Snake mine-clearing devices, lengths of explosive-packed three-inch pipe which were pushed into a minefield and detonated.

Churchills first saw action in the disastrous Dieppe raid of 19 August 1942. Only 29 of the 58 tanks of the Calgary Regiment assigned to Operation Jubilee landed; two sank in deep water;

BELOW The Churchill, though originally designed as an infantry tank, really came into its own as the basis for a number of specialised conversions. Here the AVRE, or Armoured Vehicle Royal Engineers, sports the Petard mortar.

OPPOSITE The Churchill Crocodile demonstrates its flame gun. The trailer contained the fuel and nitrogen to pressure the jet. A pipe led through the hull of the tank and the flame jet emerged from the hull machine gun port.

CHURCHILL CROCODILE

The Crocodile was the most effective flame-throwing tank of the war, and on many occasions its mere appearance persuaded troops to surrender after it had fired a few ranging shots. It consisted of Wasp flame-throwing equipment fitted to a Churchill VII, which was coupled to a jettisonable six-and-a-half ton two-wheeled armoured trailer containing 400 gallons (1800 litres) of fuel and the compressed nitrogen propellant for 80 one-second bursts. The trailer was connected to an armoured pipe on the underside of the tank and a projector that replaced the tank's BESA machine-gun. The Churchill could thus still function both as a gun tank and a flame-thrower with a range of 110 metres (120 yards). Some 800 were made during the war, of which 250 were reserved for use in the Far East. Crocodiles served in Normandy and north-west Europe.

12 became bogged down on the shingle beach; 15 made it up to and across the sea wall but found their way blocked by numerous obstacles. They returned to the beach, where they provided support for the Canadian infantry mounting the raid. All the tanks were left behind and their crews killed or captured. The Germans examining the abandoned Churchills formed a low opinion of their armour and armament, rating them below German and Soviet tanks.

A few Mark IIIs were tested at the second Battle of El Alamein in October 1942, and thereafter they were used in Tunisia and Italy. Several brigades of Churchills were deployed in north-west Europe, where their thick armour proved useful, but the tank still found itself outgunned by German armour. The Churchill remained in service until the 1950s.

CHAPTER 17

THE DESERT WAR // 1940

AFTER ITALY'S ENTRY INTO THE WAR ON 10 JUNE 1940, THE ITALIAN ARMY IN LIBYA, COMMANDED BY MARSHAL RODOLFO GRAZIANI, BEGAN LENGTHY PREPARATIONS FOR AN ADVANCE INTO EGYPT, WHICH WAS LAUNCHED BY FIVE ITALIAN DIVISIONS ON 13 SEPTEMBER 1940.

Graziani's army in Libya, with 250,000 men, outnumbered the 60,000 available to his British opponent General Richard O'Connor, the commander of Western Desert Force, but the British had a small but significant edge in armour.

The Italians had some 200 L3 tankettes, armed only with machine guns and which had been no match for Soviet armour in the Spanish Civil War. Heavier weapons were represented by the medium M11/39 and M13/40 tanks, armed respectively with 37mm (1.5in) and 47mm (1.8in) guns. However, their crews had no experience of working with larger formations.

The Italian armour was outmatched by the British Western Desert Force's A9, A10 and A13 cruiser tanks, the last being the first British cruiser to employ the Christie "big wheel"

suspension, which provided excellent cross-country speed. In June 1940, the British armour had been reinforced by 50 Matilda II infantry tanks. The main armament of all these tanks was a 2pdr gun. Most of the British tanks had radios, while the Italian vehicles did not.

Desert laboratory

The flat and deceptively featureless terrain of the Western Desert offered a laboratory in which the theories of armoured warfare developed in the 1930s could be put to the test. However, this was not an exercise in which the Italians were eager to engage. When he reached Sidi Barrani, on the Mediterranean coast near the Egyptian border, Graziani built a ring of fortified positions

ABOVE Italian Autoblinda 41 armoured cars travel down a village street in Libya. The Italian army had equipment of mixed quality. This vehicle was relatively successful with driving positions at the front and rear.

OPPOSITE British A9 tanks leave Egypt for the front. The wartime censor has obliterated the unit markings.

supported by artillery and armour, where he sat, giving General O'Connor and the General Officer Commanding (GOC) Middle East, General Sir Archibald Wavell, a chance to hit back. The odds had swung in their favour; the British now fielded nearly 300 tanks to the enemy's 120 inferior models.

Beda Fomm

On 9 December the British struck at Nibeiwa, where 7th Armoured's Matildas scythed through the Italian armour, destroying or capturing most of it and forcing the Italians into a headlong retreat that did not halt until they reached Beda Fomm, 650 kilometres (400 miles) to the west. The pursuing O'Connor strove to pin the Italians between a thrust delivered down the coast road and a "hook" exploding out of the desert. Combeforce, elements of 7th Armoured Division with armoured cars but no tanks, had been despatched across the desert to intercept the Italian columns streaming south from Benghazi along the Via Balba, the theatre's only tarmac road, which hugged the coastline. On the morning of 5 February 1941, 2,000 men of Combeforce blocked the road near Beda Fomm, while 22 cruisers and 36 light tanks of 4th Armoured Brigade raced to reinforce them.

The British armour arrived that afternoon, and its light tanks immediately launched harassing flank attacks on the extended Italian infantry column, whose 50 M13/40 tanks were straggling in the rear. Italian attempts next day to drive the light tanks off were met by the cruisers of 2nd Battalion, Royal Tank Regiment (2 RTR). At a range of 600 metres (660 yards) eight of the Italian tanks were destroyed or disabled. The British tanks,

ABOVE Here Italian Carro Veloce 33 tankettes show off in a pre-war propaganda shot. The value of them as fighting vehicles was questionable.

RIGHT An Italian helmet with a pad on the front to cushion the head as the wearer looked through the vision devices from inside. The leather neck piece was fitted to protect against bullet splash.

BELOW This Italian vehicle pennant was taken as a souvenir by a British soldier in North Africa.

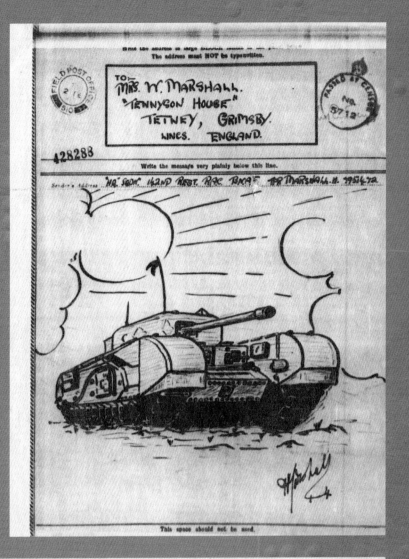

ABOVE AND RIGHT These Airgraph messages cards were sent home to Britain by Herman Marshall of 142nd Regiment Royal Armoured Corps, when he was serving in the Middle East during the Second World War. The Airgraph system was designed in the 1930s by Kodak, but took off only in the Second World War when, to speed the mail and save transport space, messages were drawn or written on a standard template form. These forms were photographed and then sent home by air and printed out on photographic paper for the recipient.

THE MATILDA

SPECIFICATION: MATILDA II

CREW: 4

WEIGHT: 26.5 tons

ARMOUR: 78mm (3.1in)

ARMAMENT: 1x 2pdr gun or 1x 3in howitzer on close-support models. 1x Vickers .303 machine-gun (Mark I) replaced by 1x BESA 7.92 mm on subsequent Marks

TOP SPEED: 24 km/h (15 mph)

ENGINE: Marks I and III 2 AEC 87hp diesel, Marks III-V 2x Leyland 95hp diesel

The shock of the German Blitzkrieg forced the British to develop faster medium and heavy tanks to fight in large multi-tank battles. The role of the infantry tank was to be supplemented by self-propelled artillery. The development of the Matilda tank illustrates this change.

The Matilda I A11 infantry tank, of which 139 were built from 1937, was armed with only one machine gun. The Matilda II was equipped with a 2pdr (40mm) gun, but was issued with non-explosive solid shot which was useless for infantry support. Both the Matilda I and II served in France in 1940, but after the Dunkirk evacuation production of the Mark I was discontinued and the Mark II became known as the Matilda after a cartoon duck of the time. In the Western Desert in 1940–41, the tank acquired the nickname "Queen of the Battlefield".

The Matilda's reign was abruptly ended by the arrival of the German Afrika Korps's dual-purpose 88mm (3.5in) guns. These could knock out the Matilda and the tank began to fade from the battlefield. Attempts to upgun it failed because the turret ring was too small to take a larger gun, and the last Western Desert action in which the Matilda was used was the first Battle of El Alamein in July 1942. However, the Matilda was an ideal vehicle to accommodate special applications and its career was by no means over.

steadily reinforced, flexibly controlled by radio and supported by artillery and anti-tank guns, held the enemy armour at bay well into the following day. Moving from one fire position to another behind ridges which ran parallel to the road, the British cruisers and light tanks inflicted heavy casualties at little cost to themselves. Cyril Joly, an officer with the RTR, watched as an M13/40 "brewed up", every tanker's nightmare: "We were horrified to see a figure with face blackened and clothes alight stumbling through the smoke. He staggered for some yards, then fell and in a frenzy of agony rolled frantically in the hard sand in a desperate effort to put out the flames. But to no avail. Gradually his flailing arms and legs moved more slowly, until at last, with a convulsive heave of his body, he lay still."

Enter Rommel

By 9 February, 7th Armoured Division had reached El Agheila in western Cyrenaica. Here, the Italians surrendered unconditionally. O'Connor, whose supply lines were overstretched, was now halted and ordered to turn his attention to Greece. In just two months, he and Wavell had achieved a remarkable victory. For the loss of just 2,000 casualties, the Western Desert Force had destroyed nine Italian divisions and taken 130,000 prisoners in a drive that had pushed the front forward by some 800 kilometres (500 miles). Greater tests lay ahead. On 12 February, Erwin Rommel arrived in North Africa.

BELOW This Matilda II, built by the North British Locomotive Company in May 1941, is painted to represent "Golden Miller", the tank commanded by Lt Colonel Henry R.B. Foote when he won the Victoria Cross in Libya in June 1942. The "Caunter" paint scheme was used only in the Middle East theatre.

OPPOSITE A Matilda II that has suffered a number of penetrations and "brewed up".

CHAPTER 18

ERWIN ROMMEL // THE DESERT FOX

ROMMEL SERVED AS AN INFANTRYMAN IN THE FIRST WORLD WAR AND WAS AWARDED THE HIGHEST GERMAN DECORATION, THE POUR LE MÉRITE, AFTER THE 1917 CAPORETTO OFFENSIVE AGAINST THE ITALIANS, IN WHICH HE DEMONSTRATED THE DYNAMIC QUALITIES OF LEADERSHIP WHICH CHARACTERIZED HIS CAREER.

As darkness fell on the evening of 12 May 1940, reconnaissance motorcyclists of 7th Panzer Division found an unguarded weir across the Meuse at Houx, north of Sedan. During the night they crossed to the west bank, a distance of some 110 metres (120 yards), where they were joined by reinforcements. The next morning, Rommel's engineers began laying pontoon bridges across the river while his tanks, waiting to cross, destroyed French bunkers. By evening, the bridges were in place and the first of his armour had crossed the Meuse.

Brushing aside a half-hearted French counter-attack, Rommel burst into open country on 15 May, advancing 27 kilometres (17 miles) for the loss of 15 German dead. Racing down the panzer corridor, Rommel was briefly checked at Arras on 21 May by a counter-attack launched under the overall command of Major-General H.E. Franklyn, using the 1st Army Tank Brigade, 6th and 8th Battalions, Durham Light Infantry and elements of the French 3rd Division Légère Méchanique. The attack struck 7th Panzer's right flank as its advanced westward south of Arras and sliced it into two, overrunning two motor rifle regiments. The German 37mm (1.5in) anti-tank guns proved ineffective against the thick armour of the British A11 Matilda infantry tanks.

Rommel succeeded in rallying his division, using the 88mm (3.5in) guns of his anti-aircraft regiment in an anti-tank role, but his report that he was under attack from "hundreds" of tanks played a significant part in the German high command's decision to halt the armoured drive to the coast for 24 hours, contributing to the eventual success of the Dunkirk evacuation.

OPPOSITE TOP **Rommel watches his tanks being offloaded at Tripoli. The Italian defeat at Beda Fomm confirmed Hitler's view that his Italian allies would need assistance and he offered to send at least one Panzer division quickly.**

OPPOSITE BELOW **The Panzers reached the English Channel on 10 June 1940 at Les Petite Dalles in Normandy. Here some German soldiers make the most of the opportunity and take a tank onto the beach for some photos.**

RIGHT **Rommel took no regard of his titular Italian superiors and little regard of orders from Berlin, but he was reliant on logistical support from mainland Europe and often it was the logistics that decided the outcome of campaigns in North Africa.**

North Africa

Early in 1941, Hitler despatched an armoured and motorized expeditionary force, the Afrika Korps, to aid the Italian invasion of Egypt. By the time Rommel arrived in Tripoli on 12 February 1941, the Italians had been driven out of eastern Cyrenaica (Libya) by the British. Technically under the command of the Italians, Rommel nevertheless went straight on to the attack, and by June the Afrika Korps had regained all the territory lost by Germany's allies and were besieging the port of Tobruk, on the Libyan coast, which was held by Australian 9th Division.

Rommel was still learning the ropes of mechanized warfare, but he possessed enormous flair and an innate grasp of mobility in a battlefield environment ideally suited to a man of his temperament. He was also a master of deception, the tactics the Red Army termed maskirovka, and which they would use so well at Kursk in 1943. Rommel had arrived in North Africa with his advance guard, the 5th Light Division, the nucleus of which was 5th Panzer Regiment, comprising 80 PzKpfw IIIs and IVs and 70 PzKpfw Is and IIs. He created the illusion of greater armoured strength with the so-called "Cardboard Division", dummy tanks built of wood and canvas on an automobile chassis. At the start of his first offensive, Rommel used the Cardboard Division to raise great clouds of dust, a ruse which persuaded the British garrison at El Agheila in western Cyrenaica to withdraw, fearing that it was about to be engulfed by an overwhelming armoured assault.

Both the British and the Germans appreciated that in the Western Desert tanks and guns were the dominant weapons. They both saw the destruction of the enemy's armour as the essential preliminary to victory, but Rommel handled his numerically inferior resources with greater skill. British commanders, in contrast, tended to imitate their horsed-cavalry forbears by mounting unsubtle charges at the enemy or failed to exploit fleeting windows of opportunity.

Like all the best panzer commanders, Rommel led from the front – often to the despair of his staff – and possessed a "sixth sense" which time and again brought him to the critical point in the battlefield where British tanks were drawn on to destruction at the hands of his 88mm (3.5in) anti-tank guns. The rapid creation of ad hoc all-arms battle groups, at which the Afrika Korps excelled, was another effective weapon in Rommel's armoury.

Nevertheless, Rommel's sixth sense sometimes betrayed him. In November 1941, German armour, adroitly concentrated and skilfully handled by commanders who enjoyed superior radio communications, took a heavy toll of the British 4th and 22nd Armoured Brigades at Sidi Rezegh, reducing their combined strength of 350 tanks to just 50 "runners". Rommel then tossed away the advantage he had gained by quitting the immediate battle zone to raid the British lines of communication in the expectation that this would force the nervous British into a

RIGHT After arriving in Libya, Rommel paraded his tanks through Tripoli. He had some drive the route more than once to make his force seem more numerous.

general withdrawal. His failure to destroy the mass of disabled British tanks allowed the British to repair them and reconstitute their armoured force at Sidi Rezegh.

When Rommel returned to Sidi Rezegh, his own force had been weakened by several bruising encounters with British artillery and his logistics system was on the verge of collapse. At the beginning of December he was forced to concede defeat and withdraw to El Agheila to lick his wounds.

The Western Desert

Commanders in North Africa's Western Desert were prisoners of the theatre's geography and climate. Both sides had arrived in North Africa with equipment designed to fight in Europe. But as the journalist Alan Moorehead observed, " ... always the desert set the pace, made the direction and planned the design".

The Western Desert was an arid waste. Over long stretches, the landward edge of the coastal plain was bounded by high ground or a steep depression which confined the movement of armies to a narrow 65-kilometre (40-mile) ribbon. The war in North Africa was characterized by a series of advances and retreats along this 1,900-kilometre (1,200-mile) strip, from Tripoli in the west to Alexandria in the east, along which a chain of small ports were the only points of military value. The war took the form of dashes from one point of maritime supply to the next, with the aim of depriving the enemy of water, fuel, ammunition and food, the essentials of desert warfare.

In this contest the British were significantly disadvantaged. Their tanks were outgunned by Rommel's Pzkpfw IIIs and IVs, whose 50mm (2in) and 75mm (3in) guns fired heavier shells over greater distances than their principal British counterparts,

ABOVE The arrival of the American M3 Stuart light tank was welcomed by the British as they came with a level of reliability and ease of maintenance. The expression "It runs like a Honey" gave the tank its nickname.

OPPOSITE The General's Charger, Tmimi. A watercolour painted in Libya, probably by Major Legrand. The tank is a Crusader. The small machine gun turret mounted on the hull next to the driver's hatch has been removed.

the American M3 Stuart, nicknamed "Honey" by the British, and the Crusader cruiser tank. It was very hard for the British tanks to get near enough to loose off a telling shot.

The Germans also benefited from the relative homogeneity of their tanks, which could roam the battlefield at matching speeds and could more easily manoeuvre en masse. Thus, while German armour worked closely together, the British, fielding a multiplicity of types – light tanks, cruisers, infantry tanks and heavy tanks – were too often scattered over the battlefield. The German tanks also worked closely with their superior anti-tank guns, although the British were persuaded to believe that it was the panzers alone, and not the artillery and panzer arms together, that were the principal desert killers.

The situation improved in the spring of 1942 with the arrival in North Africa of the American M3 Grant medium tank, which had 50mm (2in) frontal protection and carried a 75mm (3in) gun mounted in its right-hand sponson. This enabled British Eighth Army to suppress anti-tank guns at long range with HE rounds. But the Grant, with its six-man crew and an additional turret-mounted 37mm (1.5in) gun, was a tricky tank to command. One American maintenance sergeant characterized it as a "cathedral coming down the road", and it was hard to conceal behind a ridge without revealing the turret. Nevertheless, the balance of power in North Africa was beginning to tilt toward the British.

THE CRUSADER

SPECIFICATION: MARK III

CREW: 5

WEIGHT: 19.75 tons

ARMOUR: 51mm (2in)

ARMAMENT: 1x 6pdr, 1x Besa machine gun

TOP SPEED: 43 km/h (27 mph),

ENGINE: Nuffield Liberty 340hp petrol

This was a larger and heavier Cruiser tank intended to replace the earlier A9, A10 and A13 vehicles. The prototype of the Crusader was delivered in March 1940 and a total of 5,300 were built, including some Mk I and II close support models armed with a 3in howitzer in place of the tank's 2pdr gun. Its Christie suspension enabled it to move much faster than its official top speed, achieving speeds as high as 65 km/h (40 mph), a feature that troubled the Afrika Korps. The Crusader suffered from being rushed into service, and in June 1941 during Operation Battleaxe, its first engagement in North Africa, more Crusaders were captured by the Afrika Korps as a result of engine failure. Nevertheless, the Crusader was popular with its crews, fought throughout the North African campaign, and by the time of the Battle of El Alamein was armed with a 6pdr in an enlarged mantlet.

CHAPTER 19

EL ALAMEIN

AFTER ROMMEL'S RETREAT TO EL AGHEILA, HE DID NOT HAVE TO WAIT TOO LONG TO RESUME THE OFFENSIVE. ONCE FIELD MARSHAL ALBERT KESSELRING, COMMANDER-IN-CHIEF OF GERMAN FORCES IN THE MEDITERRANEAN, HAD ESTABLISHED AIR SUPERIORITY IN THE WATERS OFF ITALY, ROMMEL'S SUPPLY LINES BECAME SECURE. CONVOYS COULD NOW CROSS THE MEDITERRANEAN, BRINGING HEAVY ARMOUR AND ANTI-TANK GUNS.

In January 1942, Rommel swept down the coastal road, taking Benghazi, Derna and the western half of Cyrenaica. While the British prepared a counter-attack, Rommel beat them to the punch, routing the Free French – those elements of the armed forces which had continued resisting the Germans, largely in the colonies, after the French surrender in 1940 – at Bir Hacheim and taking Tobruk, with its vital supply harbour, and 33,000 prisoners at the end of June. Now a Field Marshal, Rommel pressed on, fired by the Axis grand strategy which envisaged a scything drive southward from the Caucasus and a north-eastward punch from Egypt in a colossal pincer movement to seize the oil riches of the Middle East.

Although his supply lines were far from secure, Rommel decided to pursue British Eighth Army into Egypt, imposing a further reverse on it at Mersa Matruh before being checked in July at the first Battle of El Alamein by the C-in-C Middle East, Sir Claude Auchinleck. The engagement ended in stalemate,

but the Eighth Army held the strategic advantage because it was operating near its base and was being reinforced at a rate that the overextended Afrika Korps could not match.

Alam Halfa

At the end of August, Rommel renewed his attack with 203 German and 234 Italian tanks, aiming to break through the southern sector of the Alamein line and then swing north to the coast, so compelling Eighth Army to withdraw. This move had been anticipated by Auchinleck, who had prepared a defensive plan that was adopted by the new commander of Eighth Army, General Bernard Montgomery. Having received substantial armoured reinforcements, he now had some 700 tanks to meet Rommel's attack.

Rommel launched his attack on the night of 30/31 August, but was halted south of the Alam Halfa Ridge by a co-ordinated defence in which tanks, artillery, anti-tank guns, ground-

ABOVE "Jock" Fraser of 6th RTR drove Montgomery's Grant tank. He thought a beret would be more practical in the confines of a tank and handed the General his own. Montgomery added the General's badge and later presented the beret to the Tank Museum.

LEFT Both sides used deception as part of their plans. Fake camps were created and false radio traffic broadcast to create an illusion of forces in places there were none. Encampments of trucks were substituted at night with tanks that were then disguised with "sunshields" or covers, therefore not giving away the build-up of armour.

attack aircraft and dense minefields all played their part. On 4 September, Rommel ordered a retreat.

The intervention of the aircraft at Alam Halfa was a sobering phenomenon for the Germans. Dr Alfons Selmayr, of II Abteilung Panzer Regiment 5, recalled:

Now the British air force began to have an effect. We had never experienced anything like it before. Without pause they came over us like squadrons at a [Nazi] Party demonstration and wherever they could see even a few vehicles together they unloaded. My panzer shook at the seams. A Company commander's tank received a direct hit on the turret in front of me. The commander and loader were badly wounded and later died; the gunner and radio operator seriously injured. And apart from a few bandages I had no more medical equipment.

El Alamein

The tables had been turned. Just as the British and French anxiously scanned the skies for Stukas in May 1940, so the Panzerwaffe of late 1942 came to fear Allied air power. Rommel was also now starved of supplies. In September 1942, he had requested 12,000 tons of fuel, 9,000 tons of ammunition and 6,000 tons of rations. In the event, he received only one-ninth of the requested ammunition, less than half the petrol and one-third of the food.

In contrast, men and machines for Eighth Army poured into the North African theatre. When Montgomery launched his offensive just before midnight on 23 October, it fielded 195,000 men; 1,029 tanks plus an immediate reserve of 200 and a further 1,000 in workshops; 2,311 guns; and 750 aircraft, of which 530 were serviceable. The Afrika Korps numbered 104,000 men (50,000 German and 54,000 Italian); 520 tanks, including 31 PzKpfw IIs and 278 Italian M13/40s, in four divisions (15th and 21st Panzer and Ariete and Littorio divisions); 1,219 guns and 675 aircraft, of which 150 German and 200 Italian were serviceable.

Rommel had long anticipated a major Eighth Army offensive, but the opposing commanders represented a contrast in styles. While Rommel was an improviser of genius, Montgomery was the polar opposite, the personification of method. Unlike his British predecessors, who had been easily seduced by the apparent freedom of manoeuvre offered by the desert terrain, Montgomery reached

the pragmatic conclusion that his British armoured divisions lacked the Blitzkrieg flair of their German opposite numbers and so was not prepared to settle for a contest of manoeuvre in which the British usually came off second best. Rather than chase the Afrika Korps back toward Tripoli, a pattern that had been repeated no fewer than three times, he intended to inflict a crushing defeat on the enemy which would entirely eliminate the Axis offensive power.

The Battle of El Alamein was to be initiated by a massive artillery bombardment followed by an infantry assault supported by heavy tanks. Only after the enemy's positions had been ground up in what he described as a "dogfight" would Montgomery launch his main body of armour into and through his positions.

When the bombardment began, at 2200, Montgomery's planning paid off. It was the prelude to an all-arms battle in which all Eighth Army's supporting elements were combined: mine-clearing by engineers, artillery, tanks, anti-tank guns and air support. Only one element was absent, Rommel, who was away on sick leave in

BELOW A briefing before the attack. Montgomery had 1,029 tanks on 23 October ready for the attack, made up of 170 Grant tanks (as seen here), 252 Sherman tanks, 294 Crusaders, 194 Valentines and 119 Stuarts, with a mix of 200 others in reserve.

BOTTOM The attritional stage of the Alamein battle meant the loss of huge quantities of armour on both sides. Here a PzKpfw IV burns. This time the German armoured force was unable to recover its tanks while the Eighth Army ground its way forward.

TYPICAL SMALL ARMS PACKING BOXES

PLATE 1.   Cal. .30 Ball in Cartons

PLATE 2.   Cal. .30 Tracer in Cartons

September, 1942

ABOVE AND OPPOSITE Ammunition manuals were issued to ensure receiving soldiers could clearly identify munitions and understand their nature, markings, colour coding and storage requirements. Given the nature of the information — literally a matter of life and death — the clarity of the drawings was of paramount importance. These pages come from a manual issued to British troops in North Africa explaining new American supplied ammunition.

37M/M GUNS, M3 (A/TK), M5 (TANK) AND M1A1 AND M1A2 (ANTI-AIRCRAFT), CONT.

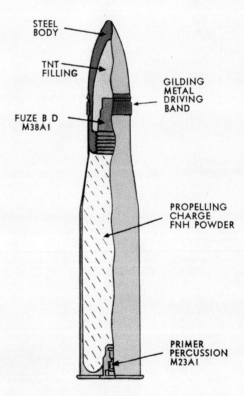

**PLATE 20.   Shell, Fixed, H.E. Mk. II
37m/m Guns, M3 and M5**

September, 1942

155M/M HOWITZERS, M1917-18, CONT.

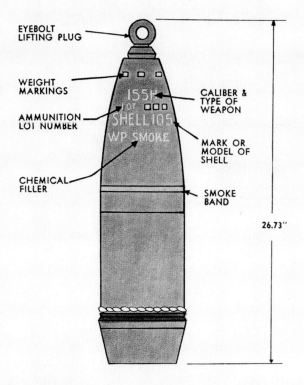

EYEBOLT
LIFTING PLUG

WEIGHT
MARKINGS

CALIBER &
TYPE OF
WEAPON

AMMUNITION
LOT NUMBER

MARK OR
MODEL OF
SHELL

CHEMICAL
FILLER

SMOKE
BAND

26.73"

155M
LOT
SHELL 105
WP SMOKE

**PLATE 27.   Shell, Smoke Phosphorus, W.P.
155m/m Howitzer**

September, 1942

155M/M HOWITZERS, M1917-18, CONT.

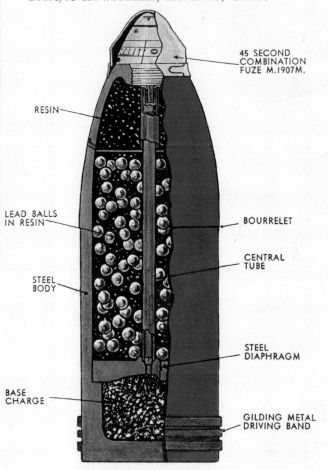

45 SECOND
COMBINATION
FUZE M.1907M.

RESIN

BOURRELET

LEAD BALLS
IN RESIN

CENTRAL
TUBE

STEEL
BODY

STEEL
DIAPHRAGM

BASE
CHARGE

GILDING METAL
DRIVING BAND

**PLATE 29.   Shell, Shrapnel, Mk. I 155m/m
Howitzer—Section**

September, 1942

M3 GRANT MEDIUM TANK

SPECIFICATION: M3 (GRANT/LEE)

CREW: 6 (Grant) 7 (Lee)

WEIGHT: 27 tons

ARMOUR: 65mm (2.6in)

ARMAMENT: 1x 75mm (sponson-mounted) gun, 1 x 37mm gun (turret-mounted), 4 x .303 machine-guns

TOP SPEED: 42 km/h (26 mph)

ENGINE: Wright radial 340hp petrol or Chrysler 5-unit multibank 370hp petrol or twin General Motors diesel producing 375hp

European battlefield experience in 1939–40 demonstrated that the 37mm (1.5in) gun of the American M2 medium tank would not be powerful enough for modern warfare and a successor emerged in the M3 Grant/Lee, which entered service in the U.S. and British armies in 1941.

In 1940, a British tank commission arrived in the United States with the intention of ordering British-designed tanks from American firms. The U.S. National Defense Advisory Committee, fearing imminent British defeat, refused to allow tanks to be produced to British designs. The British settled for a version of the M3, which incorporated a larger cast-iron turret than the standard version to conform with the British practice of mounting the vehicle's radio in the turret, where it was operated by the loader. The tank deployed a multiplicity of weapons in three tiers. The tank commander could operate the .303 Browning machine gun in the independently rotating cupola, while the turret gunner could engage armour with the 37mm (1.5in) anti-tank gun or infantry with the co-axial Browning, and the 75mm (3in) hull-mounted gun could fire either AP or HE ammunition.

Before the Grant, British tank crews' escape route from a knocked-out vehicle was by climbing out of the top. The Grant afforded an easier route through large opening side doors.

The tank first saw action in the Western Desert in the Gazala/Knightsbridge battles in 1942, the first time Eighth Army achieved any kind of parity with the 75mm (3in) gun of the PzKpfw IV. It also participated in the Battles of Alam Halfa and El Alamein and the pursuit of the Afrika Korps to Tunisia, by which time it was being gradually replaced by the Sherman. During the time when Eighth Army's fortunes were at their lowest ebb, the Grant was nicknamed the ELH, or "Egypt's Last Hope". A total of 6,258 M3s were produced, of which 3,352 rolled off the Chrysler production lines in the first example of the application of automobile production methods to the manufacture of armoured fighting vehicles.

Germany. He hurried back to North Africa, arriving on 25 October.

The first phase of the British offensive involved a diversionary attack by XIII Corps to the south, while to the north the infantry of XXX Corps strove to cut two corridors through dense belts of minefields, across which 1st and 10th Armoured Divisions could be passed. Progress was slow, but Montgomery, keenly aware of Rommel's Achilles heel, his acute shortage of fuel, decided to fight what he called a "crumbling battle", switching the Schwerpunkt from sector to sector and

compelling the Axis armour to react. The superior battlefield reflexes of the German armour ensured that the Eighth Army sustained the heavier losses but the rate of attrition could not be maintained. By 3 November, Rommel had only 30 serviceable tanks at his disposal and the next day he began to extract his remaining forces. In contrast, Eighth Army's tank armoured casualties numbered some 500, and of these many were repaired.

Aftermath

Montgomery fulfilled his orders from General Harold Alexander (who had succeeded Auchinleck in August 1942) to defeat Rommel, but the insufficient preparation he made to finish off the Afrika Korps lays his handling of the battle open to much criticism. Montgomery had brought up 7th Armoured Division from the southern sector to act as a mobile reserve. As soon as a breakthrough had been made to the depth of the Afrika Korp's defences, the division was to strike into Rommel's rear and encircle him with his back to the sea. The pursuit was poorly executed. As Liddell Hart concluded:

After the event, the rain formed the main excuse for the failure to cut off Rommel's retreat. But in analysis, it becomes clear that the best opportunities had already been forfeited before the rain intervened – by too narrow moves, by too much caution, by too little sense of the time-factor, by unwillingness to push on in the dark, and by concentrating too closely on the battle to keep in mind the essential requirements of its decisive exploitation.

However, in mitigation, Montgomery confided in his diary on the eve of battle:

… the training [of Eighth Army] was not good and it was beginning to come clear to me that I would have to be very careful … that formations and units were not given tasks which were likely to end in failure because of their low standard of training … I must not be too ambitious in my demands.

ABOVE A pause in the fighting on October 31 – here Valentine tanks and their crews of the 40th Royal Tank Regiment mingle with Australian infantry at Thompson's post – a bitterly fought-over position that drew in costly German infantry and armour counter-attacks.

OPPOSITE An M3 at Fort Knox in June 1942. The M3 was really an interim model tank as American industry geared up to make the turreted (and more complex) Sherman. For British service the M3 became the Grant Medium tank and had a new turret to house the radio and no large commander's cupola, meaning the tank was a foot lower in height.

CHAPTER 20

BARBAROSSA // TANKS ON THE EASTERN FRONT

THE INVASION OF THE SOVIET UNION, CODENAMED BARBAROSSA (AFTER THE HOLY ROMAN EMPEROR FREDERICK BARBAROSSA), WAS PLANNED TO BE THE LAST OF HITLER'S SHORT WARS AND THE GREATEST DEMONSTRATION OF BLITZKRIEG. BOTH THE GERMAN HIGH COMMAND AND MILITARY OBSERVERS IN THE WEST CONFIDENTLY PREDICTED THAT THE RED ARMY, REELING FROM THE IMPACT, WOULD BE DEFEATED IN A MATTER OF WEEKS.

The invasion began at 3.30 a.m. on 22 June 1941. Eleven new panzer divisions had been raised for Barbarossa, swelling the four panzer groups (Panzergruppen) to 19 armoured divisions spearheading seven infantry armies in the largest operation in the history of warfare. Three million soldiers, supported by 3,850 tanks, 7,184 guns and nearly 2,000 aircraft were on the move along a front stretching from Memel on the Baltic to Odessa on the Black Sea, a distance of 1,600 kilometres (1,000 miles).

Army Group North, commanded by Field Marshal Ritter von Leeb, was to attack from East Prussia toward Leningrad, aided by the Finns advancing into the Karelian Isthmus. The strongest formation, Army Group Centre, under Field Marshal Fedor von

Bock, would drive north of the natural barrier of the freshwater Pripet marshes to Smolensk, the route Napoleon had followed in 1812. To the south, Field Marshal von Rundstedt's Army Group South was to advance to the Ukraine, the Soviet Union's breadbasket, and the oil-rich industrial areas of the Donets, the Volga and the Caucasus. The cream of the Ostheer (the German Army of the East) was set to push forward into a vast area of steppe, forest and swamp.

The armoured divisions moved forward under an immense pall of dust. In the vanguard, fighting vehicles – light panzers, motorcycle troops and infantry riding in sidecars – were arrayed in wedge-like arrowheads, anticipating enemy contact.

ABOVE Soviet soldiers examine a captured PzKpfw II. Although it was considered obsolescent by 1941, due to a shortage of more modern vehicles, around 700 of the 3850 German tanks that took part in Barbarossa were PzKpfw IIs.

OPPOSITE The crew of a BT-7 survey the landscape. Communications in most pre-war Soviet vehicles were basic, often relying on flag signals with only command variant tanks carrying radios.

Next came medium and heavy panzers accompanied by lorry-borne light infantry and, bringing up the rear, motorized towed artillery.

The Red Army, in the middle of a wholesale reorganization and deployed forward to cover every curve and crevice in the Soviet frontier, was chewed up in a series of massive "cauldron battles" (Kesselschlacht). By the end of the first week in July, the Oberkommando Des Heeres (OKH, the German Supreme Army Command) concluded that 89 of an estimated 164 Soviet divisions could be struck off the Red Army's order of battle.

At Minsk and Smolensk in July, Army Group Centre had taken 400,000 prisoners, 3,100 guns and 3,200 T28, T26 and BT tanks, but at a huge cost to the Ostheer, prompting the commander of 18th Panzer Division to express fears that the loss of German men and equipment would ultimately prove insupportable "if we do not intend to win ourselves to death". Three months of

Tanks and the tyranny of distance

Two factors swung the balance on the Eastern Front. The first was technical, with the arrival in the front line of the Red Army's T-34 medium tank and KV-1 heavy tank. The T-34 proved the Red Army's battle winner and more than a match for the PzKpfw IIIs and IVs, in spite of the latter's three-man turret arrangement, compared with the T-34's two-man configuration. Colonel (later Major-General) F.W. von Mellenthin later recalled:

Guderian described how his XXIV Panzer Corps was violently attacked to the northeast of Orel on 11 October 1941 and remarked significantly, 'Numerous Russian T-34s went into action and inflicted heavy losses on the German tanks. Up to this time we had enjoyed tank superiority, but from now on the situation was reversed.

The KV-1 was the most formidable tank in the world at the time of its appearance in 1941, and the Red Army the only army equipped with heavy tanks in production. It could defeat almost every weapon that the Germans could throw at it and its reliable 600hp diesel engine gave it a range of more than 320 kilometres (200 miles). What held the KV-1 back in the early stages of Barbarossa was the poor training of the Red Army's tank crews and the inferior facilities with which they were provided.

Russia's topography and climate also proved formidable enemies for the Ostheer. The great spaces of Russia proved too big even for the Germany armies and, as they drove ever deeper into them, their supply lines and central maintenance and repair systems became progressively longer and more fragile. This hit the armoured divisions the hardest. Because the Soviet rail gauge was different to the German, and relaying the track could not match the pace of the Ostheer's advance, the back-loading of damaged vehicles became impossible and the forward transit of spares broke down.

The Russian climate took a grip as the autumnal mud season

LEFT A German officer points to an 88mm (3.5in) round wedged in a KV-1 tank. Other strike marks from rounds that have failed to penetrate can also be seen. Standard German anti-tank guns had little effect on the KV1.

ABOVE A Soviet tank commander surrenders. Stalin later had many brave soldiers who had fought well, surrendered, and miraculously survived German internment, shot for failing in their duty.

victory had cost the Germans over half a million casualties. The cauldron battles also cost the Germans unanticipated casualties as isolated Soviet pockets sought to break out of the encirclements, forcing the diversion of offensive mobile forces to defensive battles, a task for which they were unsuited. In 1941 the Ostheer lost 2,500 tanks in Russia alone, compared to a total production that year of 3,623, of which only 467 were PzKpfw IVs. The rest were already obsolescent.

(rasputitsa) dominated until the Germans were driven out of the Soviet Union. This insoluble problem, repeated every spring, was exacerbated by the wretched conditions of the Russian road system, which prompted Liddell Hart to observe:

If the Soviet regime had given her [Russia] a road system comparable to that of western countries, she would probably have been overrun in quick time. The German mechanized forces were baulked by the badness of her roads. But this conclusion has a converse. The Germans lost the chance of victory because they had based their mobility on wheels instead of tracks. On these mud roads the wheeled transport was bogged down when the tanks could move on. Panzer forces with tracked transport might have overrun Russia's vital centres long before the autumn, despite the bad roads.

Blitzkrieg breaks down

In October 1941, the first snows of winter began to fall. Hitler was now caught between driving straight for Moscow or reinforcing his extended southern flank to secure the raw materials and agricultural riches of the Ukraine. With the arrival of winter – for which the German high command had not equipped the Ostheer – the advance slowed amid temperatures so low that they welded artillery pieces into immovable blocks. Some German patrols reached a tram terminus on the outskirts of Moscow, from where they could see the domes of the Kremlin glinting in the winter sun. Then, on 6 December the Red Army counter-attacked with fresh and well-equipped divisions rushed from Siberia. Although in the battles around Moscow, the Red

CLOSE ENCOUNTER WITH THE KV-2

Two days into Barbarossa, 6th Panzer Division found its supply route blocked by an unknown tank. Believed to have been a KV-2, it stayed there for two days. Its first victims were 12 supply trucks, which were then followed by two 50mm (2in) anti-tank guns. An 88mm (3.5in) gun was knocked out at a range of over 900 metres (1,000 yards). The Germans then mounted a night raid in which two satchel charges were attached to the Russian tank. They were blown, but the tank continued to fire. Next morning, a feint attack was made by light panzers while another 88mm (3.5in) gun was brought up to finish the tank off. The tank was finally silenced when two assault engineers pushed stick grenades through a hole at the base of the turret. Only two of the 88mm (3.5in) rounds fired at the KV-2 had penetrated its armour, while the 50mm (2in) shells had succeeded only in leaving blue carbonized streak marks on its hull.

Army was unable to encircle large German groupings because it lacked the necessary tank formations (as Stavka had not yet re-established sufficient tank and mechanized corps and tank armies following their disbandment in 1940) it still drove Army Group Centre back 320 kilometres (200 miles) before the offensive slithered to a halt in the spring thaw of 1942. Blitzkrieg had met its match.

ABOVE A German column of PzKfpw II tanks stops as the Russian winter descends. The Wehrmacht was ill prepared for the temperatures they encountered in Russia which could reach below freezing, and men and vehicles suffered. Sentry duty had to be limited to 15 minute-watches to stop troops suffering frostbite.

OPPOSITE A KV-1 crewman reloads with main armament ammunition for the 76mm (3in) gun and drums of 7.62mm (0.3in) ammunition for the DT machine gun.

CHAPTER 21

T-34

THE T-34/76, THE BACKBONE OF SOVIET ARMOUR IN THE SECOND WORLD WAR, PROVIDED A SUPERB BALANCE BETWEEN MOBILITY, PROTECTION AND FIREPOWER AND IS WIDELY REGARDED AS THE FOUNDATION OF MODERN TANK DESIGN. IT WAS THE ONE OF THE WEAPONS THAT CAN BE DESCRIBED, WITHOUT RESERVATION, AS A WAR-WINNER, AND FOUGHT FROM 1941 TO 1945. INTENDED AS A REPLACEMENT FOR THE BT SERIES OF CRUISER TANKS, THE T-34'S DESIGN WAS CARRIED OUT BY A TEAM HEADED BY MIKHAIL KOSHKIN AT THE KHARKOV LOCOMOTIVE WORKS.

Rugged ride

Introduced in 1941, the T-34 made few concessions to crew comfort. Initially it lacked a radio and a turret with an all-round sight for its commander. It had a crew of four: the driver and the hull gunner, who sat in armchair-style seats in the forward part of the tank, the latter operating the T-34's gas-operated Degtyarev 7.62mm (0.3in) machine gun; and the turret crew of loader and commander (who also doubled as the gunner), laying and firing in a cramped turret.

The commander and the loader sat on padded seats mounted on a tubular support, each provided with a wide cushioned backrest fitted to the turret ring. Since the turret crew's seats were also attached to the turret ring, they did not revolve with the gun as the turret traversed, obliging both loader and commander to squirm in their seats as the gun swung around.

In battle, the tank commander shouted directions by microphone to the driver, who had only a restricted view, while bellowing orders to the loader as to the type of ammunition he wanted, ducking down to the periscope or cranked telescope sight to lay the gun, working out the range, opening fire and then keeping himself well clear of the 76.2mm (0.3in) gun as it lunged back for a full 35cm (14in) on recoil. This left him little time to see what the other tanks in his formation were doing. By using a hand trigger attached to the main armament to fire the gun, the overworked commander could remain in the turret for long periods.

Life was further complicated by an electric-powered traverse that frequently broke down, requiring the commander-gunner to haul the tank's heavy turret round with a manually operated traverse. This was so awkwardly placed that it contorted him into a crouching position, cranking away, while he strove to

ABOVE The Soviet government provided a number of tanks for inspection to the British and American forces in the Second World War and a report was written on the T34 by the School of Tank Technology in Chertsey. Here a detailed cross section from the report shows many of the component parts of the T34/76 tank.

keep his head firmly pressed against the sight's rubber eye guard which let in distracting amounts of light.

The loader had an equally stressful time. Of the 77 rounds carried by the T-34/76 (on average, 19 AP, 53 HE and five shrapnel) only nine were immediately accessible. The remaining 68 rounds were distributed in eight metal bins at the bottom of the turret, covered by rubber matting which formed the turret floor. In any action in which more than a handful of rounds were fired without an appreciable pause, the loader had to start uncovering and dismantling the turret floor in order to replenish the gun. Struggling amid a tangle of bins and matting, he faced an extra hazard every time the gun was fired, discharging a very hot shell case into the debris.

These drawbacks were outweighed by the T-34's modified suspension, a version of the same Christie system that had astonished foreign observers in the 1930s, permitting high speeds, even over rough terrain. Its broad tracks reduced ground pressure to a minimum and ensured that it remained mobile in mud or snow, ever-present seasonal factors on the Eastern Front in the Second World War. A durable all-weather diesel engine gave the tank an excellent power-to-weight ratio and a range of 300 kilometres (186 miles), three times greater than the Tiger and almost double that of the Panther, and of crucial importance in the great spaces of the Soviet Union. Sloping

armour considerably increased resistance to shell penetration and its long-barrelled 76.2mm (0.3in) high-velocity gun completed a well-balanced design which facilitated rapid mass production and easy repair and maintenance in the field.

The German View

The T-34 accounted for 68 per cent of all Soviet tank production in the Second World War. German commanders had a healthy respect for it. Major-General F.W. von Mellenthin, who served on the Eastern Front as Chief of Staff to XLVIII Panzer Corps and Fourth Panzer Army, recalled the tank's high quality: "These tanks were not thrown into the battle in large numbers until our spearheads were approaching Moscow; they then played a great part in saving the Russian capital."

Even so, the moment the fighting became fluid, Soviet tank formations were always likely to be shot up by experienced German units, even when the latter were heavily outnumbered. A tank crew member from 6th Panzer Division wrote: "We had one advantage – mobility. They were like a herd of buffalo which does not have the freedom of movement enjoyed by the leopards which prowl around the flanks of the herd – and we were the leopards."

Describing the "cauldron battles" of 1942, a German staff officer was highly critical of the Soviet armoured formations:
In tight masses they groped around in the main battle; they moved

ABOVE Cleaning the barrel of the 76mm (3in) gun. The T34, like other mass-produced tanks made at different factories, shows many variations in design and detailing, as new modifications were made and old parts used up.

IS-2 HEAVY TANK

SPECIFICATION // IOSIF STALIN 2

CREW: 4

WEIGHT: 46 tons

ARMOUR: 160mm (6.3in)

ARMAMENT: 1x 122mm gun 2x7.62mm machine guns

TOP SPEED: 37 km/h (23 mph)

ENGINE: V21S 520hp diesel

In October 1943, directions for the mass production of the new tank, the Iosif Stalin (IS), were issued. The new tank, the IS-1, was lighter than the KV-1 but had thicker, better shaped armour that provided greater protection.

Its main armament was an 85mm (3.35in) gun, the same as that carried by the T-34/85, but this left it with no more hitting power than a medium tank. At the end of October 1943, the IS-2, fitted with a 122mm (4.8in) gun, was accepted as standard and the IS-1s were upgunned. The IS-2 was a match for the Panther, and the Tiger could only penetrate its armour at under 1,750 metres (1,900 yards), a range at which it was itself vulnerable to the IS-2's 122mm (4.8in) gun. In early 1944, the IS-2 began entering service with heavy tank regiments. As more IS-2s became available, a heavy regiment was attached to each tank corps whenever possible, and eventually heavy tank brigades were formed, each comprising three IS-2 regiments. Some 3,400 IS-2s were built during the war and remained in service until well into the 1950s. The IS-3, of which some 350 were built before the end of the Second World War, did not see action before the war ended. It retained the 122mm (4.8in) gun but benefited from an improved armour layout, the principal features of which were a low, domed turret and well-angled hull armour. It remained in service with some armies until the 1960s. The final model abandoned the use of the IS prefix as the result of de-Stalinization.

hesitantly and without any plan. They got in each other's way, they blundered against our anti-tank guns, or, after penetrating our front, they did nothing to exploit their advantage and stood inactive and idle. Those were the days when isolated German anti-tank guns … would shoot up and knock out more than 30 tanks an hour.

In the autumn of 1943, the T-34 adopted an 85mm (3.35in) gun and was re-designated the T-34/85. By the end of 1943, 283 had been built, and in the following 12 months another 11,000 came off the production line. The T-34/85 remained in production into the mid-1950s and in service with other armies around the world for decades longer.

LEFT The manufacture of the T34 in wartime conditions was one of the great success stories of the Soviet Union. Whole factories were moved further East, away from the advancing Germans behind the safety of the Ural mountains.

CHAPTER 22

OPERATION ZITADELLE // THE BATTLE OF KURSK

BY JANUARY 1943 THE TIDE OF WAR HAD TURNED AGAINST THE GERMANS ON THE EASTERN FRONT. THE SURRENDER OF GERMAN SIXTH ARMY AT STALINGRAD WAS FOLLOWED BY A MASSIVE SOVIET COUNTER-OFFENSIVE BETWEEN OREL AND ROSTOV, WHICH THREATENED KHARKOV AND THE GERMAN FORCES WITHDRAWING FROM THE CAUCASUS.

This was halted in its tracks by a brilliantly weighted counterblow delivered in February-March 1943 by Field Marshal Erich von Manstein, commander of Army Group South. When the fighting died down in the mud of the spring thaw, it left a huge fist-shaped salient around the city of Kursk, jutting westward from the heartland of Ukraine into the German line.

The Kursk bulge exercised a horrible fascination on Hitler. He told Guderian, now reinstated as Inspector of Armoured Troops, that every time he thought of the impending attack on the salient his stomach turned over. To excise the bulge, the German high command planned a concentric attack against its northern and southern shoulders. This would trap the Red Army forces inside, where they could be destroyed piecemeal.

The massive German preparations for the operation, codenamed Zitadelle (Citadel), took three months. The Soviets were well informed about them by the Lucy spy network in Switzerland; by John Cairncross, a Soviet mole inside the British code-breaking station at Bletchley Park; and by a laundered version of the intelligence passed to them through official British channels.

As a result Stavka, the Soviet General Staff, had ample time to strengthen the defences of the Kursk salient, which by the end of June was held by two Red Army Fronts (Army Groups), Central and Voronezh, and was packed with 1.3 million men, with 100 guns per kilometre (60 guns per mile) on the likely axes of advance. Some 2,000 tanks and self-propelled guns had reinforced the defences, with a strong reserve held back in Steppe Front's Fifth Guards Tank Army. In the north and

south of the salient were deeply echeloned eight-line defensive networks, comprising dense minefields and trench systems linking anti-tank strongpoints. In addition, the Russians deployed a wide range of deception measures (maskirovka). These included the creation of false troop concentrations and the construction and deployment of dummy tank and air armies and some 40 false airfields, complete with dummy aircraft, runways and control towers. These were repeatedly bombed by the Luftwaffe in the run-up to the battle. The Red Army plan was to absorb the German onslaught before launching a counter-offensive.

For Zitadelle, Manstein had at his disposal two Army Groups – Centre (commanded by Field Marshal Günther von Kluge) and South, together fielding some 900,000 men and 2,380 tanks and assault guns, supported by 2,500 aircraft. The most

OPPOSITE The Kursk battle saw the introduction of the Panther. The tank had numerous teething issues causing transmission failures, and the employment of 192 of the tanks by Army Group South was a disaster. By the end of 5 of July, the first day of the attack, only 40 Panthers remained operational.

ABOVE Infantry tank riders descend and accompany KV-1 tanks into the attack. By this stage of the war the KV-1 was becoming a rarer sight on the battlefield as Soviet production switched to the T34/85 and IS series of tanks.

powerful armoured division in Manstein's order of battle was Grossdeutschland, part of Fourth Panzer Army on the southern shoulder of the salient. It was equipped with 163 tanks and 35 assault guns, plus a company of 14 PzKpfw VI Tigers and two battalions of PzKpfw V Panthers, which had arrived at the front in June. The panzer and panzergrenadier divisions which were to spearhead Zitadelle had all been rested, refitted and brought up to strength, although the loss of battle-hardened personnel and experienced leaders during the winter fighting was keenly felt. The panzergrenadier division had evolved within the German Army as a motorized infantry formation to augment the true panzer division, but as the war progressed, the distinction between the two became increasingly blurred, particularly within the SS, as their allotment of armoured fighting vehicles (AFVs) grew larger.

Manstein and General Walter Model, commanding Ninth Army on the northern shoulder of the salient, adopted different tactics to break open the Red Army defences. Model, confident that he had an adequate ratio of infantry to armour, decided to use infantry, combat engineers and artillery to open breaches in the Russian lines into which he would feed his panzers. On the southern shoulder, Manstein, anxious that he did not have enough infantry to sustain similar tactics, planned to use his armour to punch a hole in the Russian lines.

The instrument for Manstein's chosen tactical option was the Panzerkeil ("armoured wedge") with Tigers at the tip and Panthers and PzKpfw IVs fanning out behind, followed by infantry armed with automatic weapons and grenades. At the base of the wedge were more heavily armed panzergrenadiers, carried in tracked personnel carriers. Once they had broken into the Russian trench system, the momentum of the panzers was to be maintained at all costs. Tank crews were given strict orders that, in no circumstances, should they stop to assist disabled vehicles.

When Hitler launched the Zitadelle attack against the shoulders of the salient on 4 July, the German armoured spearheads were caught in the killing grounds prepared by Zhukov and mangled beyond recovery. In the south on 12 July, at the northernmost point of the advance spearheaded by Fourth Panzer Army, II SS Panzer Corps slammed headlong into Fifth Guards Tank Army, which was hastening up from the Steppe Front strategic reserve. An armoured melee which ensued at Prokhorovka was the largest tank battle in the Second World War. As armoured vehicles clashed at point-blank range, II SS Panzer Corps was stopped dead in its tracks. In an area no bigger than 8 square kilometres (3 square miles) some 300 German tanks and self-propelled guns engaged over 600 Soviet tanks.

RIGHT Panther Ausf. D are inspected ready for delivery. The cost of a Panther, less gun and radio, was calculated in June 1944 as 76,000 Reich Marks compared to 250,000 Reich Marks for a Tiger I also without gun or radio.

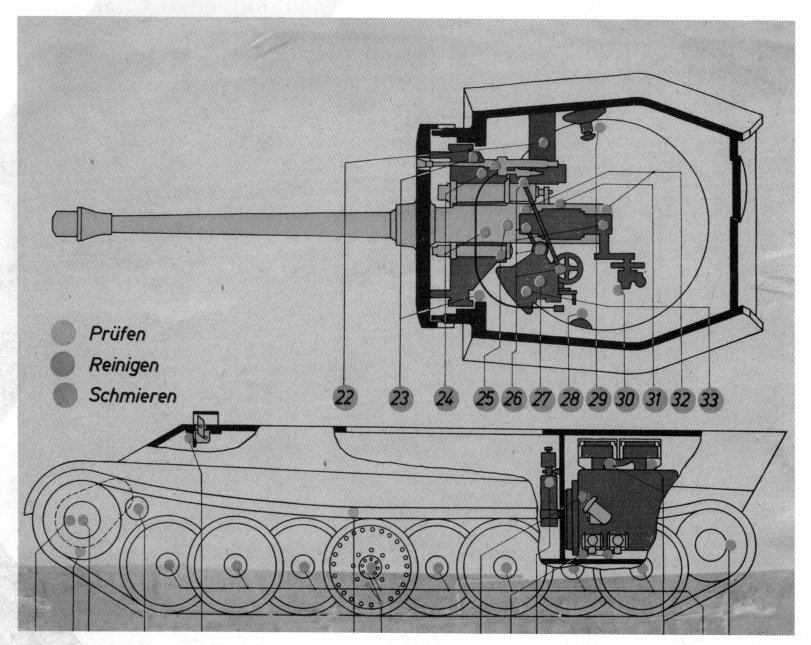

Prüfen

Reinigen

Schmieren

22 23 24 25 26 27 28 29 30 31 32 33

The fighting was ferocious. Helmut Steiner of 9th Panzer Division, driving a PzKpfw IV in his first engagement, recalled that the tank next to him blew up in an orange sheet of flame. He kept his foot pressed to the accelerator until "the bones in my foot ached under the pressure". A momentarily blinded Soviet survivor from a wrecked tank staggered across his path, and he glimpsed the wretched man's face through the vision slit, "a frozen picture compounded of shock, terror and astonishment – before he disappeared beneath the tracks".

Lieutenant Rudolf von Ribbentrop, a company commander in the SS panzergrenadier division Leibstandarte Adolf Hitler, was horrified by the number of Soviet tanks on the battlefield:

From beyond the shallow rise about 150 to 200 metres [500 to 650 feet] in front of me appeared 15, then thirty, then 40 tanks. Finally there were too many to count. The T-34s were rolling towards us at high speed, carrying mounted infantry … Soon the first shell was on the way, and with the impact a T-34 began

to burn. It was only 50 to 70 meters [165 to 230 feet] from us … The avalanche of enemy tanks rolled straight towards us: tank after tank!

At Prokhorovka, II SS Panzer Corps inflicted heavy losses on Fifth Guards Tank Army, knocking out or damaging 400 vehicles at relatively small cost to itself. However, for many of its men the battle was the last straw. The slog through the Red Army's defences in which, before the clash at Prokhorovka, it had lost 330 tanks and assault guns, had already depressed morale to the point where the will to press home attacks against strong Soviet resistance was fast slipping away. No sooner had the German thrusts in the north and south of the salient been contained than the Red Army delivered a series of crushing counter-attacks, which by September 1943 had driven the Ostheer back to the line of the River Dnieper.

ABOVE This diagram shows the key lubrication points on the Panther that would have to be attended to.

OPPOSITE While the Germans had copied the wide tracks of the T34, its sloped armour and manoeuvrability, they had failed to grasp the Soviet insistence on simplicity of manufacture, allowing large numbers to be built. This cross-section of a Panther gearbox shows the complexity of the item, despite the stated aim of simplifying the vehicle for mass production.

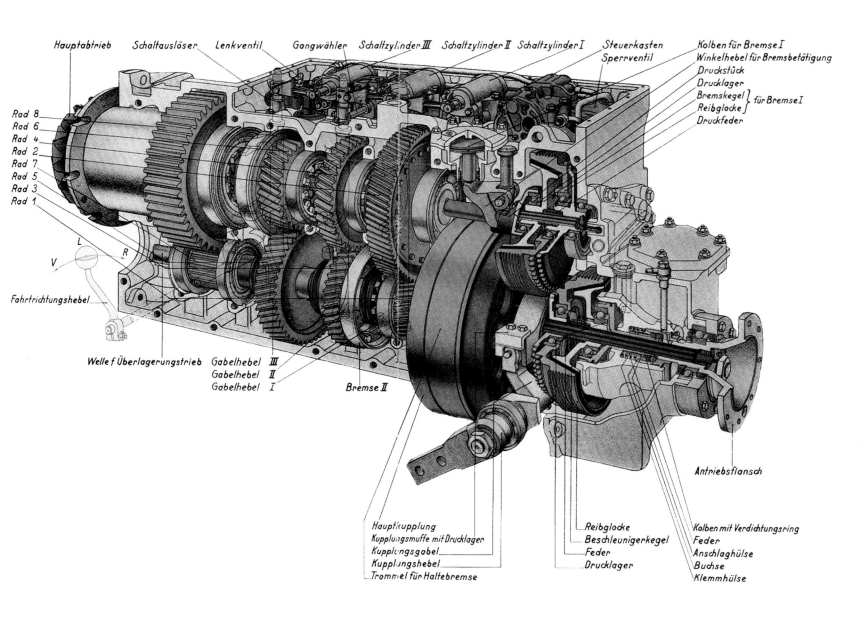

Hauptabtrieb — Schaltauslöser — Lenkventil — Gangwähler — Schaltzylinder III — Schaltzylinder II — Schaltzylinder I — Steuerkasten Sperrventil — Kolben für Bremse I — Winkelhebel für Bremsbetätigung — Druckstück — Drucklager — Bremskegel } für Bremse I — Reibglocke } — Druckfeder

Rad 8
Rad 6
Rad 4
Rad 2
Rad 7
Rad 5
Rad 3
Rad 1

L
V — R

Fahrtrichtungshebel

Welle f Überlagerungstrieb — Gabelhebel III — Gabelhebel II — Gabelhebel I — Bremse II

Hauptkupplung
Kupplungsmuffe mit Drucklager
Kupplungsgabel
Kupplungshebel
Trommel für Haltebremse

Reibglocke
Beschleunigerkegel
Feder
Drucklager

Kolben mit Verdichtungsring
Feder
Anschlaghülse
Buchse
Klemmhülse

Antriebsflansch

PZKPFW V PANTHER

SPECIFICATION // PZKPFW V PANTHER

CREW: 5

WEIGHT: 43–45.5 tons

ARMOUR: 120mm (4.7in)

ARMAMENT: 1x 75mm L/70 gun, 2 x 7.92 mm machine guns

TOP SPEED: Speed: 55 km/h (34 mph)

ENGINE: Maybach HL230 P30 700hp petrol

The Panther was the German response to the T-34. It incorporated the T-34's principal features – sloped armour, speed and manoeuvrability. Hitler took a close interest in the design stage and the first production tank rolled off the Maschinenfabrik Augsburg-Nürnberg (MAN) line in January 1943. The most notable features of the Panther were its 75mm (3in) L/70 gun, sloped glacis, wide tracks and interleaved suspension. However, the speed with which the Panther was rushed into production resulted in mechanical unreliability in the transmission and steering linkages. The engine also had a tendency to overheat, as happened when the Panther made its debut at Kursk, where it frequently caught fire. Later modifications eased the Panther's teething troubles and it went on to equip one of each Panzer regiment's two battalions. Three major versions were produced, the Model D, Model A and finally the Model G. Some 3,740 Panthers were Model Gs. The Panther's most notable derivative was the Jagdpanther tank destroyer, but command, artillery observation post and recovery versions were also produced.

CHAPTER 23

ENTER THE TIGER

AT THE TIME OF ITS INTRODUCTION IN 1942, AND FOR SOME TIME AFTERWARD, THE PZKPFW VI TIGER I WAS THE MOST POWERFUL TANK IN THE WORLD. IT WAS RIGHTLY FEARED, AND THE COUGH OF A TIGER'S ENGINES STARTING UP IN THE DISTANCE WAS SOMETHING ALL ALLIED SOLDIERS REMEMBERED WITH RESPECT MINGLED WITH APPREHENSION.

The Tiger's origins lay in pre-war concepts for the development of heavier Panzers, spurred on by encounters with heavily-armoured French and British tanks in 1940. In April 1941, it was specified to carry the 88mm (3.5in) high-velocity gun. Development was accelerated after a meeting with Hitler the next month, and further hastened by encounters with the latest Soviet tanks.

Porsche and Henschel competed for the contract. Porsche's unconventional plans for the Tiger, which included provision for electric transmission, were rejected by the Army Ordnance Office. Henschel secured the contract but, undismayed, Porsche pressed on with urgent projects for the army's artillery arm, including a new generation of tank destroyers, diverting resources from the development of the Tiger, which was prematurely committed to battle in August-September 1942 on the Eastern Front.

Disastrous debut

Like a small schoolboy with a new train set, Hitler always wanted to use his new weapons immediately they became available, forfeiting the advantage of surprise and employment en masse. The first batch of Tigers was thrown into action piecemeal in a secondary operation in the swampy forests near Leningrad where, lumbering in single file along the forest tracks, they were picked off by Soviet anti-tank guns.

Despite this inauspicious introduction, the Tiger emerged as a formidable weapon. Its gun, which had 92 rounds of ammunition, packed a heavy punch and outranged the T-34. The Tiger's 88mm (3.5in) shell could penetrate 112mm (4.4in) of armour at 450 metres (500 yards) and as a result was later much feared by the crews of M4 Shermans, the main Allied tank in Western Europe. This sharp imbalance of power reflects the differing approaches adopted by the Allies and the Germans to the trade-off between mass and technology. The Germans opted for the latter, while the Americans, with their immeasurably bigger industrial base, chose the former. This American concentration on agile, lighter tanks left British and American tank crews at a disadvantage against more heavily armed and armoured opponents.

The Tiger's armour was not well sloped, but it had a thickness of 100mm (3.9in) at the front and 80mm (3.1in) around the sides. The tank weighed 56 tons, which limited its cross-country speed to 19 km/h (12 mph) and its operational range to some 95 kilometres (60 miles), while imposing a severe strain on

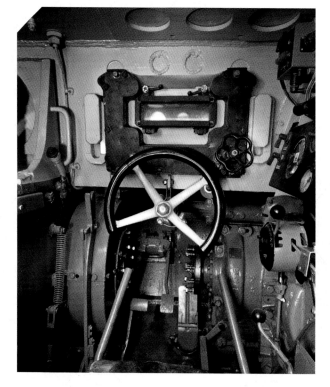

its transmission. By November 1942, production of the Tiger had reached 25 a month. By August 1944, when the Tiger I was phased out, some 1,300 had been made, a relatively small quantity set against its effect on Allied morale.

As well as on the Eastern Front, the Tiger served in Tunisia, Sicily, Italy, France and north-west Europe, equipping heavy tank battalions of about 30 vehicles under the control of an army or corps headquarters. The Tiger I was followed into service in the summer of 1944 by the Tiger II or Königstiger, known to the Allies as the Royal Tiger.

Also developed by Henschel, the Tiger II was a larger, better protected and upgunned version of its predecessor. Its armour was thicker and more scientifically arranged, using angled planes. Although ponderous and liable to be stranded in a fast-moving battle, the Tigers were capable of fighting against heavy odds and knocking out numerous enemy armoured vehicles while suffering little damage themselves.

LEFT The driver's position in the Tiger I. The crewman's hatch is offset to the left and his instrument panel to the right. The hand wheel above the steering wheel is for opening and closing the visor aperture at the front of the tank.

ABOVE An 88mm (3.5in) High Explosive round (from Tiger I).

OPPOSITE TOP This cutaway drawing of a Tiger was produced as part of the major British report on the captured Tiger 131 from Tunisia.

OPPOSITE BELOW Tiger 131 was transferred to the Tank Museum in 1951 and restored to running order in 2004. It still gives running displays and appeared in the war film *Fury* in 2014.

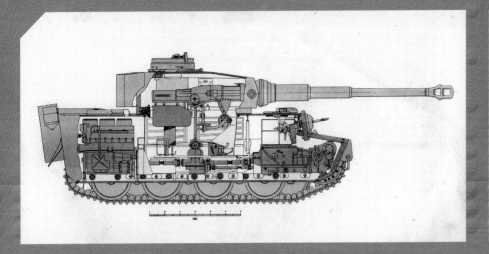

TIGER I

SPECIFICATION

CREW: 5

WEIGHT: 56 tons

ARMOUR: 120mm (4.7in)

ARMAMENT: 1x 88mm L/56 gun, 2x 7.92mm machine-guns

TOP SPEED: 45.4 km/h (28.2 mph)

ENGINE: Maybach HL230 P45 700hp petrol

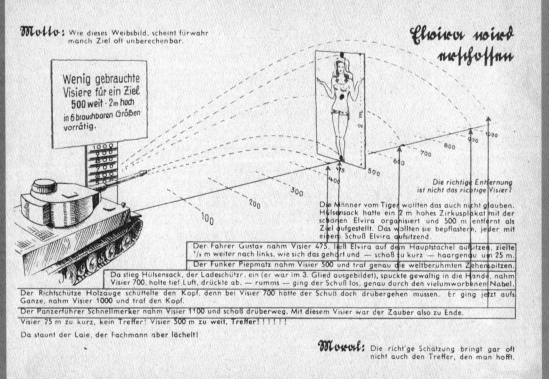

LEFT AND OPPOSITE The Tiger Fibel from 1942 was a small booklet illustrated with cartoons, mottos, ditties and useful tables to help a Tiger crewmember get the best from his tank and look after the vehicle.

Motto: Wohltätig ist des Wassers Macht,
falls Du an Glysantin gedacht.

Wasser ist ein Kühlmittel

Es umspült wie eine frische Brause unablässig das Gehäuse
und führt die Hitze, die durch Verbrennung und Reibung
entsteht, zu den Kühlern. Es speichert im Winter außerdem
die Wärme wie ein Sammler den Strom und hält dadurch
den Motor startbereit.

120 Liter braucht Dein Tiger. Bei 85° fühlt er sich sauwohl

Wasser ist ein Sprengmittel

Wenn es zu Eis friert, dehnt es sich u.n 10% aus.
Wenn die Wände nicht nachgeben können,
werden sie mit Urgewalt gesprengt. Eis sprengt
Felsen und Eisen.

Aus den 120 Litern werden dann 132 Liter, und
die haben auch in einem Tigermagen keinen
Platz.

Darum:

18

Motto: Es kommt dem alten Panzermann
sehr auf den Sitz des Schusses an.

Hülsensack trifft immer!

*Die Kanone schießt Fleck. Der Schuß geht deshalb gerade nur bis zum ein-
gestellten Visier und nicht weiter.*

*Wenn Du die Entfernung genau kennst und schießt mit Visier gleich Entfernung,
dann triffst Du den Haltepunkt.*
*Du kennst aber die Entfernung nie ganz genau. Schätzt Du auch nur um 25 m
zu kurz, dann geht der Schuß 25 m davor in den Dreck, wie beim Fahrer Gustav.*

*Die Flugbahn der 8,8 ist wundervoll gestreckt. Du brauchst also das Rohr nur
ganz wenig höher zu kurbeln, um viel weiter zu schießen. Du triffst dann mit
dem weiten Visier immer noch Dein nahes Ziel, wenn es nur genügend hoch ist.
Mit Visier 1000 triffst Du z. B. alle Ziele zwischen 0 und 1000 m, die 2 m hoch sind.
Ist das nicht wundervoll?*

*Auf Elvira mit Visier 1000 zu schießen, ist allerdings auch nicht ganz sicher, denn
wenn sie nur ein paar Zentimeter kleiner wäre, ging der Schuß drüber, wie
beim Kommandanten Schnellmerker.*

*Du hast für ein Ziel mehrere brauchbare Visiere! Das kleinste davon ist die Ent-
fernung, alle anderen liegen höher. Elvira kannst Du mit 6 verschiedenen Visieren
treffen. 500 — 600 — 700 — 800 — 900 — 1000.*

*Nicht Visier gleich Entfernung stellen! Denn, wenn Du nur um 25 m zu kurz
schätzt, schießt Du 25 m zu kurz. Mach 's wie Hülsensack, nimm das mittelste,
dann triffst Du Zielmitte, den Nabel.*

Er kann sich dann beim Entfernungsschätzen um 200 m runter und 200 m rauf ver-
geigen und trifft trotzdem. Hülsensack trifft immer, denn größere Fehler macht er
ja beim Schätzen nicht.

Moral: Die Optik stellen alte Knaben,
meist weiter, als geschätzt sie haben.

73

CHAPTER 24

TANK DESTROYERS

TANK DESTROYERS, WHICH FLOURISHED DURING THE SECOND WORLD WAR, WERE ARMOURED FIGHTING VEHICLES (AFVS) ARMED WITH AN ANTI-TANK GUN BUT WITH MORE LIMITED OPERATIONAL CAPABILITIES THAN A TANK AND DESIGNED WITH THE PURPOSE OF ENGAGING AND DESTROYING ENEMY ARMOURED VEHICLES EFFICIENTLY. SOME WERE LITTLE MORE THAN STOP-GAP IMPROVISATIONS; OTHERS BEAR THE STAMP OF MORE SOPHISTICATED DESIGN.

Of all the combatants, the Germans were the most committed to the use of the tank destroyer, and in armoured formations made little between the destroyer and the tank proper. The first generation German tank destroyers or Panzerjäger ("tank hunters") mounted anti-tank guns behind a three-sided shield on a convenient chassis. Over 200 obsolete PzKpfw Is were modified by removing the turret and then rebuilt as the Panzerjäger I, armed with a 47mm (1.8in) anti-tank gun.

The Marder (Marten) II was introduced in 1942 after the bitter fighting on the Eastern Front prompted a reassessment of armoured tactics. The first version used the chassis of the PzKpfw II Ausf A, B, C and E on which was mounted the 75mm (3in) L/46 Pak 40/2 anti-tank gun; the second version employed the chassis of the PzKpfw II Ausf D and E and was armed with a captured Soviet Model 36 76.2mm (3in) anti-tank gun re-chambered to accommodate a German 75mm (3in) round.

The most common mounting was that of the Marder III, which entered service in 1942 and was based on the chassis of the Czech-built PzkPfw 38(t). Later models mounted the German 75mm (3in) L/46 Pak 40/3 anti-tank gun. The Marder I, which perversely did not appear until 1943, was armed with the 75mm (3in) Pak 40/1 anti-tank gun mounted on the chassis of the French Lorraine tracked carrier, a lightly armoured personnel carrier (APC), or those of the French Hotchkiss light or FCM infantry tanks. A total of 716 Marder II and 1,577 Marder III conversions were made. The Marder I was regarded as second-line equipment, but the Marder II and III served with anti-tank units of front-line armoured and infantry divisions until they were replaced by more formidable tank destroyers.

Ferdinand

Tank destroyers were controlled by the German Army's artillery arm. By 1943 there was an urgent need on the Eastern Front for self-propelled tank destroyers and infantry-support guns (Sturmgeschütze) to supersede the obsolescent 37mm (1.5in) and 50mm (2in) towed anti-tank guns which were ineffective against the T-34. The Marders had partially filled the gap, but their open-topped superstructure left their crews exposed. Dr Ferdinand Porsche, who had failed in his bid to secure the contract to build the Tiger tank, now approached Hitler with a scheme for the construction of a powerful Jagdpanzer ("hunting tank"), originally called the Ferdinand (later renamed Elefant), based on the chassis of his rejected Tiger design.

OPPOSITE A Marder 2 tank destroyer advances through a Russian village. The size of the country and lack of metalled roads meant the wearing out of vehicles and a massive logistical supply problem for the Germans.

ABOVE The Panzerjäger I mounted a 47mm (1.8in) anti-tank gun on the PzKpfw I chassis. The vehicle gave the crew some protection and the gun a mobility hard to match when in its usual towed configuration.

Hitler immediately saw that the production of the Jagdpanzer might be quicker and cheaper than that of tanks and would also provided a fast road to boosting the strength of the Panzerwaffe. In this he received partisan encouragement from the artillery arm, which was determined to retain the assault guns and tank destroyers within its command structure.

The Ferdinand heavy tank destroyer carried an 88mm (3.5in) gun on a fixed superstructure at the rear of the hull and was protected at the front by 200mm (7.9in) of frontal armour. At first sight, it was a formidable beast weighing 67 tons, but it was more expensive to produce than the Marder, whose narrow field of fire it shared, and lacked secondary armament.

Essentially a mobile pillbox and a symbol of the growing gigantism which had infected the Panzerwaffe, the Ferdinand was formidable in defence but less suited to a mobile offensive role. In July 1943, at the Battle of Kursk, where 76 Ferdinands were deployed in two tank battalions on the northern shoulder of the salient, their brutal firepower and heavy armour enabled them to break into the Soviets' defensive zones with ease. But they soon found themselves marooned in a maze of slit

trenches, where they were separated from the tanks needed to cover their flanks. Lacking secondary armament, the Ferdinands frequently fell victim to Soviet infantry who emerged from their foxholes, boarded them on the move and played flamethrowers over their ventilation slats.

Reviewing their performance at Kursk, Guderian judged that the Ferdinands were:

… incapable of close-range fighting since they lacked sufficient ammunition (armour-piercing and high-explosive) for their guns and this defect was aggravated by the fact that they had no machine gun. Once (they) had broken into the enemy's infantry zone, they literally had to go quail-shooting with cannon. They did not manage to neutralize, let alone destroy, the enemy infantry and machine guns, so that our infantry was unable to follow up behind them. By the time they reached the Russian artillery they were on their own.

After coming to grief at Kursk, the Ferdinand/Elefant had a more agreeable afterlife. Fitted with a hull machine gun, the survivors of Kursk were despatched to Italy, where they

ABOVE Captured vehicles are taken for evaluation in the United States. On the left is a Marder II fitted with the 7.5cm anti tank gun while on the right is a Wespe, which used the same basic chassis (from a PzKpfw II), but mounted a 10.5cm howitzer.

acquitted themselves well in semi-static positions, their thick armour proving almost impenetrable to Allied anti-tank guns.

Replacing the Marders

The Jagdpanzer IV was introduced toward the end of 1943, replacing the Marders in tank destroyer battalions of panzer divisions. At 24 tons, it was based on the chassis of the PzKpfw IV, with a fully enclosed fighting compartment and a superstructure of well-angled plate extending to the vehicle's rear, which prompted the nickname "Guderian's duck". Later versions of the Jagdpanzer IV were armed with a 75mm (3in) L/70 KwK 42 and a machine gun, and its frontal armour was 80mm (3.1in) thick. Side skirts were frequently fitted as a defence against shaped charges and toward the end of the war a coating of Zimmerit hard-drying paste was applied to counter magnetic charges. It had a maximum speed of 39 km/h (24 mph). Thought by many to be the best tank destroyer of the war, the Jagdpanther, which entered service in 1944, was based on a Panther tank chassis and was armed with an 88mm (3.5in) L/71 Pak 43/3 gun in a well-angled superstructure.

Weighing 45 tons, it was capable of attaining 45 km/h (28 mph) and had a crew of five. Its drawbacks were a limited traverse and a height of almost 3 metres (9 feet), which made it difficult to conceal in an ambush. The Jagdpanther replaced the open-topped Nashorn (Rhinoceros) heavy tank destroyer, which equipped 30-strong heavy tank destroyer battalions controlled by army commanders.

Allied tank destroyers

The Red Army based the SU-85 tank destroyer on a T-34 chassis with its D-5T 85mm (3.35in) gun thrusting forward from an enclosed superstructure. An upgunned version, the SU-100, with a 100mm (4in) gun, was introduced in 1944 and equipped many of the Soviet Union's allies and client states after the war.

American tank destroyer (TD) battalions were intended to be concentrated and mobile, to counter a German armoured breakthrough on a narrow front. In the event this happened on only one occasion, in Tunisia at El Guettar in March/April 1943, where 50 of 10th Panzers's tanks overran US 1st Infantry Division before running into a minefield and then being

ABOVE The Jagdpanther. Hitler had a particular liking for tank destroyers — arguing at the demonstration of the first Jagdpanther in December 1943 that the vehicle had lower production costs, lower weight and greater mobility than the Tiger II, which was armed with the same gun.

GUN MOTOR CARRIAGE M10

SPECIFICATION // M10

CREW: 5

WEIGHT: 29.4 tons

ARMOUR: 37mm (1.5in)

ARMAMENT: 1 x 3in gun M7, 1x .50 Browning machine gun

TOP SPEED: 48 km/h (30 mph)

ENGINE: Twin GMS6/71 Diesels (M10), Ford GAA V8 petrol (M10A1) 375 hp

The M10 was a tank destroyer based on the chassis of the M4A2 Sherman medium tank with angled hull armour and was fitted with an open-top turret capable of all-round traverse and mounting a 3in high-velocity gun. In June 1942, the design was standardized and the Sherman M4A3 chassis was employed to increase production in the version known as the M10A1. Nearly 5,000 M10s and 1,413 M10A1s were built, and a number of turretless M10A1s were later converted for use as heavy artillery tractors (M35s). The M10 entered service during the closing stages of the war in North Africa.

checked by U.S. artillery, anti-tank guns and 31 M10 tank destroyers.

American tank destroyers were termed Gun Motor Carriages. They were mobile, heavily armed and usually open-topped. The M10 Wolverine was based on an M4 Sherman hull and transmission and carried a 76mm (3in) gun. Probably the most successful U.S. tank destroyer was the fast, hard-hitting M18 Hellcat, also armed with a 76mm (3in) gun. Just over 2,500 were built by the Buick division of General Motors between July 1943 and October 1944. However, only the later M36, mounting a larger turret which housed a 90mm (3.5in) gun and armour 50mm (2in) thick, could vie on equal terms at long range with German armour. By 1945, some 1,700 had been built.

In common with their German counterparts, the British artillery arm remained jealous controllers of their domain. The British also encountered difficulties in accommodating the 17pdr anti-tank gun in suitable standard tanks. The result was the Archer tank destroyer, built from the hull and chassis of a Valentine tank on which a 17pdr was mounted in a fixed open-top structure over the vehicle's rear. This meant that, in addition to its limited traverse, the Archer had to be reversed into position. Another drawback was that the gun recoiled directly over the driver's seat. Introduced in the autumn of 1944, the Archer remained in service after the war. It later saw action with the Egyptian army in the 1956 war with Israel.

ABOVE An Archer being used by its Royal Artillery crewmen in the fire support role – lobbing 17-pounder high explosive shells at enemy targets in the winter of 1944.

OPPOSITE The US M10 tank destroyer in Germany in 1945. The thin armour and open top turret of tank destroyers meant they had to be handled in a very different manner than a conventional tank by their crews.

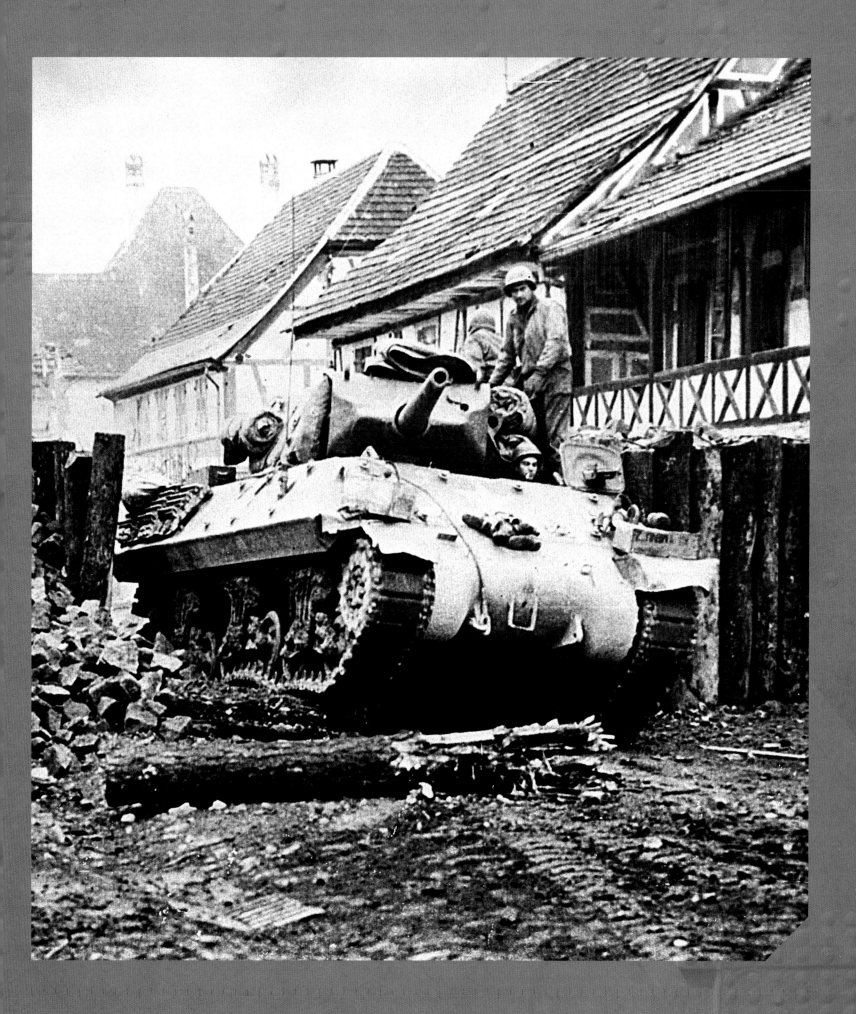

CHAPTER 25

HOBART'S FUNNIES

THE DIEPPE RAID, A DISASTROUS "RECONNAISSANCE IN FORCE", HAD NEVERTHELESS GIVEN THE ALLIES A SALUTARY WARNING ABOUT THE DANGERS OF A PREMATURE INVASION OF NORTH-WEST EUROPE. IT WAS CLEAR THAT THE INVASION FORCE WOULD NEED TO OVERCOME THE OBSTACLES AND COASTAL FORTIFICATIONS ON THE NORMANDY BEACHES RAPIDLY, AS THE INLAND TOPOGRAPHY LENT ITSELF TO A COUNTER-ATTACK BY GERMAN ARMOUR.

The Allied High Command needed no reminding of the Salerno landings in Italy in September 1943, in which a well-planned assault had almost come to grief because of the rapidity of the German reaction.

The invasion of north-west Europe in 1944 required the development of a wide range of modified tanks and armoured vehicles. They were needed for bridging ditches and rivers, clearing minefields, as flamethrowers, for destroying pillboxes and emplacements and for crossing rivers. However, none of this could be achieved if the Allied armies failed to get ashore and establish a lodgement on French soil. A formation, 79th Armoured Division, was raised to tackle this task under the command of General Sir Percy Hobart, universally known as "Hobo". The vehicles they developed were given an affectionate nickname, "Hobart's funnies".

Swimming tanks

The starting point was the invasion beaches. Hobart's command developed a range of ingenious weapons to clear a way through minefields and beach obstacles and to punch holes in the sea walls overlooking the invasion beaches. The primary need was for tanks that could be launched from ships to swim ashore to support the assault infantry. This was a concept which had been taken up by the ingenious J. Walter Christie in 1924, when he designed an armoured amphibious vehicle that swam from a battleship on to a Puerto Rican beach. In the early 1930s, Vickers-Armstrong had built two prototypes of amphibious light tanks, and some 4,000 had been manufactured in the Soviet Union between 1933 and 1939 as the T-37 and T-38. However, these were small vehicles armed only with a machine gun and capable only of navigating calm inland waters.

The problem was solved by a Hungarian engineer, Nicholas Straussler, who had become a British citizen in 1933. He had worked on armoured cars, artillery tractors and bomb trolleys used by RAF Bomber Command. In 1941, he devised a canvas flotation screen and fitted it to a Tetrarch light tank equipped with a marine propeller that took its drive from the tank's engine. The two forms of propulsion, propeller and tracks, gave the system its name, Duplex Drive or DD.

The DD Tetrarch underwent successful trials at Brent Reservoir and off Hayling Island, and the go-ahead was given for the conversion of 600 Valentine infantry tanks which were used for trials and training. The tank chosen for Operation Overlord, the landings in Normandy, was the M4 Sherman, which in its DD form was to equip three U.S., three British and two Canadian armoured battalions.

Overlord

On 6 June 1944, the DD Shermans crossed the Channel in Landing Craft Tanks (LCTs). The British and Canadian LCTs each carried five tanks, the Americans four in their shorter LCTs. In the Bay of the Seine, the Shermans met with mixed fortunes. On Juno Beach, 21 of 29 Shermans landed on the invasion beach. On Gold Beach, eight tanks of the Sherwood Rangers Yeomanry foundered on the way in, and by the time the remainder landed, Sherman Crab tanks (see below) had overrun the German artillery positions and machine-gun nests which had been their objectives. On Utah, the US 70th Tank Battalion launched 27 DDs but, confused by dense smokescreens, the great majority came ashore some 1,800 metres (2,000 yards) from their objectives. One hundred and twelve DDs had been assigned to Omaha, with 56 tanks each in U.S. 741st and 743rd Tank Battalions. At 05.40, 5 kilometres (3 miles) offshore, 741st launched 29 DDs, of which 27 sank. The remainder were landed directly on the beach an hour later. At Utah Beach the waves had been too high for the swimming tanks. Their aiming point was a church on the horizon and, in order to keep it in sight, the DDs were forced progressively to turn away from the shoreline, thus flooding their flotation devices.

OPPOSITE A Churchill fitted with a small box girder bridge, or SBG. Usually used to cross a gap up to 9 m (30 ft) wide, these bridges were used as ramps on D-Day to allow vehicles to exit the beaches across the protective sea wall.

TOP A Sherman DD tank is launched from a Landing Craft Tank. It was concluded that in choppy seas the risk should be taken of approaching closer to shore before launching the DD tanks.

ABOVE The badge of the British 79th Armoured Division.

RIGHT The Davis escape apparatus, as issued to DD crews.

RIGHT A Sherman BARV or Beach Armoured Recovery Vehicle awaits a task on the Normandy beaches. The BARV could pull flooded vehicles ashore to safety or push lighter landing craft back out to sea from the beach.

OPPOSITE A Sherman DD tank collapses its floatation screen. Compressed air was pumped into canvas tubes and these in turn were supported by metal struts to hold the rubberized screen in position.

Hobart's menagerie

The DD Shermans were the only "funny" wholeheartedly adopted by the Americans. Nevertheless, by the end of the war, 79th Armoured Division had developed an entire family of combat engineering vehicles. The majority were based on modified forms of the Churchill and Sherman tank, the latter in particular noted for its mechanical reliability.

These included the "Crocodile", a flame-throwing Churchill, and the AVRE (Armoured Vehicle Royal Engineers), a Churchill adapted to overcome German defensive fortifications. The AVRE's main gun was replaced by a Petard mortar firing an 18kg (40lb) HE-filled projectile (nicknamed the "Flying Dustbin") to destroy concrete obstacles. The "Crab" was a modified Sherman tank fitted with a flail, a rotating cylinder of weighted chains which exploded mines in the path of the tank. The BARV (Beach Armoured Recovery Vehicle) was a waterproofed Sherman whose turret had been replaced by an armoured superstructure. Capable of operating in water up to 2.7m (9 feet) deep, it was designed to clear beaches of swamped and sunken vehicles. The Canal Defence Light was an ingenious device, with a deliberately misleading name, fitted to a tank turret and intended to dazzle enemy soldiers during a night attack with a powerful carbon-arc searchlight. It was not used on D-Day but was employed in Germany in the closing stages of the war.

The 79th Armoured, which consisted of seven brigades and 17 regiments, never operated as a single division. Its vehicles were distributed in small parcels to formations tasked with such operations as opposed landings and river-crossings. To smooth out any difficulties, liaison officers from 79th Armoured were assigned to the units to which its elements were despatched. Once the operation was completed, the vehicles were returned to 79th Armoured Division.

GENERAL SIR PERCY HOBART

1885–1957

Influenced by Fuller and Liddell Hart, Hobart became a passionate advocate of the armoured idea. In 1931, he took command of the 2nd Royal Tank Regiment, where he pioneered the use of radio-telephony to command armour in action. In 1933, he became Inspector of the Royal Tank Corps and a year later took command of the 1st Tank Brigade. In an exercise on Salisbury Plain, he demonstrated that a large armoured formation could move 240 kilometres (150 miles) in three days, deploying along selected routes from one position to another, making use of every vestige of natural cover and the welcome cloak of darkness in an anticipation of Blitzkrieg. Hobart pressed for the full mechanization of the British Army, an institution in which he succeeded in making himself extremely unpopular. His 1937 suggestion for an armoured division consisting of a tank brigade, a cavalry brigade of one or two light tank regiments and a holding group of motorized rifles, anti-tank and anti-aircraft guns, field artillery and Royal Engineers, resembled a British tank division of 1944. This proposal earned Hobart a rebuke from the War Office. He found rather more favour in Germany with Heinz Guderian. In 1938, Hobart was packed off to Egypt to form a mobile division and set up the force that became 7th Armoured Division, the "Desert Rats". In 1939, however, he was relieved of his command and returned to England, where he was placed on the retired list, joining his local Home Guard as a corporal. Churchill rescued Hobart from retirement, and secured him command of the newly formed 11th Armoured Division. In the summer of 1942, he was appointed the commander of 79th Armoured Division. The vigorous and combative Hobart received support in this role from his brother-in-law, General Montgomery, who convinced General Eisenhower, Supreme Commander of the Allied Expeditionary Force, of the importance of specialized armour in the planning of Overlord.

ABOVE A Sherman Crab demonstrates its flail. The flailing chains would detonate mines ahead of the tank and serve its primary purpose, but it could also rip up barbed wire entanglements as can be seen here.

OPPOSITE Bert, a Churchill tank that shed a track in front of the Casino at Dieppe is inspected by German troops. The raid was costly in men and material and gave the Germans a number of Churchill tanks to evaluate.

CHAPTER 26

NORMANDY // THE CHANGING BATTLEFIELD

THE NORMANDY LANDINGS, WHICH TOOK PLACE ON 6 JUNE 1944 AND OPENED A SECOND
FRONT AGAINST GERMANY IN THE WEST, MARKED A TURNING POINT IN THE SECOND WORLD
WAR. IN THE FOUR YEARS SINCE IT HAD BEGUN, THE NUMBERS AND ROLE OF TANKS IN THE
ARMIES OF THE MAJOR COMBATANTS HAD CHANGED RADICALLY.

In 1943–44 the United States produced 47,000 tanks, almost all of them M4 Shermans. In 1940, still at peace, it had produced only 346 tanks. In 1943–44 Germany manufactured 29,600 tanks and assault guns; with the exception of the Tiger, the Germans made little distinction between the two. Over the same period the Soviet Union's output of tanks was 29,000, almost all of them T-34s and all of them made at the enormous works at Chelyabinsk nicknamed "Tankograd". In contrast, during the same period Britain's armoured "cottage industry" produced only 5,000 tanks. The British came instead to rely on the US M4 Sherman as the mainstay of their armoured divisions.

At Bulson in 1940, during the Battle of France, the mere rumour of approaching bodies of German armour had been enough to send waves of panic running through an experienced French infantry division. By 1944, experienced troops fighting on the same soil in France were well aware that flight was more dangerous than holding their positions. German tank formations no longer operated as independent spearheads but advanced in concert with specialist infantry – panzergrenadiers – and supported by artillery.

Defending infantry who abandoned their positions exposed themselves to a range of fire. If they chose to hold their ground, they could keep their attackers at bay while calling on artillery support and air strikes and, in theory at least, an intervention from their own armour. The tank, by itself, was no longer an autonomous instrument of strategy. Rather

ABOVE Metal from redundant German anti-tank defences were shaped into four-pronged teeth and attached to a tank to allow them to cut through field banks and hedges.

OPPOSITE The production of the Sherman played on the strength of the automobile industry.

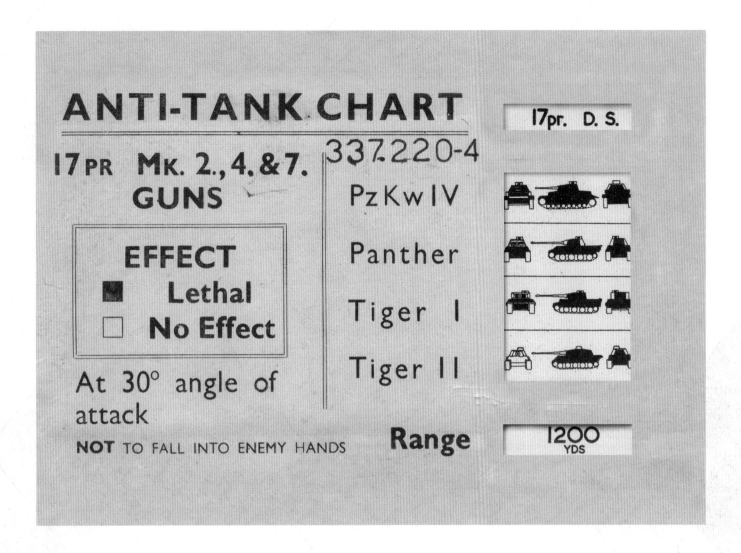

ANTI-TANK CHART

17 PR MK. 2., 4. & 7. GUNS

337.220-4

EFFECT

�■ Lethal
☐ No Effect

At 30° angle of attack

NOT TO FALL INTO ENEMY HANDS

	17pr. D. S.
PzKw IV	
Panther	
Tiger I	
Tiger II	
Range	1200 YDS

it had become a constituent part of tactical attrition which aimed to wear down the enemy instead of slicing through his line with the single rapier-like thrust envisaged by Liddell Hart and Fuller.

A window shuts

Immediately after the Allies came ashore in Normandy, the briefest of windows opened for German armour to make a telling riposte. The nearest Panzer Division to the Allied lodgement on 6 June was 21st Panzer, part of Rommel's Army Group B, positioned near Caen, on the eastern flank of the British Sword Beach.

Rommel was away on sick leave, but his chief of staff, Lieutenant-General Hans Speidel, gained permission from OKW for a counter-attack. However, two more hours elapsed before his immediate superior, General Erich Marcks, issued an operational order for the tanks to probe into the gap between Sword and Juno Beaches. He hoped this would halt the British advance on Caen, which was only 13 kilometres (8 miles) from the sea, and roll up the British bridgehead. Marcks warned, "If

you don't succeed in throwing the British into the sea, we shall have lost the war."

At 1800, a British infantry brigade, accompanied by tanks of the Staffordshire Yeomanry, was advancing on Caen when it encountered the vanguard of 21st Panzer. As 22nd Panzer Regiment moved forward to attack the British bridgehead, the German PzKpfw IVs ran into the Staffordshire Yeomanry's Fireflies (Shermans armed with 17pdr guns) and were extremely roughly handled. Having been overflown by gliders of 6th Airborne Division and fearful of being cut off, they withdrew.

On 7 and 8 June, 12th SS Panzer (Hitler Youth) attacked the Canadians in their bridgehead but failed to break though to the sea. The Allies, able to reinforce their bridgeheads at a faster pace than the Germans, who were under constant air attack, could muster forces for a telling counterblow. The commander of the Allied invasion land forces, General Montgomery, had hoped to take Caen by 6 June, but encountered stiff resistance from 12th SS Panzer on 7–8 June,

OPPOSITE ABOVE 147 Regiment Royal Armoured Corps prepares for the breakout in Normandy. Most of the tanks sport track draped over the vehicles, to give extra protection.

OPPOSITE BELOW Prior to the Allied invasion Rommel inspects self-propelled guns of Major Becker's unit.

ABOVE These simple charts were issued to British tank crews to help them estimate the effect of certain types of ammunition on the key German tanks in service. The 77mm (3in) gun was fitted to the Comet tank and this chart, from 1944, details the possible performance at various distances of the two main anti-tank rounds carried. DS stands for Discarding Sabot.

GOODWOOD

Montgomery intended that Operation Goodwood, launched on 18 July south-east of Caen, would open the road to Paris beyond the Bourguébus Ridge. Goodwood involved the Guards, 7th and 11th Divisions and was preceded by a massive aerial bombardment the heaviest in the Normandy campaign, which left the German survivors in a state of shock. Tigers weighing 56 tons were turned upside down by the concussion and Pzkpfw IVs were buried under mounds of earth. By mid-morning, British tanks were halfway to their objectives and success seemed assured. Commander of a Battle Group of 21st Panzer Division, Colonel Hans von Luck sighted the mass of advancing Shermans. He quickly improvised a defensive line of surviving tanks and 88mm (3.5in) guns, which knocked out

12 Shermans. Then a Company of the 503rd Heavy Tank Battalion encountered the Guards Armoured Division and accounted for nine more Shermans. By early afternoon, British tanks were at the bottom of Bourguébus Ridge, but at its the top were the engineer battalions of 1st SS Panzer Division, rushed into battle as infantry and supported by their tanks and those of 12th SS Panzer. As the Fife and Forfar Yeomanry deployed to take the ridge, they were met with heavy 75mm (3in) and 88mm (3.5in) fire from above. One hundred and twenty-six Shermans were lost in the battle, more than half the Yeomanry's strength. In the earlier encounters, the Guards Armoured Division had lost 60 tanks. Goodwood, which had opened so well, had turned into a disaster for the Allied armour.

ABOVE The use of the bombers to clear a path ahead of the main advance caused much political wrangling within the Allied High command. For the German forces, the effect was devastating – as can be seen by this Tiger of the 503rd Battalion.

PANZERFAUST, BAZOOKA AND PIAT

The Panzerfaust was a German hand-held recoilless anti-tank weapon fired by one man. It consisted of a short steel tube containing a propelling charge and with the tail stem of a shaped charge bomb inserted in the mouth of the tube. The firer tucked it under his arm, took aim across the top of the bomb and pressed the trigger to fire the charge, which in turn blew the bomb forward while expelling gases from the rear of the tube to counteract the recoil.

The first model appeared in 1942 but had a very short range of 30 metres (100ft). By the end of the war, the hundreds of thousands of Panzerfausts issued to the Volkssturm (German Home Guard) were effective against tanks at up to 150 metres (500ft). It was most effective against thinner side or rear armour, but could also penetrate the frontal armour of most Allied tanks. In terms of cost-effectiveness, a Panzerfaust in the hands of a determined soldier was one of the most successful weapons of the war.

The U.S. equivalent was the Bazooka. It was a shoulder-fired 60mm anti-tank rocket, designated M1, M1A1 or M9. A lightweight tube (in two pieces in the M9) was placed on the firer's shoulder and aimed with a simple sight. A fin-stabilized rocket with a shaped charge warhead was inserted into the rear end of the tube and fired electrically. The Bazooka's effective range was about 135 metres (450ft) and the warhead could penetrate approximately 200mm (8in) of armour.

The British PIAT (Projector, Infantry, Anti-Tank) was a spigot discharger in which a heavy steel rod propelled by a spring shot fired a bomb with a shape-charged warhead over a range of 110 metres (360ft). It entered service in 1943, and was first used in the Allied invasion of Sicily. Combat analysis established that the PIAT could achieve a hit 60 per cent of the time at a range of 90 metres (300ft), but faulty fuses meant that only 75 per cent of the hits detonated on target. In Normandy about seven per cent of knocked-out German tanks were disabled by PIAT.

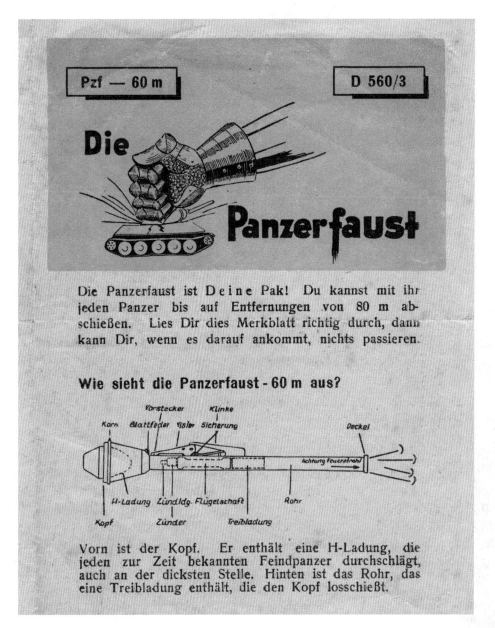

Attrition

It took the Allies six weeks of hard fighting to break out of the Normandy bridgehead. On Montgomery's right, American forces advanced through the Cotentin peninsula toward Cherbourg, badly needed for its port facilities, which was taken on 27 June by U.S. 7th Corps. Joined by 8th Corps, it then turned south and fought its way through the bocage country, a chequerboard of fields, dense hedgerows and sunken lanes which made the perfect terrain for ambush.

The extremely difficult nature of the country through which they were fighting confined tanks to the roads. The first Sherman of 737th Independent Tank Battalion that tried to

during which an armoured attack on the city was beaten off by one of the few Tiger battalions in Normandy. Another drive, codenamed Epsom, by 15th Scottish Division, was halted by 9th and 10th Panzer Divisions, and after five days of heavy fighting the operation was called off.

ram its way through a hedgerow was flipped onto its back like an upended turtle. One solution was to fit "hedgedozer" Shermans with front-mounted bulldozer teeth, which enabled the tank to gouge its way through the steep, confining lane banks. One unanticipated advantage conferred by this problematic landscape was that it neutralized the long-range advantage enjoyed by German tank gunners. Nevertheless, they lay in wait for Allied tanks which were forced to break cover to advance.

Losses on both sides were heavy. Panzer Lehr Division, commanded by General Fritz Bayerlein, lay in the path of US 7th Corps as it launched its assault on St Lô, which was some 19 kilometres (12 miles) from Omaha Beach. The assault was preceded by carpet bombing, and Bayerlein testified to the weight of the attack: "After an hour I had no communications with anybody, even by radio. By noon nothing was visible but dust and smoke. My front lines looked like the face of the moon and at least 70 per cent of my troops were knocked out –

ABOVE This is a user instruction guide for the Panzerfaust from the Second World War. When fired, the hollow charge warhead could travel up to 30m (100ft) and could penetrate 200mm (8in) of armour if detonating at the right angle (it had less effect on sloped armour surfaces). The mass-produced Panzerfaust was simple to use and very effective, and is one of the forerunners of the ubiquitous Rocket Propelled Grenade of current times.

dead, wounded, crazed or numbed."

Bayerlein had been promised an SS battalion of 60 Tigers. Just five arrived. With only 14 tanks remaining, he withdrew on the night of 17 July, and St Lô was taken on the following day. Panzer Lehr had once been arguably the strongest armoured division in the German Army and its parlous state was testimony to the bitter fighting in Normandy.

Burnt-out tanks were always a grim sight. Trooper Austin Baker of the Royal Dragoons Guards was looking for a friend, Wally Walters, in a burned-out Cromwell:

... the outside is usually a dull, dirty, rust colour and inside it is a blackened shambles. There is a queer indescribable smell. The bottom of Jonah's tank had been blown right out, and we could peer inside from underneath. There was no trace of anybody in the turret, but some stuff in the driving seat that must have been Walker. There was a body on the ground by the left-hand track. Somebody had thrown a ground sheet over it, but we lifted it off. It was probably Brigham Young, but it was impossible to recognise him – he was burned quite black all over, and one part of his anklets remained of his clothes. Nobody ever found any sign of Wally.

ABOVE One Tiger tows another. This was officially forbidden, as the extra strain it placed on the towing Tiger's engine meant this tank could end up disabled as well. The need to recover such powerful vehicles meant the rule was often ignored.

BELOW A sketch of a knocked-out Panther in Normandy painted by Christie Fyffe. The painting is mis-labelled "Tiger". Many servicemen had actually seen very few German tanks "in the flesh" and didn't have the overview that we have today.

DISABLED "TIGER" AUG. 1944 F. Christie.

CHAPTER 27

THE FALAISE GAP

THE FIRST AND LAST DEMONSTRATION BY AN ALLIED ARMY IN THE SECOND WORLD WAR OF BLITZKRIEG, A TECHNIQUE PIONEERED BY THE GERMAN ARMY IN FRANCE IN 1940, CAME AT THE BATTLE OF FALAISE GAP IN AUGUST 1944.

When the German containment of the Allied bridgehead in Normandy collapsed, a torrent of mechanized and motorized columns burst into the narrow corridor between Mortain and the sea, only 32 kilometres (20 miles) away, precipitating the last major tank battle in France. Hitler, grasping at straws, saw the Allied break-out as another opportunity. He told his OKW operations staff:

We must strike like lightning … When we reach the sea the American spearheads will be cut off … We might even be able to cut off their entire beachhead. We must not get bogged down in cutting off the Americans who have broken through. Their turn will come later. We must wheel north like lightning and turn the entire enemy front from the rear.

Four armoured divisions 2nd, 116th, 1st and 2nd SS Panzer, moved on to the flank of U.S. 1st Army as it raced south from Brittany. However, the Allies possessed an advantage in the regular receipt of decrypted German transmissions (code-named Ultra) which had pinpointed the German movements. As a result, four U.S. divisions – 3rd Armoured, 30th and 44th, with 2nd Armoured in reserve – were tasked with blocking Operation Lüttich, the German drive to the Atlantic down the See valley. On the night of 6/7 August, 2nd Panzer was halted by 30th Division, whose tank destroyers shot up 14 panzers before waiting for daylight to bring in air support.

By the summer of 1944, each British and American infantry division had up to 100 anti-tank guns and hundreds of hand-held anti-tank rockets. In general, armour is penetrable by rounds equal in diameter to its thickness, and only the thickest German armour exceeded 100mm (4in). German armour was no longer invincible.

In 1940, German armour had also been largely untroubled by Allied air intervention. Now the balance had swung here too in the Allies' favour and the skies were clear of the Luftwaffe. On 7 August, rocket-firing Typhoons subjected the German armour to eight-and-a-half hours of attack. As a 2nd Panzer commander remarked. "Your fighter bombers simply nailed us to the ground."

The air attacks dealt a heavy psychological blow to the Panzerwaffe. Subsequent operational research by 21st Army Group investigated the damage inflicted on some several

PZKPFW IV MEDIUM TANK

SPECIFICATION // PZKPFW IV MODEL H

CREW: 5

WEIGHT: 25 tons

ARMOUR: 80mm (3.1in)

ARMAMENT: 1x 75mm L/48 gun, 2x 7.92mm machine guns

TOP SPEED: 42 km/h (26 mph)

ENGINE: Maybach HL120 TRM 300hp

The PzKpfw IV was the only German tank to stay in continuous production throughout the Second World War. It stemmed from a German specification of 1935 which envisaged that two principal armoured types would shoulder the burden of battle: the first, armed with a high-velocity gun, was the PzKpfw III; the second, a support tank firing a large-calibre HE shell, was the PzKpfw IV. Deliveries began in 1939 and the Model D took part in the Polish and French campaigns. The PzKpfw's IV's original gun was the short-barrelled 7.5cm KwK 37 L/24, and its layout closely resembled that of the PzKpfw III. There were three compartments for the crew; the driver and radio operator occupied the front compartment, with the hull machine-gun on the right side and set slightly back from the driver. The turret in the fighting compartment contained the commander, gunner and loader. The PzKpfw IV's turret was traversed by electric motor (as against that of the PzKpfw III which was hand-operated). The IV could carry 80 rounds of ammunition and 2,800 belted rounds for the machine guns.

Operational experience indicated the need to increase the IV's armour, and the process began with the Model E. In 1943, the fitting of a long-barrelled 75mm (3in) L/43 gun to the Model F2 radically changed the role of the IV, which became a fighting tank and, along with the up-armoured Model G with side skirting plates, gradually took over from the PzKpfw III.

The later Model Gs carried a more powerful 75mm (3in) L/48 gun, enabling the PzKpfw IV to take on the T-34 on roughly equal terms. The larger gun meant a larger up-armoured turret.

The final model was the J, which appeared in 1944 and had much in common with the tank which had begun the war. By 1945 over 8,000 had been delivered. A few were still running with the Syrian army in the 1967 Arab-Israeli war.

ABOVE The badge of the Polish 1st Armoured Division. It shows a helmet adorned with wings.

hundred German panzers, assault guns and other armoured vehicles in the Falaise pocket. It concluded that only 4.6 per cent were destroyed by rockets and bombs, while almost 40 per cent were destroyed by their crews to avoid capture and around 30 per cent were abandoned undamaged. It was the unnerving effect of non-stop air attack which had cracked German morale rather than the physical damage inflicted.

The Falaise Pocket forms

A pocket was on the point of being formed south of Falaise in which German 7th Army, 5th Panzer Army and Panzer Group Eberbach were in imminent danger of being trapped by Canadian 1st and British 2nd Armies advancing from the north, and the northward-pushing U.S. 1st and 3rd Armies, the latter commanded by General George S. Patton.

For Blitzkrieg to succeed, its victim must unwittingly acquiesce in his own destruction. In 1940 it had been the French and British High Commands who had put their heads in the noose. Hitler, who had presided over the triumphs of 1940–41, now became the Allies' accomplice, ordering Operation Lüttich to be renewed on 11 August. Six panzer divisions were to attack south-west, under the command of General Hans Eberbach.

Hitler's C-in-C West, Field Marshal Günther von Kluge, who had urged a withdrawal, was only too well aware of "the incredibility of a large military force of twenty divisions blissfully planning an attack while far behind it an enemy is busily forming a noose with which to strangle it." Kluge, implicated in the July bomb plot to kill Hitler, committed suicide on 17 August.

The Falaise Pocket had begun to form on 13 August and the jaws snapped shut six days later, although fighting continued until 21 August. Of the 80,000 German troops in the pocket, only 20,000 escaped. Of the remainder, 10,000 were killed and 50,000 surrendered. Amid the shambles after the pocket's fall, the Americans found 380 tanks and self-propelled guns, more than 700 artillery pieces and 5,000 vehicles. In the British and Canadian sectors, 187 tanks and self-propelled guns, 157 armoured cars and armoured personnel carriers (APC), 252 artillery pieces and 2,500 motor vehicles were found. The Allied Supreme Commander, General Eisenhower, toured the battlefield two days later, encountering "scenes that could only be described by Dante. It was literally possible to walk for hundreds of yards at a time stepping over nothing but dead and decaying flesh."

ABOVE A PzKpfw IV from the 21st Panzer Division, knocked out in Normandy. The side skirt armour was added to help disrupt an incoming solid shot, making it less effective. It could also detonate a High Explosive round and had the advantage of detonating hollow charge rounds fired from a Bazooka or PIAT away from the main armour of the vehicle and therefore weakening their effect.

FOLLOWING PAGES The devastation in the Falaise pocket was remarked upon by all who saw it. The desperation of German troops to escape the attacks from the air and artillery fire from three sides led to units abandoning much of their equipment.

CHAPTER 28

PATTON

GEORGE S. PATTON WAS THE OUTSTANDING APOSTLE OF THE ARMOURED IDEA AMONG THE WESTERN ALLIES' SECOND WORLD WAR GENERALS AND A MAN WHO, TO THE VERY END OF HIS CAREER, WAS UNAFRAID TO COURT CONTROVERSY.

In Sicily in 1943 and in north-west Europe in 1944–45 Patton was a masterful handler of large armoured formations, prompting General Günther Blumentritt, the post-war biographer of Gerd von Rundstedt, to describe him as "the most aggressive panzer general of the Allies".

Patton served as an aide to General John J. Pershing in the campaign against the Mexican bandit Pancho Villa in 1916. After the United States joined the First World War in 1917, Patton served on the staff of the American Expeditionary Force (AEF), but in November of that year he was placed in command of a training school for tank crews. The AEF's aim was to create a tank corps of 200 heavy British Mark Vs and 1,000 Renault light tanks. This ambitious scheme was scaled down, and eventually eight heavy and 21 light battalions were raised, of which only four battalions saw combat.

In December 1917 Patton met Colonel J.F.C. Fuller, who briefed him on the use of tanks at the Battle of Cambrai. Patton first went into action commanding 304th Tank Brigade (326th and 327th Tank Battalions), part of U.S. First Army, at the Battle of St Mihiel, the pinching out of a salient that had threatened Allied movements in Champagne. Patton personally reconnoitred the area before the attack went in.

The armoured idea

Two weeks later, Patton was wounded during the Meuse-Argonne offensive and saw no more action before the war ended. In 1920, while serving on a committee charged with writing a manual on tank operations, he began to develop the idea that tanks should not be used merely as infantry support, but could operate as an independent fighting force.

Patton also became a fervent supporter of the American engineer J. Walter Christie and his M1931 suspension system, which enabled armoured vehicles to travel at speed across country. However, in the post-war climate of military cutbacks and American isolationism, Patton's ideas obtained little traction until the late 1930s, when another world war seemed imminent. Patton chafed at his peacetime duties, but in 1939, while commanding 3rd Cavalry, he met the U.S. Army Chief of Staff, General George C. Marshall, who marked him out as an ideal candidate for promotion to general.

In 1940 Patton served as an umpire in military manoeuvres, during which he met General Adna Chaffee, another American advocate of the armoured idea and commander of US I Armored Corps. In April 1941, promoted to Major-General, Patton became the commander of 2nd Armored Division. He was now the U.S. Army's most prominent expert on armoured warfare, a tireless advocate of offensive movement; and, in his flamboyant persona, sporting ivory-handled revolvers (relics of his Mexico days), the epitome of the all-American soldier.

North Africa and Sicily

In 1942, during the invasion of North Africa as part of Operation Torch, Patton commanded the Western Task Force which came ashore at Casablanca. In March 1943, after Rommel had routed the raw US II Corps at Kasserine Pass, in Tunisia, Patton assumed personal command of the formation, restoring its discipline and morale. He initiated wholesale changes, ordering all the troops to wear clean, pressed uniforms, setting rigorous schedules and insisting on absolute adherence to military protocol, before relinquishing the command to General Omar Bradley in order to participate in the planning of Operation Husky, the Allied invasion of Sicily.

During Husky, Patton commanded 7th Army which occupied the western half of Sicily. It was during this operation that Patton's career nearly came to an abrupt end when, in two separate incidents, on 3 and 10 August 1943, he struck hospitalized soldiers suffering from battle fatigue. The incidents were brought

LEFT Patton first encountered armoured vehicles in November 1917, when he was placed in command of the training of the fledgling American armoured force in France. Having been trained to drive a Renault at the factory, he personally backed tanks off the train on their arrival at the new training centre at Langres.

ABOVE The badge of the American 2nd Armoured Division.

OPPOSITE An American propoganda poster from the Second World War.

YOUR METAL

keeps 'em shooting

U. S. ARMY

146-147

COMBAT LESSONS

No. 9

man should be given a ride in a buttoned-up tank. One such ride does a lot to counteract the infantryman's dread of a tank attack and to increase his faith in his own ability to resist tanks."

Tank-Infantry Team Plays

States a report from the *752d Tank Battalion:* "At certain times the burden of carrying the attack must, because of the terrain and the situation, fall on the infantry. At other times, the tanks are best qualified to bear the brunt of the attack. Both units must know this and learn to recognize the situations in which one or the other unit should lead."

The following extracts from field reports describe team plays used by some tank-infantry units in specific situations.

—In General

From a *36th Infantry Division* training memorandum: "When infantry and tanks are used together, the tanks' primary targets are enemy machine guns and riflemen. Tanks will also make paths through wire and anti-personnel mines and break up any counterattack . . .

"If infantry does not come up with tanks within a reasonable time, a section or more of tanks should be sent back to investigate. The delay will usually have been caused by enemy MG's previously overlooked by the tanks."

From the *XXIV Corps* on LEYTE: "Infantrymen must protect the tanks by fire to prevent the enemy from ambushing the tanks. Ground distance between tanks and infantry is dependent upon the ability of the infantry to cover the tanks by effective fire."

"When possible, the tanks moved off the trails and covered one another. On each tank the bow gunner covered the area to the left, and the coaxial gunner covered the area to the right.

"Two infantrymen rode each tank; one was an automatic rifleman and the other manned the tank anti-aircraft gun. Both carried grenades and used the turret for protection. It was found best to assign a definite field of fire to each.

"Four mines and fuzes to be used by the infantry for local protection were carried in each tank."

—In Heavy Undergrowth

A report from *Headquarters XIV Corps* includes these comments on target designation: "Jap pillboxes are usually extremely well hidden and tanks are almost blind in thick vegetation or undergrowth. For these reasons, prime consideration should be given to target designation. Tank obstacles as well as targets should be designated to the tank commander by the infantry squad leader whenever possible.

"Tracer fire proved unsatisfactory for designating targets to the tanks. The best method was the use of red or violet smoke grenades. The full-charge grenade produces too much smoke and obscures the target. However, if the fuze is unscrewed from the grenade and half the charge removed, an adequate amount of smoke will be produced."

"Rifle projection of the grenade is desirable for longer ranges. Best results are obtained by arming the grenade before firing as this will then give a trail of smoke to the target."

Common Errors That Impair Teamwork

From the *36th Infantry Division:* "Platoon and squad leaders frequently forget during attacks that tanks are supporting them.

"Infantry leaders frequently go to a tank commander and tell him an enemy machine gun is holding them up but can give no idea of its location. Even giving four or five possible locations helps the tanks to reduce such a target.

"Lack of communication between tanks and front-line infantry often makes real coordination impossible. (See p. 16.)

"Time for tank reconnaissance and orders is often not provided.

"Failure to use enough tanks sometimes reduces the effectiveness of the combined assault.

"Tank timidity is frequently encouraged. Tanks must expect losses as do the riflemen."

"Failure to give tanks the complete plan of maneuver reduces the effectiveness of tank support."

"Failure to give tanks the plan of maneuver . . ."

Third Division doughboys ride to the front.

Technique of Transporting Infantry on Tanks

Load Allocation

Says *Lieutenant Colonel Kinne, 781st Tank Battalion,* after working with six infantry divisions during European campaigns: "In an infantry mission, a maximum of 10 men may be carried.

"It is imperative that before mounting the infantry, thorough plans are made by the infantry commanders and tank commanders who are to ride together. It is the duty of the infantry commander to mount infantry personnel in such manner as to preserve unit tactical integrity. This insures that no time is lost in organizing for combat after dismounting.

"Heavy-weapons units as well as riflemen may be transported. A complete machine-gun or mortar crew with weapon can be carried on a tank.

ABOVE AND LEFT The original booklet was part of a series issued by the US War Department in an attempt to ensure the latest information and experience of fighting reached the serving soldier. As the introduction states, "Since, to be effective, they must reach the soldier promptly, publication is not delayed to insure that they always represent the thoroughly digested views of the War Department." Contributions from serving soldiers were invited.

OPPOSITE Mobile artillery helped maintain the momentum of Patton's breakout to Avranches. Here M12 155mm (6.1in) self-propelled guns fire as a battery. The loader in the foreground holds one of the bag charges full of propellant.

to light by the journalist Drew Pearson and the resulting row ensured that Patton did not command a force in combat for the next 11 months. The more cautious and self-effacing General Omar Bradley, then Patton's junior, was appointed to command 1st US Army preparing for the invasion of Normandy.

The German High Command's continued respect for Patton meant that he played an important role in the Allied deception plan, codenamed Fortitude, which preceded Overlord. The Germans were led into believing that Patton had been appointed commander of the First United States Army Group (FUSAG) which was readying itself for an invasion in the Pas de Calais, but which was in fact an entirely fictitious unit. As a result German 15th Army remained in that area to meet the phantom threat.

Breakout at Avranches

Patton returned to active duty at the end of July 1944, commanding US 3rd Army, part of Bradley's 12th Army Group in north-west France. His leadership in the breakout toward Avranches showed his version of Blitzkrieg at its best. Third Army used forward scout units to establish the enemy's strength and dispositions. Self-propelled artillery moved forward with Patton's advanced units and engaged the enemy with indirect fire. Light aircraft operated over the battlefield, spotting artillery and providing reconnaissance. Once the enemy had been fixed, mechanized infantry went into the attack supported by armour. More armoured units then sought a breakthrough, exploiting any breach while preventing the enemy from recovering his balance. The efficient execution of this sequence depended on

761st TANK BATTALION

Before and during the Second World War, federal law prevented African-American soldiers from serving alongside white troops in the U.S. Army. The U.S. military establishment also harboured serious reservations about committing African-American troops to combat. Nevertheless, in 1941 General Lesley J. McNair, commander of Army Ground Forces, suggested that the Army should experiment with African-American combat units. The 761st Tank Battalion was activated on 1 April 1942 at Camp Clairborne, Louisiana, and began training on M5 Stuart light tanks. It moved on to M4 Shermans at Fort Hood, Texas, and was deployed to Europe in the autumn of 1944. The battalion had trained for almost two years while seeing white units deployed overseas after as little as two months training.

The battalion had its baptism of fire on 8 November 1944, sustaining 105 battle casualties and losing 14 tanks and another 20 damaged in combat. It took part in the relief of Bastogne in December and then crossed the Siegfried Line with 4th Armoured Division. At the end of the war it joined hands with the Red Army's First Ukrainian Front in Austria. The battalion, known as the Black Panthers, adopted the motto "Come out fighting".

For his extraordinary heroism in action between 15 and 19 November 1944, Staff Sergeant Ruben Rivers was awarded a posthumous Medal of Honor in 1997. The so-called "baddest man in the 761st", tank commander Sergeant Warren G.H. Crecy, a quiet easy-going fellow, was nominated for the Medal of Honor after knocking out an anti-tank position and a number of German machine-gun positions under heavy fire while armed only with a machine gun. He received a battlefield commission and retired with the rank of major.

On 24 November 1947, the 761st was reactivated as an integrated unit and served until 1955, when it was deactivated. It was awarded the Presidential Unit Citation by President Jimmy Carter in January 1978, and in 2005 a monument to the unit was unveiled on 761st Tank Battalion Drive, Fort Hood, during a ceremony attended by surviving veterans.

air reconnaissance and massive tactical air support co-ordinated at the point of contact with the enemy by an air traffic controller in one of the leading tanks.

Patton's rapid advance from Avranches to Argentan – some 100 kilometres (60 miles) – was achieved in two weeks and was also made possible by the receipt of Ultra intelligence on German movements, which enabled Patton to concentrate his forces for counter-moves. By mid-August 1944, Patton was outrunning his fuel supplies, but was champing at the bit to "bounce" the Rhine. On 21 August he wrote in his diary: "We have at this time the greatest chance to win the war ever presented. If they will let me move on with three corps … we can be in Germany in ten days". But the Allied Supreme Commander, General Dwight D. Eisenhower, favoured a "broad front" strategy, which would allow Patton's 3rd Army, on the right flank, to maintain its drive to the Saar, while Montgomery's 21st Army Group, on the left, seized the Channel supply ports and overran the enemy's V-1 launching sites. Patton did not get his way.

On the surface Patton and Montgomery were a study in opposites. Montgomery was prim, teetotal and schoolmasterly, a stringy birdlike man. Patton was the embodiment of all-American aggression, firmly of the belief that you grabbed the enemy by the nose, "the better to kick him in the pants". Both men had developed a hearty dislike for each other after their race to Messina in the campaign for Sicily. But they had more in common than they would have cared to admit. Both were instinctive showmen – Patton's revolver was matched by Monty's motley collection of cap badges – who concealed complex characters behind an all-too-evident egotism. They prompted mixed emotions in the men they led, some of them less than complimentary. Patton's nickname of "old Blood and Guts" was often said to stand for "our blood, his guts".

Battle of the Bulge

In December 1944, the Germans launched their last major offensive in the West, in the Ardennes. It was Hitler's last gamble – too little, too late. As Sepp Dietrich, commander of 6th SS Panzer Army, one of the two armies committed to the offensive, observed: "All Hitler wants me to do is to cross a river, capture Brussels and then go and take Antwerp. And all this in the worst time of the year through the Ardennes when the snow is waist deep and there isn't room to deploy four tanks abreast let alone armoured divisions."

Nevertheless, Operation Wacht am Rhein (Watch on the Rhine) gave the Allies a massive shock before they recovered their poise and attempted to deal with the German salient which had developed – the so-called Bulge. Patton, whose 3rd Army was locked in heavy fighting near Saaarbrucken, grasped the situation immediately and ordered his staff to prepare three separate contingency orders to cover the despatch of 3rd Army northward to slice into the southern shoulder of the German salient.

At a meeting of the Allied high command held near Verdun on 19 December, Eisenhower asked Patton how long it would

RIGHT Cavalry pass the machines that were shortly to eclipse them.

take to disengage six divisions of 3rd Army to relieve US 101st Airborne Division, which was trapped in Bastogne. Patton told the astonished Eisenhower he was ready to go with three divisions as early as 21 December. Eisenhower gave him the go-ahead to attack with 4th Armoured and 26th and 80th Infantry divisions on 22 December.

Patton had not lost his flair for colourful phraseology, telling Bradley on 21 December, "Brad this time the Kraut's got his head in the meat grinder and this time I've got hold of the handle". He was as good as his word. In one of the best-executed manoeuvres of the war, completed within four days, he disengaged and realigned three divisions to drive into the southern flank of the lengthening salient. Bastogne was relieved by 4th Armoured Division on 26 December. The Allies went on the offensive on 3 January 1945 in rapidly improving weather conditions, and by 16 January the salient had been eliminated. The cost to the German Army had been 100,000 men killed or wounded and some 800 tanks destroyed.

Third Army began crossing the Rhine on 22 March 1945. On the night of 26/27 March 1945, Patton sent an armoured column deep behind German lines to a POW camp at Hammelburg, east of Frankfurt. The column reached the camp but suffered heavy casualties as it made its way back to American lines. Patton claimed that his aim had been to confuse the enemy, but it emerged that his son-in-law, Lieutenant John K. Waters, who had been captured by the Germans in North Africa in 1943, was an inmate of the Hammelburg camp. The suspicion remains that Patton's principal purpose was to rescue him. In this he failed, as Waters was wounded during the operation.

Patton ended the war with another whirlwind advance, into Czechoslovakia. He then requested but failed to obtain a command in the Pacific. In July 1945, he was appointed military governor of Bavaria but was obliged to step down after making a number of remarks favourable to the Nazis. He died after a road accident on 9 December 1945.

M4 SHERMAN

SPECIFICATION // M4 SHERMAN

CREW: 5

WEIGHT: 30.2 -33.6 tons

ARMOUR: 75-105mm (3-4.1in)

ARMAMENT: 1x 75mm gun, 2x .30 Browning machine guns

TOP SPEED: 38-47 km/h (24-29 mph)

ENGINE: (M4 and M4A1) Wright Continental R-975 petrol radial 353hp

More Shermans were manufactured during the war than any other single tank of the Western Allies, a tribute to the American genius for mass production. When production ceased in June 1945, 49,234 had been built. Combat experience quickly revealed that the Sherman was undergunned in comparison with the German Tiger and Panther, and later models were armed with a 76mm (3in) gun, which improved armour-piercing capability but nevertheless fell short of that possessed by the British Sherman conversion, the Firefly, which had a 17pdr gun. Although Shermans were no more vulnerable to "brewing up" if penetrated by a German shell than other tanks, their ammunition could and did catch fire. "Wet" stowage was introduced to reduce the likelihood of this, with the ammunition bins being surrounded by water jackets. As well as providing the backbone of the U.S. armoured force during the war, the Sherman was also the mainstay of British armoured divisions.

BELOW LEFT A 75mm (3in) shell as fired by the M4 Sherman. Shells were colour- coded so soldiers could tell at a glance what they contained. Black meant Armour Piercing, a solid shot containing no explosive.

BELOW RIGHT M4A2E8. A later model version of the Sherman showing wider tracks and a larger 76mm (3in) high velocity gun in a redesigned turret. This vehicle was used for the 2014 war film *Fury*.

OPPOSITE A Sherman of the US 9th Army in German mud, early 1945. Tracks distribute the weight of a tank, biting into the mud with the drive sprocket. However, if the tank becomes stuck, a tow rope or shovels and timber are needed to give the tracks purchase.

CHAPTER 29

TANKS IN THE FAR EAST AND PACIFIC

THE JAPANESE BEGAN EXPERIMENTING WITH TANKS AT THE END OF THE FIRST WORLD WAR, BUYING A BRITISH MARK IV TANK AND SOME 12 MONTHS LATER A HANDFUL OF MEDIUM A WHIPPETS AND FRENCH RENAULT FTS. THE FIRST JAPANESE TANK UNIT WAS FORMED IN 1925, BUT THE ONLY FOREIGN TANKS THEN AVAILABLE WERE OBSOLESCENT RENAULT FTS, PROMPTING THE DEVELOPMENT OF AN INDIGENOUS TANK.

The First Japanese tank

The Japanese design team, led by Captain (later Lieutenant-General) Hara, completed their assignment within 21 months. The first Japanese tank, built at the Osaka Arsenal, was demonstrated at the Fuji training ground in 1927. It weighed 18 tons, had a road speed of 20 km/h (12.5 mph) and three turrets: a central two-man turret armed with a low-velocity 57mm (2.2in) gun; and two one-man machine-gun turrets, one at the front of the hull and the other at the rear behind the engine compartment. It impressed on its demonstration but was not adopted by the Japanese army.

Instead the army issued a specification for a 10-ton infantry-support vehicle, which became the Type 89 medium tank, with a single two-man turret armed with a 57mm (2.2in) gun. Its original petrol engine was later replaced by a six-cylinder air-cooled diesel in the Type 89B, which performed more efficiently in Manchuria (which from 1932 had been the Japanese colony of Manchukuo and an important industrial base). Between 1931 and 1939 some 400 Type 89s were built. Its combat debut came in 1932 in the so-called "Shanghai Incident", a series of brutal engagements between Japan and China which preceded the

ABOVE War with China in 1937 led the Japanese command to choose the Type 97 or Chi-Ha tank over a rival design – the Chi-Ni that was lighter in protection and armament. The Chi-Ha had similar design features to the Type 95 Ha Go light tank but with a two-man turret and thicker armour.

LEFT The design of the Type 89 tank was influenced by imported tanks from Europe – in particular the Vickers Medium C. Early models had a petrol engine but Japan started a Dieselization programme for its vehicles in the mid 1930s, leading to a new variant the Type 89 B.

Second Sino-Japanese War that began five years later. The Type 89 performed well in the Sino-Japanese War, albeit against an enemy who possessed few anti-tank weapons. However, it was outclassed by Soviet armour in the 1939 clash between Japan and the Soviet Union at Khalkin Gol. The Japanese had been pushing across the Nomonhan River and precipitated a major battle with a Soviet armoured force commanded by General Zhukov, who surrounded and destroyed Japanese Sixth Army in a cauldron battle which anticipated the Blitzkrieg of 1941.

Infantry support

The reverse at Khalkin Gol accelerated the production of the Type 97, although it did little to change Japanese armoured philosophy. Influenced by tank developments pioneered in Britain by Hobart in the early 1930s, a Japanese combined arms mechanized brigade had been created, promising more than a philosophy of infantry support. However, after the outbreak of war with China in 1937, the brigade was broken up and its tanks were parcelled out to infantry formations. It was only in 1942 that the Japanese had second thoughts, concentrating their tanks into three divisions whose main weapon was the Type 97.

Japan organized the empire it had acquired by 1940 into a Greater East Asia Co-Prosperity Sphere. Both the Japanese conquests before and after its entry into the Second World War following the attack on the U.S. naval base at Pearl Harbor on 7 December 1941 were largely achieved with capital ships, notably

TYPE 97 CHI-HA MEDIUM TANK

SPECIFICATION // TYPE 97 CHI-HA

CREW: 4

WEIGHT: 15 tons

ARMOUR: 25mm (1in)

ARMAMENT: 1x 57mm gun, 2x 7.7mm machine-guns, one in bow, one in rear

TOP SPEED: 38 km/h (24 mph)

ENGINE: Mitsubishi 170hp air-cooled diesel

The Type 97, most of which were built by Mitsubishi, entered service in 1937 and was the mainstay of the Japanese tank arm. Experience in clashes with Soviet armour in 1939 indicated that Japan was falling behind the West in terms of tank design and the Type 97 was rearmed with a 57mm (2.2in) high-velocity gun housed in a larger turret, which increased the tank's weight to 15.75 tons. This version began to reach regiments in 1942. The tank usually carried approximately 120 rounds (80 HE and 40 AP) and 2,350 rounds of machine-gun ammunition. The higher proportion of HE ammunition compared to other tanks of the period stemmed from the Japanese belief that the tank's principal role was that of infantry support rather than a weapon to be used against enemy armour. The Type 97 chassis was used in small numbers in three self-propelled mountings: the Ho-Ni I tank destroyer armed with a 75mm (3in) gun; the Ho-Ni II with a 105mm (4.1in) howitzer; and the Ho-Ro with a 150mm (6in) howitzer.

aircraft carriers, bomber and fighter aircraft and the Japanese infantry. The technological thrust of Japanese war industry was focused on warships and aircraft rather than on tanks. Japan managed to produce only about 500 medium tanks a year, and in 1944 and 1945 the devastation wrought by U.S. bombers on its war industries brought tank production to a virtual halt. General Hara ended the war working in an aircraft factory.

Throughout the Second World War, infantry support remained the principal role of Japanese armour. This mattered little in the six months of victory which Admiral Yamamoto, commander-in-chief of the Japanese Combined Fleet from 1939, guaranteed the Emperor Hirohito in 1941. The Allies at the time had few tanks in the Far East and Pacific theatres. Whereas General Yamashita had 200 tanks in the force with which he took Singapore in February 1942, his British opponent, General Percival, had none and few anti-tank guns. It was a Japanese detachment of 15 Type 97 medium and Type 95 light tanks which burst through the British defences along the Slim River and opened the way to the city's fall.

Once the Japanese drive had been checked at the Battle of the Coral Sea in May 1942 and halted at Midway in the following June, the Allies also began to employ tanks in infantry support roles in their long, hard fightback on mainland Southeast Asia and in the islands of the Pacific. The British used Grants and the Americans Shermans, both of which were superior to their Japanese opposite numbers, many of which were used in static defensive roles, as in the defence of Iwo Jima In February/March 1945.

Principal Operations

The main offensive operations carried out by Japanese tanks included included Operation Ichi-Go in southern China in the summer of 1944, where 3rd Tank Division, deploying 255 Type 97s and Type 95s, played a significant role against the hapless Chinese. South of Imphal in June 1944, 14th Tank Regiment had a sharp encounter with British M3s in which it lost almost all its tanks. It was reconstituted at approaching half its original strength and was destroyed at Meiktila in February/ March 1945. At Luzon, Yamashita, the victor at Singapore, used 1st and 2nd Tank Divisions to cover his withdrawal into the interior in March 1945.

The last battle in which Japanese tanks took part was on the island of Shimushu, after the Soviet invasion of Manchuria. After the German surrender the previous May, four Soviet armies had been rapidly transferred to Siberia and Mongolia, and a massive offensive was launched on 8 August 1945 along four axes by 1.5 million men and 5,500 tanks, the bulk of them T-34/85s. The Soviet Union occupied Manchuria within two weeks.

RIGHT Australian Bren gunner Corporal G.G. Fletcher fires on Japanese troops as they flee from a pill box at Giropa Point, Buna in Papau New Guinea in January 1943. The tank, an M3 Stuart, knocked out the pill box, while the infantry from D Company, 12th Battalion advanced with it through the palm groves. The use of armour in the Far East needed excellent infantry/tank co-operation in the restricted, close country position.

CHAPTER 30

WAR IN PEACE

AT THE END OF THE SECOND WORLD WAR, THE EXHAUSTED VICTORS BEGAN TO DISMANTLE THE ENORMOUS MILITARY APPARATUSES THAT THEY HAD ASSEMBLED TO BRING ABOUT THE DEFEAT OF THE AXIS POWERS.

In 1945, the United States Army fielded 16 armoured divisions, comprising 52 tank battalions and 65 independent non-divisional tank battalions. By 1948, it had a single tank division with a paper strength of 373 tanks. The remainder of the Army's tanks were distributed among the infantry divisions' tank battalions and regimental tank companies. A division had a nominal strength of 147 tanks. There were no independent tank battalions or tank destroyer battalions. Tank Destroyer Command had been

scrapped and was not mourned, as it had exercised a baleful influence over tank development during the war years.

The Korean War
Relations between the Soviet Union and the Western Allies soon degenerated into mutual suspicion and then outright hostility, ushering in a period known as the Cold War, in which large land forces of the US-led NATO alliance faced

those of the Soviet-dominated Warsaw Pact in Central Europe. The threat of a catastrophic nuclear conflict held the peace there, but a series of proxy wars broke out elsewhere as the United States and the Soviet Union (and its ally China, after the communist revolution there in 1949) sought to establish a geostrategic advantage over the other.

At the end of the war, Korea, which had previously been occupied by Japan, had been divided along the 38th Parallel, with Soviet forces occupying the north and those of the United States the south. The North Korean president, Kim Il Sung, claimed the entire country, but elections in the south produced a government which was friendly to the United States and by 1949 both Soviet and U.S. troops had withdrawn. Diplomatic efforts to resolve tensions between North and South Korea faltered and a series of border clashes broke out. In June 1950, secure in the

knowledge of support from China (where Mao's communists had come to power in 1949), the North Korean People's Army (KPA) invaded the south, pinning a predominantly American force under the banner of the United Nations within the Pusan perimeter in south-east Korea.

The KPA had deployed some 250 T34/76s and T34/85s in infantry support roles, while the South was reinforced by U.S. armour. At the time of the invasion the four U.S. infantry divisions in Japan each had a company of M24 Chaffee light tanks, which had entered service in Europe in 1944. They were rushed to Korea. The Chaffee's 75mm (3in) gun was unable to penetrate the armour of the T-34/85 and its own armour was not proof against the guns of the Soviet tanks.

More American medium tanks began arriving in Korea at the end of July 1950, but no armoured division was despatched

OPPOSITE A captured T34/85 is inspected by UN soldiers. The T34/85 formed the spearhead of North Korea's invasion of the South in June 1950. The Americans rushed more modern vehicles and weapons such as the M26 Pershing to the country, which proved superior to the older Soviet tank.

ABOVE An M-46 tows another out of the mud. Water-filled paddy fields made tank movement more difficult in Korea. The aim of the bright tiger-stripe patterns was to frighten Chinese soldiers, who were considered to have a superstitious fear of tigers.

M26 PERSHING

CREW: 5

WEIGHT: 41.1 tons

ARMOUR: 102mm (4in)

ARMAMENT: 1x 90mm gun, 1x .50 machine gun, 1x .30 machine gun

TOP SPEED: 48 km/h (30 mph)

ENGINE: Ford GAF V-8 500hp petrol

The Pershing was conceived as the T26E3, a counter to the Tiger and Panther with a 90mm (3.5in) gun capable of penetrating their armour, a low silhouette and overall battlefield mobility. However, the Pershing had a fractious development as disagreement flared between the U.S. Ordnance Department, the Armored Force and the Army Ground Forces over the need for a heavy tank. The head of Army Ground Forces, General Lesley McNair saw the introduction of a new heavy tank as introducing unnecessary complications into an already overstretched trans-Atlantic supply chain. Moreover, many in the U.S. tank arm believed – incorrectly as it transpired – that the M4 Sherman was a match for German heavy armour.

General George Marshall, the U.S. Army Chief of Staff, gave the go-ahead for the T26E3, which went into production in November 1944 and acquired the name Pershing after the First World War U.S. Expeditionary Force commander. The first shipment of 20 Pershings arrived in Antwerp in January 1945. Another 310 arrived in Europe before war's end, but only the original 20 saw combat. Twelve Pershings were despatched to Okinawa in August 1945, but Japan surrendered before they were committed. The Pershing was subsequently re-classified a medium tank and in a re-designated form gave sterling service in the Korean War as the M46 Patton.

The M26 Pershing, a significant departure from previous American tank designs. Twenty M26s were rushed to Europe in January 1945 and supported by the Zebra Mission. They were followed by 310 more before the end of the war in May, but only these first 20 saw combat.

to the theatre because commanders on the ground considered the terrain generally unfavourable to large-scale armoured operations. Nevertheless, 309 M26 Pershing tanks were sent to Korea in 1950, and the shortfall in regimental tank companies made good by reconditioned M4 Shermans.

On 15 September 1950, the UN commander-in-chief, General Douglas MacArthur, mounted an amphibious landing at Inchon, high up on the west coast of South Korea, which combined with a successful breakout from Pusan to drive the KPA back into North Korea. During the subsequent fighting there were a total of 119, mostly small-scale, tank versus tank actions involving U.S. Army and Marine units in which some 97 T-34s were knocked out. After November 1950, North Korean tanks were seldom encountered.

Vietnam

Just as in Korea, the long war in Vietnam had its origins in the opening for nationalists which emerged after the Japanese defeat in a former European colony, and led to an equally dangerous indirect confrontation between superpowers. It began in 1946 with Vietnamese nationalists (Viet Minh) fighting the restored French colonial power and ended with the defeat in 1975 of the U.S.-backed South Vietnamese forces (ARVN) by the North Vietnamese Army (NVA). Tanks played a relatively minor role in the conflict. The land war in Vietnam was dominated by infantry and firepower, in large part because the North Vietnamese initially had few tanks of their own and their opponents, the French and later the Americans and their allies, saw the struggle as a guerrilla war in country unsuited to armoured warfare. It was not until November 1967 that an American feasibility study revealed that tanks could operate in some 60 per cent of Vietnam during the dry season and 46 per cent in the monsoon season, while armoured personnel carriers (APCs) could operate in 65 per cent of Vietnam all year round.

The principal role of tanks in Vietnam was that of supporting the infantry, and the major threat to them was posed by mines and infantry anti-tank weapons. The tanks employed in the conflict were, on the American side, the M48 Patton medium tank, the M551 Sheridan light tank, and a few Sherman M4A3–M4A6 medium tanks. From late 1968, the Australian armoured contingent in Vietnam consisted of three squadrons of the 1st Armoured Regiment, Royal Australian Armoured Corps (RAAC), equipped with Centurions. The North Vietnamese Army and the regular units of the Viet Cong (Communist insurgents) were supplied with Soviet tanks: T-34/85 medium tanks, the T-54 main battle tank and the PT-76 light amphibious tank. The Chinese provided the NVA with the Type 59 main battle tank (a version of the T-54), the Type 62 light tank (a smaller version of the Type 59) and the Type 63 light amphibious tank, their version of the PT-76. The major ARVN tank was the American M41 Walker Bulldog, which replaced the M24 Chaffee light tanks that the South Vietnamese had inherited in 1954 from the departing French. The Chaffee had been well-liked by its Vietnamese crews, small men who were not bothered by its cramped interior, a feature which made it unpopular with American crews.

ABOVE A fleet of PT-76 light tanks crossing a river. The PT-76 was a reconnaissance vehicle. It was able to swim, which gave it exceptional mobility but made it larger than equivalent vehicles and lightly armoured. The North Vietnamese made use of the PT-76 during the Vietnam War. It had heavy firepower, but was vulnerable to anti-tank weapons.

RIGHT An example of the colourful tiger and dragon imagery painted on some American tanks in Korea during 1951.

Ben Het

There was only one tank-on-tank engagement in Vietnam between NVA and U.S. armour, a skirmish at Ben Het on the night of 3 March 1969. Two PT-76s of the NVA's 202nd Tank Regiment were glimpsed through thick mist at a range of 1,000 metres (1,100 yards) by M48s of 1st Battalion, 69th Armor. Their infrared searchlights could not penetrate the murk, but the American tanks used the muzzle flashes of the PT-76s to pin the enemy, hitting one of them with the second round fired by Specialist Frank Hembree. The resulting blaze illuminated a second PT-76, which suffered a similar fate.

Throughout most of the war the NVA, which lacked air cover, was reluctant to commit large bodies of tanks to battle and also placed great emphasis on camouflage. However, in the spring of 1972, during the protracted battle for An Loc, attacks on the ARVN-held town were launched by T-54s and PT-76s ahead of dense masses of infantry. They were blunted by ARVN infantry, US anti-tank helicopters firing TOW (Tube-launched, Optically tracked, Wire-guided) missiles and massive USAF air strikes, including "Arc Light" missions flown by B-52 bombers, during which the NVA lost some 80 armoured vehicles in the course of the six-week battle. It has been estimated that overall NVA tank losses in the spring offensive of 1972 were approximately 700.

The United States withdrew from Vietnam in 1973 and a North Vietnamese victory followed in April 1975 after the NVA had launched a crushing offensive against the demoralized ARVN. At noon on 30 April 1975, an NVA T-54 burst through the gates of Saigon's presidential palace, bringing the 30-years' war to an end.

BELOW The American M-24 light tank was used by the French and the South Vietnamese during the war. In 1954 ten were even flown in pieces into Dien Bien Phu to try and defeat the Vietnamese siege. By the mid 1960s, the ARVN's M24s were crippled by a lack of spare parts and they were replaced with M41 Walker Bulldogs.

OPPOSITE The Australian forces in Vietnam were supported by a Squadron of 26 Centurions. They first deployed in 1968 and operated until the tanks were withdrawn in 1971. A number of extra features were added to the tanks, including extra storage for ammunition and equipment. They also had their armoured side skirts removed, as it was found that the dense jungle could get caught in the tracks. The tanks were Mark 5/1s, armed with the 20pdr gun.

OPPOSITE BELOW LEFT Centurions sent to Vietnam received modifications to allow them to fit better into the American logistic system. A good example is the .30-calibre M1919 machine gun mounted on the commander's hatch.

OPPOSITE BELOW RIGHT An M48A3 in Vietnam. The main threat to tanks in Vietnam were mines and light anti-tank weapons such as rocket-propelled grenades (RPGs). The crew of this vehicle have added a large number of sandbags to provide extra protection from RPGs. This was common when tanks were used to escort convoys, as they could be expected to attract heavy enemy fire.

CHAPTER 31

BRITISH TANKS OF THE COLD WAR

THE BRITISH HABIT OF CLASSIFYING TANKS AS INFANTRY OR CRUISER TOOK A LONG TIME TO CHANGE. YET AS EARLY AS 1943, WHEN THE DEVELOPMENT OF THE CENTURION BEGAN, GENERAL (LATER FIELD MARSHAL) SIR BERNARD MONTGOMERY NOTED THE ADVANTAGES OF A SINGLE "UNIVERSAL" TANK, WHICH HE CALLED A "CAPITAL" TANK – A THEME TO WHICH HE RETURNED IN 1946, WHEN HE BECAME THE CHIEF OF THE IMPERIAL GENERAL STAFF.

This idea of a "universal" tank anticipated the emergence in the 1960s of the Main Battle Tank (MBT), a single tank that would combine the functions of the different classes of armour – light, medium and heavy – which had dominated the "armoured idea" before and during the Second World War.

This development did not meet with universal approval in the War Office, but a candidate was waiting in the wings: the

Centurion. The A41 Centurion was originally intended to be a cruiser tank, but after the war it adopted many of the features of the A45, a 55-ton infantry support tank which never got beyond the prototype stage. In the late 1940s, the A45 re-emerged, in modified form, as the FV214, the 65-ton Conqueror. This was armed with an American 120mm (4.6in) gun firing tungsten-cored Armour-Piercing Discarding Sabot (APDS) ammunition,

which replaced traditional full-calibre armour-piercing shot, and High Explosive Squash Head (HESH) rounds, which succeeded conventional high-explosive ammunition. The Conqueror, which was in part a response to the Soviet IS-3 heavy tank, underwent trials in 1952 and was intended to serve alongside the Centurion, the first Mark I examples of which had arrived in northern Europe less than a month after Germany's unconditional surrender. Only 180 Conquerors were built, but they continued in service with the British Army until 1966. By then, the Centurion had established itself as the British Army's main battle tank.

The first Centurions to go into service in 1945 were armed with the wartime 76mm (3in) 17-pounder gun. In 1948, the Mark III Centurion was upgunned to carry an 83.8mm (3.3in) or 20-pounder gun, a weapon influenced by the 88mm (3.5in) KwK 43 L/71 gun of the Tiger II, which many rate as the finest tank gun of the Second World War. The gun was electronically stabilized in elevation and azimuth, an enormous boost to gunnery control and shooting. Along with conventional full-calibre armour-piercing projectiles, the Centurion carried APDS ammunition with a higher muzzle velocity than any other tank gun ammunition and the most powerful of its day.

In 1955, the Centurion's 83.8mm (3.3in) gun was replaced by the 105mm (4.1in) L7 gun. The tank's glacis plate was also thickened – a lesson learned from British tanks' inferiority in firepower and protection to the German tanks of the Second World War – and infrared night-fighting lights were added and a ranging gun installed. The 105mm (4.1in) gun and its derivatives armed an estimated 35,000 tanks worldwide, including the German Leopard 1, the Israeli Merkava, and the

Swedish S-tank, making it the most widely used post-war tank gun outside the Soviet bloc. When the Centurion itself began to go out of British service in the 1960s, other nations, notably Israel, stepped forward to purchase Centurions with more powerful new engines and transmissions.

The Centurion made its debut in the Korean War with three squadrons of the 8th King's Royal Irish Hussars. Operating in sub-zero temperatures in the winter of 1950–51, the 8th Hussars quickly learned how to park on straw to prevent the tank's tracks from being frozen to the ground. During the Battle of the Imjin River in April 1951, Centurions covered the withdrawal of 29th Brigade with the loss of five tanks, most of which were recovered and repaired.

In the 1950s, Centurions equipped three British armoured divisions in Germany and during the 1950s and 1960s, they were bought by 16 countries, with more than half the total production of 4,432 tanks being exported.

The Chieftain

The Centurion was followed into service by the Chieftain main battle tank (MBT), the development of which had run through the 1950s, although a prototype was not built until 1959. Among the Chieftain's innovatory features was the supine position of the driver, which lowered the height of the hull, making it a less conspicuous target for enemy armour. A by-product of this reconfiguration was the reduction in the weight of the Chieftain to 55 tons – compared with the 65 tons of the Conqueror – despite its thicker frontal armour.

The Chieftain's 120mm (4.7in) rifled gun made it NATO's most powerful tank. In contrast to the Centurion and Conqueror, which were both powered by Rolls-Royce engines, Chieftain was

OPPOSITE In common with most tanks, Centurions received continuous upgrades throughout their service. One of the most significant was the introduction of the 105mm (4.1in) L7 gun. This upgrade began in 1959 and the result can be seen here. When it was introduced it could defeat any Soviet tank.

ABOVE A tank is not a comfortable environment to live or fight in. This Centurion has been cut in half to show the turret crew. The commander sits behind the gunner on the right of the turret, with the loader on the left. The loader is the only crewman with any space to move about in. The fourth crewman, the driver, is alone in the hull.

CHIEFTAIN MAIN BATTLE TANK

SPECIFICATION // CHIEFTAIN MAIN BATTLE TANK

CREW: 4

WEIGHT: 55 tons

ARMOUR: (glacis) 120mm (4.7in); (hull sides) 38mm (1.5in); (turret) 195mm (7.7in)

ARMAMENT: 1x L11A5 120mm rifled, 2x 7.62 machine guns

TOP SPEED: (road) 48 km/h (30 mph)

ENGINE: Leyland L60 750hp multi-fuel

powered by an aero-engine based on one developed in Germany before the Second World War. This could tolerate a wide range of fuels, a significant factor following the 1957 NATO decision that fighting vehicles be powered by multi-fuel engines.

The problems associated with meeting this requirement delayed the introduction of the Chieftain into service until 1966. The Chieftain's initial fire control system was a 12.7mm (0.5in) ranging gun mounted over the main gun. This fired ranging shots to a maximum of 2,400 metres (2,600 yards), when the tracer in the ranging round burned out, although its HE tip nevertheless created a visible "splash" on impact. From the early 1970s, the ranging gun was replaced with a laser rangefinder with a 10-kilometre (6.2-mile) range, enabling more rapid engagements of a greater number of targets at increased range. Later models were equipped with an improved fire control system boosted by a digital ballistic computer and many had their infrared searchlights replaced by TOGS (Thermal Observation Gunnery Sight). The Chieftain was also fitted with schnorkel deep-wading equipment.

The Chieftain was supplied to at least six countries, including Iran, Kuwait, Oman and Jordan. There was significant Israeli input into ensuring that the Chieftain operated successfully in a hull-down position in a desert environment, co-operation which spurred the development of the Israeli Merkava. And it was the IDF's General Tal who recommended the purchase by the Iranian government of 707 Chieftains in 1971. The tank was used extensively by the Iranians in the Iran–Iraq war of 1980–88. Later, Kuwaiti Chieftains saw combat in the First Gulf War, in which 136 were lost.

RIGHT Whatever the reason, tanks seem to fascinate all ages. Here three West German children encounter a Chieftain during a training exercise. These took vehicles out of their usual training areas and made encounters with the civilian population much more frequent. The 12 tubes above the main gun were used during exercises as an economical alternative to firing a shell.

CHAPTER 32

SOVIET TANKS OF THE COLD WAR

IN CONTRAST TO ITS WARTIME ALLIES, THE UNITED STATES AND BRITAIN, THE SOVIET UNION HAD AN UNWAVERING BELIEF IN THE VALUE OF ARMOUR AS A DOMINANT ELEMENT IN GROUND FORCES. FAR FROM REDUCING THE NUMBER OF TANKS AND ARMOURED DIVISIONS AT THE END OF THE SECOND WORLD WAR, IT RETAINED LARGE NUMBERS OF T-34S – ESTIMATED AT SOME 25,000 IN SOME 50 TANK DIVISIONS – AND MAINTAINED A HIGHLY PRAGMATIC POLICY OF BASING EACH NEW TANK OF THE POST-WAR ERA ON PREVIOUSLY SUCCESSFUL MODELS.

In the years following 1945, tanks of the Soviet Army (as the Red Army had been renamed in 1946), dominated the scene, particularly given the Soviet Union's aggressive posture during the Cold War. At the beginning of 1989, two years before the collapse of the Soviet empire, the Soviet Union and its satellites in Eastern Europe , who were organized into the Warsaw Pact alliance (Bulgaria, Czechoslovakia, East Germany, Hungary, Poland and Romania) could put more than 57,300 tanks into the field compared with the 22,224 tank strength of NATO (the North Atlantic Treaty Organization, comprising the United States, Canada, the United Kingdom and 13 Western European nations).

The T-34's successors

The T-34/76, possibly the single most successful tank design in history, was capable of considerable stretch. From 1943, its classic hooded turret with a 76mm (3in) gun was replaced by a new turret mounting a more powerful 85mm (3.35in) gun. In 1945, the T-44 was introduced, marrying the T-34/85 turret with a new lower hull and suspension. The first batch arrived just in time to be despatched to the Far East for the offensive against the Japanese in Manchuria in August 1945.

The T-44 was succeeded by the T-54 and the more powerful T-55, the major Soviet tanks of the mid-20th century. Eventually some 100,000 T-54s and T-55s were built in Poland, Czechoslovakia and China (the last as the Type 59). T-54s played a large part in the suppression of the Hungarian uprising in 1956 and both tanks fought in many other conflicts, including the Arab-Israeli Six Day War of 1967, the last stages of the Vietnam War, the 1980s conflicts in Afghanistan and Angola and the Second Gulf War of 2003.

The T-62 was introduced in 1961 and mounted a U-5T smoothbore 115mm (4.53in) gun with integrated fire control. Based on the T-55, the T-62 nevertheless took tank design another step forward. Its gun fired arrow-like, Armour Piercing Fin Stabilized Discarding Sabot projectiles (APFSDS), at a higher muzzle velocity (1,680m/s: 5,500 ft/s) than any other contemporary tank weapon, achieving greater penetration. Subsequently, the APFSDS armament was almost universally adopted by armies worldwide. By the time production of the T-62, in modified form, ceased in the Soviet Union in 1983

SECRET

SECRET 20

approximately 20,000 had been built.

The T-62 was succeeded by the T-64, which introduced the 125mm (4.93in) smoothbore gun. The T-64 was highly capable, but complex and expensive. Its counterpart the T-72 was simpler to manufacture and operate, and some 30,000 were built, of which about 6000 were exported. The T-72 incorporated new features. From 1978, laser rangefinders were fitted, replacing parallax optical rangefinders which could not be used for distances under 1,000 metres (1,100 yards). After 1985 all T-72s had their 125mm (4.93in) guns upgraded to fire guided anti-tank missiles from the barrel as well as standard main gun ammunition, including HEAT (High Explosive Anti-Tank)

ABOVE The Soviet T-55 is one of the most common tanks of the post-war era. More than 50,000 were built and they were exported to dozens of countries. Both sides in the Cold War put a great deal of effort into gathering intelligence on their opponent's vehicles. Many details were highly classified. This image was used to help soldiers identify the T-55. The photo was likely taken clandestinely, and the "SECRET" stamps show how closely guarded such material was.

BELOW These identification cards, issued by the US Army, were part of a massive effort by NATO forces to ensure that servicemen knew both what Soviet vehicles looked like and what their Allied compatriot's vehicles looked like to ensure there were as few "blue on blue" incidents as possible if the Cold War turned Hot. To this day, vehicle recognition is still a key part of military training for very similar reasons.

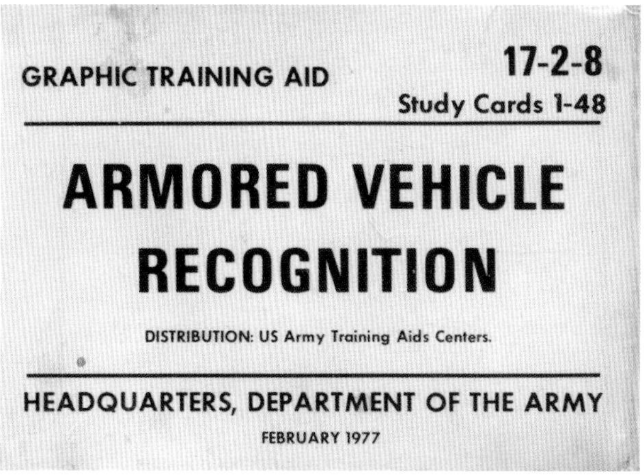

GRAPHIC TRAINING AID 17-2-8

Study Cards 1-48

ARMORED VEHICLE RECOGNITION

DISTRIBUTION: US Army Training Aids Centers.

HEADQUARTERS, DEPARTMENT OF THE ARMY

FEBRUARY 1977

TANKS AND NUCLEAR WEAPONS

The armies with the most sophisticated modern arsenals in the 1970s were those of the Soviet Union and members of NATO. Tanks were developed in accordance with contrasting strategies, although their weapons show many similarities. Soviet determination to avoid a repetition of the casualties suffered in the Second World War gave rise to a strategy of offensive operations. This involved massive firepower and rapid manoeuvre, to soften up defences before tanks and mechanized infantry formations moved quickly to exploit any opening created and to seize objectives, so that tactical nuclear weapons used against them would end up destroying the things they were supposed to protect. In January 2006, the Polish government published a declassified Soviet 1979 battle plan, "Seven Days to the Rhine", which envisaged a Blitzkrieg-style attack on Western Europe and the use of nuclear weapons in response to a NATO nuclear first strike. This remained Warsaw Pact doctrine until the late 1980s and explains why up to 250 tactical-range nuclear warheads were based in Poland. NATO's ability to withdraw and counter-attack in the face of an offensive was constrained by the need to protect the territory it was designed to defend. In the days when a Soviet offensive was a possibility, NATO's defensive strategy involved the use of everything from long-range artillery to short-range missiles and rockets, with tanks, supported by infantry and tactical air assets.

GTA 17-2-8
FIG. 43

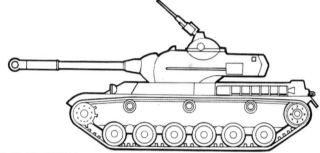

TK 61–JAPANESE
REAR OVERHANGING TURRET WITH PROMINENT CUPOLA
6 ROAD WHEELS, 3 SUPPORT ROLLERS
90-MM GUN TUBE WITH BORE EVACUATOR AND FLASH DEFLECTOR

GTA 17-2-8
FIG. 22

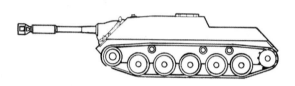

JP KANONE–WEST GERMAN
NO TURRET
BORE EVACUATOR AND MUZZLE BRAKE AT MUZZLE
LOW FLAT-TOPPED SILHOUETTE WITH STEP BETWEEN FIGHTING COMPARTMENT AND REAR DECK
5 ROAD WHEELS WITH SUPPORT ROLLERS.

GTA 17-2-8
FIG. 14

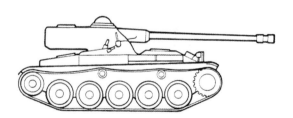

AMX13–FRENCH
SMALL TURRET SET WELL TO REAR WITH LARGE FLAT OVERHANG
BLAST DEFLECTOR AT MUZZLE
LOW SQUARE HULL
5 ROAD WHEELS WITH SUPPORT ROLLERS.

GTA 17-2-8
FIG. 39

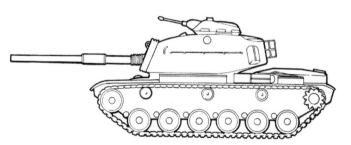

M60–UNITED STATES
HIGH REAR DECK
TORTOISE SHELL SHAPED TURRET
6 ROAD WHEELS WITH 3 SUPPORT ROLLERS
PROMINENT CUPOLA

and APFSDS rounds. The T-72, in common with the T-64 and all subsequent Soviet tanks, had an automatic loading system, which decreased the size of the tank, eliminating the need for a dedicated loader, reducing the crew to three.

Threat to the tank

In the early 1970s, the tank's dominance of the battlefield was put into question by the apparent lethality of missiles which was demonstrated in the early stages of the 1973 Arab-Israeli war, when many Israeli tanks were destroyed or disabled by the Egyptians' shoulder-launched missiles. However, counter-measures in the form of tank armour and air-launched infrared decoys sent the missile designers back to the drawing board to work on multiple or top attack warheads for anti-tank missiles. From 1985, the T-72 was fitted with explosive reactive armour (ERA) as standard. ERA consists of sandwiches of two steel plates with an explosive interlayer which detonates when the sandwich is penetrated by a shaped charge jet, disrupting its progress by as much as 70 per cent. The T-72 has been used by more than 40 countries worldwide and was followed by a third-generation MBT, the T-80, a development of the T-64, and the first production tank equipped with a gas turbine engine.

Maintaining pace with developing Western tank technology, the T-80 incorporated composite armour, advanced computerized fire control and a 125mm (4.93in) smoothbore main armament firing high-velocity APFSDS ammunition. It was introduced in 1976, when the T-64 and T-72 were already in production, leading to the situation in which the Soviet

Union had three tanks which were armed with the same 125mm (4.93in) gun and possessed similar combat capabilities, but were powered by different engines and had different hulls, running gear and fire control systems. In addition, the T-80 cost twice as much as the T-72, which prompted a refocusing on the T-72, although scaled-back production of the T-80 was maintained to provide work for the factory in Omsk that built it. A new diesel-powered version, the T-80UD, was introduced in 1985, but after the collapse of the Soviet Union the T-80 was no longer available to the Russian Army, because it was built in Ukraine.

The T-90, which entered modest production in 1993, is a significantly upgraded T-72. Its main armament is a 125mm (4.93in) smoothbore gun capable of firing APFSDS, HEAT and HE-FRAG (High-explosive fragmentation) ammunition as well as anti-tank guided missiles, which can penetrate 950mm (37in) of steel armour. Its 12.7mm (0.5in) remotely controlled anti-aircraft gun can be operated from within the tank by its commander. The T-90 has a layered protection system: composite armour and third-generation Kontakt-5 ERA in the turret. It has a counter measures suite which includes active infrared jammers, laser warning receivers, smoke grenade discharging systems and a computerized control system. The T-90 is also protected by nuclear, biological and chemical (NBC) protection equipment, mine sweeps and automatic fire suppression systems.

ABOVE T-62s in Prague during the Soviet invasion of 1968. The lead tank is being pelted with bricks by Czech civilians. The T-62 was the Soviet replacement for the T-55. It mounted a new 115mm (4.5in) smoothbore gun that was intended to defeat the latest Western tanks.

OPPOSITE The BMP-1 was the first Infantry Fighting Vehicle (IFV) designed for combat on a nuclear battlefield. It carried both a 73mm (2.9in) gun and an AT-3 Sagger anti-tank missile, allowing it to fight without exposing the infantry onboard to dangerous conditions. Despite its design impact it was insufficiently armoured, vulnerable to catching fire and cramped inside.

CHAPTER 33

FRENCH AND GERMAN TANKS OF THE COLD WAR

THE UNITED STATES AND BRITAIN WERE NOT THE ONLY NATO COUNTRIES WITH THEIR OWN TANK DEVELOPMENT PROGRAMMES. IN FRANCE, TANK DEVELOPMENT RESUMED AFTER THE SECOND WORLD WAR WITH THE AIM OF PRODUCING A TANK MORE POWERFUL THAN THE M4 SHERMAN WITH WHICH THE THREE RE-CREATED FRENCH ARMOURED DIVISIONS WERE EQUIPPED AT THE END OF THE WAR. AFTER GERMANY'S DEFEAT IN 1945, THERE WERE NO MORE TANKS BUILT UNTIL DEVELOPMENT BEGAN IN 1956 ON A MODERN TANK TO REPLACE THE BUNDESWEHR'S (WEST GERMAN ARMY'S) FLEET OF M47 AND M48 PATTONS.

French Tanks

The first post-war French tank, the ARL 44 was a hasty improvisation, armed with an adapted 90mm (3.5in) anti-aircraft gun, and running gear which resembled that of the Char B-1 of the 1930s. Only 60 were made between 1947 and 1949 and work was soon underway on a more modern tank, the AMX 50, planned as the French Army's only battle tank.

The AMX 50 was intended to be mobile, heavily armed and easy to mass-produce. A novel feature of its design was the oscillating turret consisting of an upper part mounted on trunnions in the lower part. The gun was fixed in the upper part so that the entire upper turret moved as it was elevated or depressed. This facilitated an autoloader in the turret bustle, as there was no relative movement between it and the gun mounting. One drawback of the oscillating turret was that it was not well sealed against nuclear or chemical contaminants.

The AMX 50 never entered service. Instead, large numbers of M47s were supplied to France to replace their elderly Shermans. But the oscillating turret and bustle autoloader were incorporated into the AMX 13 light tank, some 2,800 of which were exported to more than a dozen countries in the 1950s and 1960s. They were used by the Israelis in the Suez campaign of 1956 and the Six-Day War of 1967. In 1964, the French Army re-armed the AMX 13 with a 90mm (3.5in) gun. They remained active with the French Army until 1987 and continued in service with other armies, notably Singapore and Indonesia.

AMX 30

Initially conceived as a joint Franco-German project in 1957, the AMX 30 was in the end developed only by France and entered service in 1966, displacing the M47. By 1977, the French Army had received 1,084 AMX 30s, and almost 900 had been built for other countries.

The AMX 30 had a conventional turret mounting a 105mm (4.1in) gun. This fired Obus G ammunition, a HEAT projectile which used ball bearings within the shell to prevent the spin imparted by the rifling of the gun from degrading performance. An upgraded fire control system, a laser rangefinder and

APFSDS ammunition were incorporated into the AMX 30B2, which was introduced in 1982.

The German Leopard

Germany's first post-war tank venture came as a collaborative project between West Germany, France and later Italy. However, after a series of competitive trials, each country decided to proceed with its own design. The project came at a time in the late 1950s when the emergence of HEAT warheads had thrown a question mark over the future of the tank. In response, Porsche, who won the German trials to build the new tank, focused on its firepower and cross-country performance. The adoption of the British 105mm (4.1in) L7 gun and an 830hp V-10 diesel engine met these requirements. However, the Leopard was significantly less well armoured than the M60 and the Soviet T-55 and T-62.

The first batch of tanks was delivered to the Bundeswehr from September 1965 and eventually it fielded 2,237 Leopard 1s; 2,537 were purchased by the Belgian, Dutch, Norwegian, Australian, Canadian, Danish, Greek, Turkish and Lebanese armies. The Bundeswehr disbanded its last Leopard 1 battalion in 2003.

Leopard 2

In 1963, the Bundeswehr entered into a joint programme with the U.S. Army to develop a new, more powerful tank. The Germans pulled out of this in 1969, but continued development on their own, leading to the construction of 16 prototypes in 1971 of what became the Leopard 2, armed with a Rheinmetall 120mm (4.7in) smoothbore gun.

After a delay, caused in part by second thoughts on the part of the Bundeswehr, 1,800 Leopard 2s were ordered in 1977. The first of these, with increased armour protection on the front of the hull and manufactured by Krauss-Maffei Wegmann, was delivered at the end of October 1979. Production for the Bundeswehr came to an end in 1992, by which time 2,125 had been built.

BELOW Early versions of the Leopard 1. This was the first tank developed by West Germany after the end of the Second World War. Unlike their wartime Tigers and Panthers, the West Germans emphasized mobility and firepower with the Leopard 1 at the expense of armour protection, which was thin even by the standards of the day.

LECLERC MAIN BATTLE TANK

SPECIFICATION // LECLERC

CREW: 3

WEIGHT: 56 tons

ARMOUR: Armour: modular composite armour

ARMAMENT: 1x GIAT CN 120-26/52 120mm gun, 1x 12.7mm coaxial machine gun, 1x 7.62mm machine gun

TOP SPEED: 72km/h (45 mph)

ENGINE: 8-cylinder diesel SACM (Wartsila) 1,100kW (1,500hp)

The tank's design was finalized in 1986 and deliveries to the French Army began in 1992 and continued to 2006, by which time 406 had been completed and 388 sold to the army of the United Arab Emirates. The Leclerc's main armament is a 120mm (4.7in) smoothbore cannon capable of firing the same rounds as German Leopard 2 and the US M1 Abrams. The tank's turret was designed around its auto-loading system and, by eliminating the human loader, reduced the crew to three. It has a rate of fire of 12 rounds a minute and can handle up to six different types of ammunition, although it cannot change ammunition types once a round has been loaded. The Leclerc is fitted with state-of-the-art fire-control and battle-management systems, including a digital fire-control system providing real-time integrated imaging, and the combination of the gunner's primary sight and the commander's panoramic sight gives the Leclerc a hunter-killer capability.

The Leclerc remains one of the lightest MBTs in the world, with an excellent power-to-weight ratio, and one of the fastest accelerations, going from 0 to 32km/h (20 mph) in under six seconds. It has been deployed in a number of peace-keeping operations and low-intensity conflicts in Kosovo and Lebanon. Leclercs of the United Arab Emirates deployed in combat in Yemen during 2015.

BELOW The latest French main battle tank is the Leclerc. It entered service in the 1990s and 2000s. The tank features an autoloader, meaning the crew has been reduced to three. It has seen service during peace-keeping in Kosovo and Lebanon. Leclercs operated by the United Arab Emirates have been involved in combat in Yemen.

RIGHT At over 55 tonnes, modern tanks are often too heavy for bridges in the areas they operate. One solution is demonstrated by this Leopard 2. The tank is specially sealed, and the commander climbs to the top of the tower. The tank then drives, completely submerged, along the river bed. Although not quick to set up, this vastly improves the vehicle's mobility.

There were two major developments of the Leopard 2. The first, the Leopard 2A4, the most numerous member of the Leopard family, incorporated an automated fire and explosion suppression system, an all-digital fire-control system, and a modified turret with flat titanium/tungsten armour. The Leopard 2A5, which entered service with the Bundeswehr in the summer of 1998, enhanced the 2A4's armour, most noticeably with wedge-shaped spaced armour on the turret front that dramatically changed the tank's appearance. It also introduced an all-electric turret and an improved gun braking system. All the 2A5s were then converted to the Leopard 2A6, which introduced the new 120mm (4.7in) L/55 smoothbore gun, with its longer barrel giving increased muzzle velocity and greater armour penetration. A further upgrade, the Leopard 2A6M, has additional protection under the chassis against mines. The collapse of the Soviet Union in 1991 led to an immediate lowering of international tension and a reduction in the size of Western armies, particularly their tank fleets. The Bundeswehr, which at the height of the Cold War had a tank force of 85 battalions fielding over 5,000 tanks, had reduced by 2015 to four battalions and some 250 Leopards.

Overall production figures are 3,480, and Leopard 2s are serving with the armies of Austria, Canada, Chile, Denmark, Finland, Greece, Indonesia, Norway, Poland, Portugal, Singapore, Spain, Sweden, Switzerland and Turkey. The Royal Netherlands Army withdrew the Leopard in 2011, but reactivated a small unit in 2015.

Leopards saw in action in Kosovo with NATO forces in 1999 and with the US-led coalition in Afghanistan in 2007–08. The first fatality suffered by a Leopard crew occurred on 25 July 2008, when a Danish Leopard 2A5 hit an improvised explosive device (IED) and the driver was killed.

LEOPARD 2A7

SPECIFICATION // LEOPARD 2A7

CREW: 4

WEIGHT: 62.5 tons

ARMOUR: third-generation composite, including hardened steel, tungsten and plastic fitted with ceramic component

ARMAMENT: 1x 120mm smoothbore, 1x 12.7mm machine gun, 1x 7.62 machine gun

TOP SPEED: (max road) 72 km/h (45 mph)

ENGINE: MTU MB 873 Ka501 1,500hp diesel

The Leopard 2A7 is the latest in the series of Leopard upgrades. The first batch of 2A7s was delivered to the Bundeswehr in 2014. The 2A7 features the latest generation of passive armour and belly armour, which provides protection against mines and IEDs and is fitted with adapters for mounting extra armour modules or protection systems against RPGs. The modular armour facilitates the easy replacement of damaged modules in battle conditions. The tank's main armament is the Rheinmetall 120mm (4.7in) L/55 smoothbore gun. The gun is loaded manually and is compatible with all standard NATO ammunition as well as newly developed programmable HE munitions which enable the tank to engage targets behind cover and within buildings. These multi-purpose rounds can be used against enemy troops, armoured vehicles and low-flying helicopters. The tank's driver has a front and rear thermal imaging system, and commander and gunner have additional cameras for long-range surveillance. The tank is fitted with advanced command and control equipment and a battlefield management system.

CHAPTER 34

TANKS IN THE MIDDLE EAST

THE ARMOURED ELEMENT OF THE IDF (ISRAELI DEFENCE FORCES) HAD MODEST BEGINNINGS. IN 1948, WHEN THE NEWLY FORMED STATE OF ISRAEL WAS THREATENED WITH DESTRUCTION BY ITS ARAB NEIGHBOURS DURING THE FIRST ARAB-ISRAELI WAR, IT COULD MUSTER ONLY A SOLITARY M4 SHERMAN, TWO CROMWELLS, 12 HOTCHKISS H35 LIGHT TANKS AND A FEW LOCALLY ARMOURED TRUCKS AND CARS. FROM THESE UNPROMISING BEGINNINGS EMERGED ONE OF THE FINEST ARMOURED FORCES IN THE POST-WAR WORLD.

LEFT A British soldier inspects a captured Egyptian SU-100 assault gun during the 1956 Suez Crisis. The Soviet-made SU-100 is an example of an assault gun or tank destroyer. It mounts a gun powerful enough to destroy a tank, but does not have the complicated, expensive turret. This makes them cheaper and easier to manufacture but less versatile. The Soviets and Germans made great use of assault guns during the later years of the Second World War.

The 1956 War

It was not until the war of 1956 that that the emphasis in the IDF began to swing toward armour. In 1955, France had begun exporting arms to Israel and the latter had acquired some 100 Shermans and AMX 13 light tanks armed with a 75mm (3in) gun. In the same year, the Egyptian army's miscellany of Shermans and British armour was augmented by 230 T-34/85s and 100 Czechoslovak SU 100 tank destroyers. Thus, when Israel attacked Egypt in Sinai on 29 October

1956 as part of a joint campaign with Britain and France aimed at reversing Egyptian President Nasser's nationalization of the strategic Suez Canal, the two opposing sides deployed armour of Second World War vintage. This was inferior to the Centurion tanks landed by the British at Port Said in early November as part of the joint British and French operations against the Suez Canal.

During the campaign in the Sinai, the Israelis husbanded their tanks, reconnoitring their way around the Egyptian armour, much of which was allocated to the infantry and dug in, which enabled their armoured task forces to take the enemy in the rear. The Egyptian tanks were destroyed where they stood or shot up by the Israeli armour when they attempted to move. By the time a ceasefire was declared on 6 November, the Israelis had captured 125 Egyptian tanks and 60 armoured troop carriers and occupied the Sinai (from which they withdrew in March 1957).

Israel's sweeping success in 1956 gave a huge boost to the IDF's armoured corps, and in 1960 it acquired 30 new and used Centurions from the British armed with the 84mm (3.3in) gun. In 1962, the IDF acquired more Centurions, this time armed with the 105mm (4.1in) L7 gun, which was also used to rearm the first batch. By 1967, the IDF had acquired 385 Centurions, the most significant element in its tank fleet.

Under the tough discipline of Major-General Israel Tal, commander of the armoured corps and an admirer of Guderian, the long-distance gunnery skills of the IDF's Centurion and M48 crews (the latter purchased in 1965) were rigorously refined. In March 1965 Tal, riding in an M50 Super Sherman carrying a high-velocity 75mm (3in) gun, took two minutes to destroy five Syrian tractors (which were diverting water into the River Jordan) at a range of 2,000 metres (2,200 yards).

The Six-Day War

Tal's finest hour came on 5 June 1967, the second day of the Six-Day War (a pre-emptive series of strikes by Israel against its Arab neighbours after a period of heightening tensions between them), when as commander of 84th Armoured Division, he made a series of breakthroughs along the Mediterranean coast road between Gaza and El Arish. This was the reward for his insistence on superb gunnery allied to supreme self-confidence in the men and machines under his command. Across the entire Sinai battle front, the tanks of Tal's, General Joffe's and General Sharon's respective divisions drove deep into the Egyptian rear areas in a classic demonstration of Blitzkrieg. At one point, near Nakhle, Sharon's tanks overran the Egyptian 125th Armoured Brigade, part of 6th Division, whose vehicles were neatly drawn up by the road, their crews having fled with no attempt to deny them to the enemy, as they had received no orders to do so. A few hours later, Sharon overhauled the rest of 6th Division, destroying another 60 tanks, 100 guns and 300 vehicles.

By 8 June, the Israelis were on the Suez Canal. Some 820 of the 935 tanks deployed by the Egyptians had been lost, hundreds of guns and over 10,000 vehicles – more than 80 per cent of the Egyptian army's inventory – had fallen into

BELOW The Israeli Defence Force bought several hundred M48s from the United States during the 1960s and 1970s. They also captured around 100 from Jordan in the 1967 Six Day War. After the war the Israelis upgraded their M48s in several different ways. The most obvious was the installation of the 105mm (4.1in) gun. They named these tanks Magach (ramming hit).

Israeli hands at a cost to the IDF of 1,300 casualties, of whom 300 were dead. On Israel's eastern flank, there was a bitter armoured clash with Jordanian tanks in Samaria before an IDF breakthrough at Nablus precipitated a Jordanian collapse. To the north, on the Golan Heights in Syria, disciplined IDF infantry and armour punched gaps in the enemy's defended positions, recalling the battle plan at Cambrai in 1917, before the Syrian infantry took to their heels and the armoured crews abandoned their vehicles.

Of the 373 T-54s and T-55s lost by the Egyptian army in the Six-Day War, many were taken into Israeli service, equipping an entire IDF armoured brigade. The Israelis also captured some 100 Jordanian M48s, which were assimilated into the Israelis' tank formations.

The Yom Kippur War

On 6 October 1973, Israel faced a new war with her Arab neighbours as Egyptian and Syrian forces launched a surprise attack on the Jewish holiday of Yom Kippur, the Day of Atonement. Their simultaneous attack prevented the Israelis from concentrating on one before dealing with the other, while the great attention paid by the Syrians and Egyptians to marrying tactics to terrain initially caused the IDF great difficulties.

In the north the Syrians, with 1,000 tanks, some of them T-62s with infrared night vision equipment and smoothbore 115mm (4.5in) guns, possessed an initial advantage of 5:1 (and 12:1 in certain sectors). They made inroads into the Golan Heights but failed to seize the bridges across the River Jordan, the absolute keys to Israeli security. The Syrians were kept at bay by 170 Centurion tanks of two IDF tank brigades, some of which were emplaced, while others were used to plug gaps as they threatened to open. The Israeli high command favoured the employment of the Centurion, with its rugged suspension and all-steel tracks, on the rocky Golan Heights. Superior Israeli gunnery and strict economy of effort held the line while reinforcements were rushed up piecemeal.

By combining Anti-Tank Guided Weapons (ATGW) tank-hunting teams with armour, the Syrians eliminated the first line of Israeli defences inside 24 hours and advanced to within 10 minutes' tank-travelling time of the River Jordan and the Sea of Galilee. Then, like the Red Army T-34s of 1942, they lost their cohesion and began to mill about. In four days of fierce fighting, IDF Centurions and Super-Shermans accounted for about 400 Syrian AFVs before rolling the enemy back with sustained air and armoured counter-attacks.

On 12 October, 300 Jordanian and Iraqi tanks launched a flank attack on the IDF as it thrust beyond the Golan and toward Damascus. The result was two hectic days of close-range (200-300m/220-330 yards), tank-versus-tank combat which left 60 burning hulks on the battlefield, most of them Iraqi. On the northern front of the Yom Kippur War, the Arabs lost overall nearly 1,200 tanks against the Israelis' 250, of which over half were capable of being repaired.

The Egyptian front

To the south, the Egyptians achieved a signal tactical and strategic success. They had convinced Israeli military intelligence that the massive preparations for the crossing of the Suez Canal were no more than training operations and military manoeuvres, a feat of deception in the league of Operation Fortitude which preceded the Normandy invasion in June 1944. The crossing itself, which involved the simultaneous transfer of five divisions within 24 hours – over ten bridges for tanks and vehicles and another ten for infantry – while engaged in battle with the surprised enemy was another organizational and technical feat of the first rank.

The Egyptians had also anticipated the Israeli response – massive, rapidly deployed air and armoured counter-attacks – and had armed the infantry with quantities of Sagger anti-tank rockets and Strela SA-7 light anti-aircraft missiles. The counterblow, when it came on 8 October, was made by tanks of the Israeli 162nd Division unsupported by artillery and infantry and as a consequence suffered heavy losses – 165 of its 268 tanks – while failing to prevent the Egyptians from expanding their lodgements into a continuous bridgehead.

The situation was retrieved by the IDF's superior battlefield reflexes on both the northern and southern fronts. The Syrian and Egyptian attacks were ground down on armoured "anvils" which combined with mechanized infantry and artillery to slow down and then defeat the enemy. In the north this reached a peak on 9 October with the encirclement of the Syrian 1st Armoured Division on the Golan Heights. On

OPPOSITE The Israelis renamed their Centurions Sho't (whip). They were upgraded to carry Israeli 105mm (4.1in) cannons and American engines and machine guns. This turret mounts an M2 .50 calibre machine gun.

CENTURION MARK 3

SPECIFICATION // CENTURION MK 3

CREW: 4

WEIGHT: 49 tons

ARMOUR: 152mm (6in)

ARMAMENT: 1x 84mm, 1x .50 Browning ranging gun, 1x .30 Browning machine gun

TOP SPEED: 34 km/h (21 mph)

ENGINE: Rolls Royce Mk1VB 12 petrol 650hp Meteor

Manufacture of the Centurion commenced in January 1945, and it first saw combat with the British Army during the Korean War, where it demonstrated its hill-climbing ability. The Centurion was the first attempt to produce a "universal" tank and so do away with the old distinction between "cruiser" and "infantry" tanks. It had a sloped glacis plate and improved turret shape. The Mk I was fitted with the obsolete 76.2mm (3in) gun, but the Mk 3 was armed with the more effective 84mm (3.3in) which was electronically stabilized in elevation and azimuth, improving gunnery control and shooting. When fitted with the L7 105mm (4.1in) gun, along with improved ammunition, the Mk 9 Centurion was able to penetrate the thickest Soviet armour. Between 1946 and 1962, 4,423 Centurions were produced, including 25 different marks and numerous variants, equipping armies worldwide. In 2006, the IDF still used heavily modified Centurions as armoured personnel carriers (APC) and combat engineering vehicles.

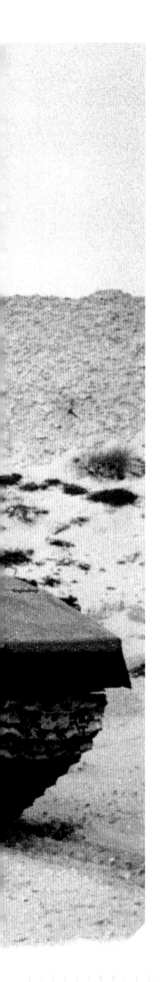

MERKAVA IV

SPECIFICATION

CREW: 4

WEIGHT: 65 tons

ARMOUR: classified composite

ARMAMENT: 120mm (4.7in) smoothbore capable of firing LAHAT ATGM, 1 x 12.7mm (.50in), 2 x 7.62mm (.30in) machine-guns

TOP SPEED: 64 km/h (40 mph)

ENGINE: 1,500hp turbocharged diesel

OPPOSITE A Merkava Mark III. Introduced from 1989, this version was the first to be armed with a 120mm (4.7in) smoothbore gun in a re-engineered turret. It also featured a more powerful engine, improved armour and upgraded fire- control system over earlier versions.

14 October, the Egyptians launched six armoured columns – some 1,000 tanks supported by artillery – from their bridgehead in an attempt to carve out a penetration to a depth of 50 kilometres (30 miles), reaching the Gidi and Mitla passes. In the largest tank battle since the Second World War, the Egyptian armour was met and defeated by 750 Israeli M48s and M60s, which destroyed around 250 Egyptian tanks. The IDF was subsequently rapidly reinforced by U.S.-supplied armour which brought the size of its tank fleet back up to 2,000. Overall, IDF tank losses on both fronts have been estimated at around 850, of which probably about 400 were recovered from the battlefield and repaired.

On 16 October, it was the Israelis' turn to cross the Suez Canal. When the Egyptians counter-attacked on 17 October, their tanks were sent on a death ride. The armoured battle on the west bank had been won, the ATGW threat on the east bank had been neutralized, Cairo was under threat and, on 24 October, a ceasefire was arranged. Subsequently there was much debate about the effectiveness of ATGW weapons in the early stages of the war, but post-war analysis demonstrated that the great majority of tank losses could be credited to tank guns and that the majority of kills by missiles had occurred during the initial stages, before the Israelis fully appreciated the threat they posed. More than 3,000 Arab tanks had been lost to an enemy who depended almost entirely on the gun and who, after the opening exchanges, displayed a grasp of decisive manoeuvre worthy of Guderian.

The Merkava

After the Six-Day War, high priority was given by the Israeli Defence Forces (IDF) to the development of an indigenous tank, and the project was overseen by General Israel Tal, drawing also on lessons from the Yom Kippur War. The first prototypes of the Merkava (Chariot) were built in 1974, and the first tanks were delivered to the Israeli army in April 1979.

The constant threats to its northern and southern borders that Israel had experienced from its Arab neighbours since 1948 made the country a leading exponent of armoured warfare. Tal decided that survivability should be at the heart of the Merkava's design, offering maximum protection to its crew and ammunition. This entailed a departure from the customary layout of a main battle tank, placing the engine and transmission at the front of the Merkava, shielding the crew from frontal attack. Ammunition for the 105mm (4.1in) gun was stored at the rear of the hull, where it was less vulnerable, and a clamshell rear access door was included, allowing for better protected resupply and crew evacuation.

The Merkava made its combat debut during the 1982 Lebanon War, during which it also performed as a makeshift armoured personnel carrier (APC) housing 10 soldiers or walking wounded, although at the expense of ammunition capacity. The Merkava Mark II entered service in April 1983, with adaptations made for urban warfare as a result of IDF experience in Lebanon. This included relocating the roof-mounted 60mm (2.4in) mortar to inside the hull, protecting the operator from small arms fire, anti-rocket netting against infantry armed with RPGs; and an improved fire control system.

The Merkava Mark III arrived in December 1989 and incorporated further improvements, including the Israeli-manufactured IMI 120mm (4.7in) gun; the addition of laser designators; and the incorporation of the Kasag modular armour system, which facilitated rapid replacement and repair in combat. In 1995, the Mark III BAZ (Shining Light) fire control system was introduced, which increased the tank's ability to engage moving targets while on the move itself.

The Merkava Mark IV entered service at the end of 2004. It had a more powerful 1,500hp turbocharged diesel engine, reshaped turret. a combination of passive and active armour and a thickened steel belly plate to protect it against heavy mines. During the 2006 war against Hezbollah (Party of God), the Shia Muslim organization operating on Israel's northern border with Lebanon, the IDF faced a new generation of anti-tank missiles, notably the Russian-manufactured, laser-riding Kornet, claimed to be capable of penetrating up to 1,200mm (47.2in) of steel armour with ERA protection. Some 50 Merkava II, III and IVs were hit during the campaign (14 being disabled by rockets), a toll which accelerated the introduction, in 2010, of the Trophy Active Protection System. This uses radar to detect incoming missiles and a shotgun-style projectile to intercept them. Since 1979, 2,270 Merkavas have been produced – 250 Mark Is, 580 Mark IIs, 780 Mark IIIs and 660 Mark IVs.

CHAPTER 35

THE GULF WARS

THE STRENGTHS AND WEAKNESSES OF NATO AND SOVIET TECHNOLOGY WERE PUT TO THE TEST IN THE FIRST GULF WAR, SPARKED WHEN IRAQI DICTATOR SADDAM HUSSEIN INVADED KUWAIT AFTER A DISPUTE INVOLVING RIGHTS TO OIL-FIELDS ALONG ITS BORDER WITH IRAQ.

The Iraqi army which invaded and occupied Kuwait on 2 August 1990, was principally Soviet- and Chinese-equipped and trained, although it departed from Soviet practice in its grim determination to fight from static positions, a legacy of the Iran–Iraq War (1980–88). Iraq faced a coalition composed of American, Arab, British and French forces, which were in the main equipped and indoctrinated in highly mobile tactics by NATO.

The coalition began military action against Iraq on 17 January 1991, and within four days it achieved its first objective of gaining air supremacy. The systematic air and artillery pummelling of Iraq's ground forces which followed degraded its dug-in T-55s, T-62s and T-72s and dismantled key elements of its command and control system. Simultaneously, coalition ground forces were secretly redeployed from east to west. By

ABOVE In the pre-digital and mobile phone world of the First Gulf War tank soldiers were given these cards to send home to stay in touch.

LEFT A captured Iraqi T-72M. The T-72 was the most advanced Soviet tank in the Iraqi Army. It was used by the elite Republican Guard and its successful combat record in the Iran–Iraq War led it to be perceived as a very real threat by the Coalition forces. In fact, the American M1A1 Abrams proved to be far more capable.

OPPOSITE An American M1A1 Abrams during the 1991 Gulf War. The M1A1 was a major step forwards for the US Army when it was introduced in the 1980s. It boasted improved firepower and armour over the M60, as well as a highly capable fire control system and unprecedented speed for a main battle tank.

M1A1 ABRAMS

SPECIFICATION // M1/M1A1/M1A2

CREW: 4

WEIGHT: M1 54 tons, M1A1 57 tons, M1A2 62 tons

ARMOUR: M1, M1A1 Burlington composite armour, M1A2 depleted uranium mesh-reinforced composite armour

ARMAMENT: Armament M1 105mm L/52 M68 rifled gun, M1A1. M1A2 120mm L/44 M256A1 smoothbore gun; secondary armament 1x 12.7 mm M2HB heavy machine gun, 2x 7.62mm M240 machine guns

TOP SPEED: 72 km/h (45 mph)

ENGINE: Honeywell AGT1500C multi-fuel turbine engine 1500hp

In 1972, the U.S. Congress gave the go-ahead for the production of a new main battle tank which would replace the M60. A Chrysler design was approved and in 1980 the production of the M1 Abrams began. The first 2,374 tanks were armed with a 105mm (4.1in) L7 gun, but after 1985 the M1A1 version was armed with an M256 120mm (4.7in) smoothbore Rheinmetall gun, firing fin-stabilized rather than spin-stabilized projectiles, which had been developed for the Leopard 2. The M1A2 represented a further improvement, with a commander's independent thermal viewer, weapon station, position navigation equipment, and a full set of controls and displays linked by a digital data bus.

The M1 adopted British Chobham armour and further protection was later provided by a special armour incorporating depleted uranium. The Abrams's fire control systems compute solutions for the gunner or commander to achieve more than a 95 per cent certainty of a hit. They are fed by sensors which determine wind speed and direction, air temperature and pressure, barrel wear and temperature, and even when rain is falling on one side of the barrel, all factors which critically effect performance.

Some 1,850 M1A1s were shipped to the Gulf before the start of the First Gulf War, where the tank's thermal imaging sights enabled crews to detect targets. In Desert Storm, friendly fire proved a greater danger than that posed by Iraqi armour, and subsequently combat vehicles, were fitted with Combat Identification Panels on the sides and rear of the turret to reduce friendly fire incidents. Fewer M1A1s were used during the 2003 invasion of Iraq. In that operation they once more outgunned the opposing Iraqi T-55s, T-62s and T-72s, but proved vulnerable to mines and close-quarter attacks by RPG-7 rocket-propelled anti-tank grenades, descendants of the Panzerfaust.

DEFENSIVE OPERATIONS

Listed below are some of the key elements in Iraqi defensive operations:

* **SECURITY ZONE FORWARD OF FLOT**

* **RECCE UNITS REINFORCED BY INFANTRY ARTILLERY**

* **STRONG FORWARD DEFENSIVE POSITIONS**

* **DEFENCE IN DEPTH AND OBSTACLES IN DEPTH**

* **MAXIMUM USE OF NATURAL AND <u>MANMADE</u> OBSTACLES**

* **MAXIMUM USE OF TANK DITCHES AND <u>BERMS</u>**

* **MINEFIELDS COVER FORWARD POSITIONS**

  ** **UP TO 350M DEEP**

  ** **MIX NORMALLY 3 AP AND 1 ATK PER CLUSTER**

  ** **MIXED WITH BARBED WIRE**

* **TANK HEAVY RESERVE USED FOR COUNTER ATTACK**

* **ATGM DEPLOYED FORWARD**

* **TANKS DEPLOYED FORWARD WHEN NEEDED IN ANTI-TANK ROLE**

* **ANTI-TANK TACTICS**

  ** **EMPLOY ANTI-TANK WEAPONS IN DEPTH**

  ** **CHANNEL ENEMY TANKS INTO 'KILLING ZONES'**

* **COMMANDOS USED IN REAR AREAS TO AMBUSH TANKS**

"Oh shit! - I've really blown it this time!"

PRODUCED BY

**HEADQUARTERS
7 INTELLIGENCE COMPANY**

**INTELLIGENCE AND
SECURITY GROUP (GERMANY)**

SEPTEMBER 1990

ARMY EQUIPMENT
MBTs

T-72

Crew: 3

Weapons	-	Calibre	Range
Main	-	125mm	2000m
Secondary	-	7.62mm	1000m
AAMG	-	12.7mm	

RECOGNITION FEATURES

1. 6 large road wheels with 3 return rollers.
2. Flexible, full-length skirting over return rollers (May be removed).
3. "V" shaped splash plate.
4. IR searchlight usually to right of barrel.
5. Fume extractor one third of way down barrel, with jointed thermal sleeve.
6. Schnorkel tube carried at rear of turret.
7. Slim AAMG on commander's cupola. Stowed pointing rearwards.

Associated Equipment: KMT mine plough series T-55 series ARVs, T-72 series ARVs, MTP and MT-55.

T 62

Crew : 4

Armament	Calibre
Main	115mm
Secondary	7.62mm MG
AAMG	12.7mm

RECOGNITION FEATURES

1. 5 large road wheels gaps between 3rd and 4th, 4th and 5th.
2. Slack track, no return rollers.
3. Straight splash plate.
4. Curved hand rails on turret.
5. Fume extractor 1/3rd way down barrel.
6. AAMG on commander's cupola.

CHIEFTAIN

Crew : 4

Weapons	Calibre
Main	120mm
Secondary	7.62mm MG
AAMG	7.62mm MG

RECOGNITION FEATURES

1. 6 evenly spaced road wheels.
2. 3 return rollers.
3. Straight splash plate.
4. Straight side skirts.
5. Searchlight on left hand side of turret.
6. Smoke grenade dischargers on either side of turret.
7. AAMG on commanders cupola.

OPPOSITE ABOVE A British Challenger 1 crew have constructed a home away from home using camouflage nets, tarpaulins and their vehicles. Operations in the desert make resupply harder, meaning crews had to carry much more with them and there was little space in a tank.

OPPOSITE BELOW A Scimitar reconnaissance vehicle accompanied by a sniper team during the invasion of Iraq in 2003. Scimitars serve alongside Challengers in British Army Armoured Regiments. This photograph demonstrates how armoured vehicles still cooperate with infantry. The snipers gain protection from the Scimitar, while offering the vehicle better awareness of its environment, and a much less damaging weapon system.

RIGHT British tank soldiers were given much intelligence prior to deployment. This publication contained vital information to help tank crews identify Iraqi armoured vehicles and aircraft. It also covered rank insignia worn on enemy uniforms and tactics employed by their tank and infantry units.

23 February, the coalition had placed two corps on the Iraqi extreme right flank. The Iraqis had positioned 26 divisions forward in a prepared defensive belt, behind which were nine more experienced mechanized divisions and eight supposedly elite Republican Guard divisions deployed well to the rear.

The coalition ground offensive, Operation Desert Storm, was launched on 24 February and swiftly breached the minefields, ditches and berms screening the Iraqi frontier. The lead elements, two U.S. Marine divisions, plunged into the defensive belt near the coastal highway while the main coalition effort, by VII and XVIII Corps, made a single envelopment of the Iraqi forward defences, which promptly collapsed, opening the way to the Republican Guard units.

Battle of 73 Easting

The armoured fighting in the war during which the M1A1 Abrams main battle tank made its combat debut, was often very one-sided. For the best part of two days, VII Corps fought its way through the blocking Republican Guard. On the afternoon of 26 February, the U.S. 2nd Armored Cavalry Regiment (2nd ACR), a reconnaissance and security element attached to VII Corps, emerged from a sandstorm to engage the Iraqi Tawakalna Division in a stretch of featureless desert near a map reference known as "73 Easting". The regiment's lead scouting troop, consisting of 9 M1A1 Abrams tanks and 12 M3 Bradley armoured personnel carriers (APC) commanded by Captain H.R. McMaster, destroyed the entire defensive belt in front of them. In a little over half an hour they hit 37 Iraqi T-72s and 32 other armoured vehicles. The scouting troops on either side of McMaster enjoyed similar success; between them the three troops destroyed an entire Republican Guard brigade. An Iraqi counter-attack was snuffed out, leaving 113 Iraqi armoured vehicles destroyed at a cost of one Bradley.

2nd ACR had kept a tight, efficient combat formation in the middle of a fierce sandstorm with no significant mechanical failure. In the engagement, its crews' gunnery was exceptional. The first three kills by Eagle troop were recorded in three single shots by a single M1A1 over an interval of less than 10 seconds. Eighty-five per cent of 2nd ACR's shots struck their targets at ranges of up to 2,000 metres (2,200 yards), well below the Abrams' effective range of 2,500 metres (2,750 yards). The Iraqi armour, having suffered constant air and artillery bombardment, denied intelligence and with their signals communications ruined or jammed, had no answer.

RIGHT As tank armour increased in effectiveness, ammunition improved to match. This is a British L27 Armour Piercing Fin Stabilised Discarding Sabot round, as fired by Challenger 2. It features a longer penetrator to defeat thicker armour. Fin Stabilised refers to fins being used to keep the round accurate, such as on a dart, rather than spinning, like a bullet. This allows the round to travel faster, again defeating thicker armour.

CHALLENGER

SPECIFICATION // CHALLENGER 2

CREW: 4

WEIGHT: 61.5 tons

ARMOUR: Chobham/Dorchester Level 2

ARMAMENT: 1x 120mm L30A1 20mm rifled, 1x coaxial 7.62mm chain gun, 1x 7.62mm cupola machine gun

TOP SPEED: (road) 59 km/h (37 mph)

ENGINE: Perkins CV-12 diesel 1,200hp

The most significant aspect of the Challenger was its Chobham armour. Its precise composition remains secret, but it is composed of ceramic tiles encased within a metal matrix and bonded to a backing plate and several elastic layers. This provides improved resistance against HEAT rounds and shatters APFSDS ammunition.

The Challenger 1's Rolls Royce 1,200hp engine conferred excellent mobility. Less satisfactory features were the tank's 120mm (4.7in) L11 rifled gun, not as powerful as the M1A1's 120mm (4.7in) smoothbore, and its fire control system, unchanged from the Chieftain design.

In the First Gulf War, 221 Challenger 1s of 1st (UK) Armoured Division were deployed to Saudi-Arabia. They were modified for desert operations with additional Chobham armour, ERA on the nose and front glacis plate, external fuel drums and smoke generators. The British force was placed under the command of US VII Corps. In the space of almost 100 hours, 1st (UK) Armoured Division destroyed the Iraqi 46th Mechanized Brigade, 52nd Armoured Brigade and elements of at least three infantry divisions of Iraqi 7th Corps, capturing or destroying approximately 200 tanks and a significant number of other vehicles. The Challengers' Global Positioning System (GPS) and Thermal Observation and Gunnery Sight (TOGS) proved effective, enabling attacks to be made at night and in poor visibility. Not a single Challenger was lost in action and one made the longest range tank kill in history, destroying an Iraqi tank with an APFSDS round at a distance of over 5,100 metres (3 miles).

By the late 1980s Chieftain needed to be replaced. The Ministry of Defence commissioned an improved Challenger 2 from Vickers Defence Systems. It featured a new turret, fire control system and 120mm (4.7in) L30A1 rifled gun which could also be retrofitted to Challenger 1. However, the collapse of the Soviet Union in 1991 and subsequent downsizing of the British Army resulted in an order for only 127 Challenger 2s.

The Challenger 2 is one of the best protected tanks in the world. Second generation Chobham armour, known as Dorchester, protects the turret and hull. The turret and gun are moved by a solid-state electric drive instead of more dangerous hydraulics.

The Challenger 2's first taste of combat came in March 2003 during the invasion of Iraq. Tanks of 7th Armoured Brigade provided fire support for the British infantry and engaged Iraqi armour around Basra. No Challengers were lost to enemy fire, although one was destroyed in a friendly-fire incident. Two crew members died when the attacking Challenger's HESH rounds hit the open commander's hatch, sending hot fragments into the turret. This set off an explosion in the tank.

OPPOSITE ABOVE This beret was worn by Brigadier Patrick Cordingley during the Gulf War. He commanded 7th Armoured Brigade, one of two Brigades contributed by the British Army. His cap badge is the design worn by Colonels and Brigadiers across the Army.

BELOW This preserved Challenger 1 was commanded by Lieutenant Colonel Arthur Denaro during the 1991 Gulf War. He led the 57 Challengers of the Queen's Royal Irish Hussars, one of three British armoured regiments to take part in the war. His tank is named "Churchill", and his radio callsign 11B (pronounced one one bravo) has been painted on the side of the tank.

CHAPTER 36

TANKS AND THE FUTURE

IN ONE SENSE, THE TANK STORY COULD BE TOLD AS A CONSTANT STRUGGLE, NOT TO INCREASE FIREPOWER, PROTECTION OR MOBILITY, BUT SIMPLY TO SURVIVE. TIME AND TIME AGAIN, THE TANK HAS BEEN DECLARED REDUNDANT ONLY TO RE-EMERGE IN YET MORE ADVANCED AND LETHAL FORMS.

At the end of the First World War it was hoped that there would never be another like it, and therefore that there would be no more need for tanks. Many were scrapped or handed out to towns as memorials. During the Second World War bigger and more expensive tanks were developed – and yet by 1945 cheap weapons such as the Panzerfaust meant a single soldier could destroy them. Was the age of the tank over?

It was soon clear that tank forces would play a major role if the Cold War turned hot. Many nations developed their own, or bought vehicles from the superpowers. Anti-tank missiles, used to devastating effect by ground forces in the Yom Kippur War of 1973, raised the question again, as did the fitting of missiles to attack helicopters shortly afterwards. However, new defensive measures were quickly developed. Combined arms tactics using tanks, infantry, artillery and mobile air defences working together were re-emphasized. Add-on Explosive Reactive Armour provided extra protection against missile warheads.

The end of the Cold War seemed likely to slow or end tank development, especially in the West. Many thousands of tanks were scrapped or sold off cheaply. For western militaries, most operations since 1990 have required forces to deploy over long distances, and then operate amongst and win the support of civilians. It was assumed that tanks, with their tremendous weight, would be difficult to deploy and probably cause damage to buildings and infrastructure, alienating the local population. At first this led to designs for smaller and lighter "medium weight" vehicles that were easier to transport.

After 2003 the counter-insurgency campaigns in Afghanistan and Iraq saw a high threat from improvised explosive devices (IEDs). This moved the emphasis onto heavier troop-carrying vehicles with high levels of underbelly and all-round protection.

It soon became clear that the tank still had a role to play – although not necessarily the one for which it was designed. Tanks brought a level of protection few other vehicles possessed and they could provide long-range surveillance and fire support with their all-weather sights and highly accurate gun. A tank's mere presence as could also in itself act as a deterrent to the enemy. More recently, the conflicts in Lebanon, Georgia, Ukraine, Syria and Yemen have reinforced the continued usefulness and potency of the tank in its traditional combat role.

Throughout this period some countries have continued to design and manufacture their own tanks, such as the South Korean K2,

Chinese Type 99 and Israeli Merkava Mark IV. Many nations have taken advantage of Germany and Holland downsizing their Leopard 2 fleets to cheaply replace their older vehicles. Others have designed their own tanks for the first time. Turkey's Altay is intended to replace their German and American tanks from 2018. Other nations have instead chosen to upgrade older tanks at a fraction of the cost of building a new one. Since the end of the Cold War thousands of American M1 Abrams have been rebuilt to keep them viable on the battlefield.

This fits the increasingly common view of the tank as a "platform"; something that is expected to go through many changes in its service life; including rebuilds and upgrades to encompass newer technology and additional equipment to enable the tank to deal with a new or predicted threat. New technology has brought alternatives to heavier and heavier armour – Active Protection Systems can detect incoming munitions, then either shoot them down with a projectile, as on the Israeli Trophy, or trigger jammers or smoke, as with the Russian Shtora.

Armour itself continues to develop; laminates, ceramics and plastics are now widely used and can give greater protection

TOP An improvised armoured vehicle made by Kurdish forces battling insurgents in Syria. The creation of "home made" armoured vehicles on the chassis of bulldozers and excavators clearly shows the continuing desire for heavy armoured vehicles in fighting forces.

ABOVE The advantages of medium weight armoured vehicles, such as this CV 90, built in Sweden, in terms of costs and mobility are clear to both Governments and the military. However, as with so many other military vehicles the urge to improve protection levels and add further improvements such as defensive aid suites has meant the weight of the vehicle has on some models markedly increased from 23 to 35 tonnes.

than traditional steel. Lightweight "bar" armour has been developed to defeat lighter weapons. Networked battlefield management systems allow the immediate sharing of information about the locations of friendly and enemy forces. Electronics are also becoming more widely used in place of mechanical or hydraulic systems on board vehicles.

Unmanned vehicles are already in operation and bring the very desirable feature of not having to risk a crew's life in combat. Exercises have shown that commanders have a different attitude to risk when none of their soldiers are in the deployed vehicles.

The use of new technologies brings with it the risk of new things that could potentially go wrong. This could be through Programming errors might introduce problems, the technology could be hacked or jammed, or the more vulnerable command centres and satellites vital for control could be targeted.

Whether the tank can really be replaced on the battlefield is still unclear. While they continue to face a range of threats – from other tanks, aircraft, missiles and IEDs – the actual use of tanks in contemporary conflicts seems to indicate they do still have a role to play. Where forces, such as the Kurds in Syria, do not have tanks they appear keen to acquire or improvise them.

The lesson of the tank's first century seems to be that new ways will always be developed to defeat them, only for tank users to adapt the vehicle and their tactics to neutralise this new threat – the constant action and counter-action of technology in war. However too tight a focus on technology can mean overlooking the human element of warfare. The sheer size and presence of a tank still gives a significant morale boost to friendly troops and has a psychological impact on the opposition – just as it did in the First World War.

As a British peacekeeper in Bosnia put it: "you turn up in a Land Rover and they throw stones at you, you turn up in a Challenger and people back off quick with 'well, maybe not today …'." Now over a century old, the tank, for good or ill, will remain a potent weapon for decades to come.

T-14 ARMATA

SPECIFICATION // T-14 ARMATA

CREW: 3

WEIGHT: 48 tons

ARMOUR: Unknown

ARMAMENT: 1 x 125mm Smoothbore, 1x 12.7mm Kord machine-gun, 1 x 7.62mm PKTM machine-gun

TOP SPEED: 80–90 km/h (50–56 m.p.h.)

ENGINE: 1,500hp ChTZ 12H360 (A-85-3A) diesel engine.

The new T-14 tank is part of a family of heavy Russian armoured vehicles that will have the advantages of common parts and maintenance systems. Key to the design is an unmanned turret with a new autoloader that can handle a longer kinetic penetrator round than fired by previous Russian tanks. The longer the penetrator, the more armour it can defeat. The autoloader holds 32 ready rounds that can be fired with a 5 second reload cycle; 13 extra rounds are carried but the crew have to exit the vehicle to load these. The tank shows a new respect for crew survival, with the three crew members – Driver, Gunner and Commander – now in a single crew compartment at the front of the vehicle. Active Protection Systems to jam missile guidance systems and shoot down incoming munitions are fitted or will be fitted as the technology matures. Speculation as to the effectiveness of the many new systems continues, but the Russians hope to help fund this expensive tank with foreign exports.

LEFT A T-14 Armata was first shown to the public at the 2015 May Day parade on Red Square in Moscow. It features an unmanned turret fitted with a roof-mounted commander's independent sight and multiple Active Protection Systems. The commander is standing in his hatch behind the gun. The gunner and driver sit side by side to his left.

INDEX

CREDITS

THE TANK MUSEUM

The Tank Museum in Dorset brings the story of tanks and tank crews to life. With over 300 tanks from 26 nations, The Tank Museum holds the finest and most historically significant collection of fighting armour in the world. Powerful exhibitions tell the story of armoured warfare spanning a century of military history.

Bovington is the "home of the tank". In October 1916 it was appointed as the new home of the Heavy Branch Machine Gun Corps, the title of the first unit to use tanks. It was here that the pioneers of armoured warfare were trained and it remains home to The Royal Armoured Corps today.

Following the First World War, hundreds of redundant tanks were shipped back to Bovington to await the attention of the scrap man. It is believed that Rudyard Kipling suggested the foundation of The Tank Museum following a visit to Bovington. He petitioned the War Office in 1923 that one of each vehicle type was set aside. The fruits of this foresight form the basis of the collection today, but The Tank Museum wasn't officially opened to the public until the 1950s.

The Tank Museum's curatorial staff are leaders in their field. They are frequently called upon to advise and support other institutions with historical vehicle collections around the world. Their expertise is often sought by the media in factual entertainment programmes and recently in the production of the Hollywood production *Fury*, starring Brad Pitt.

The Archive and Reference Library is the world's foremost research centre on the subject of armoured warfare, with an extensive collection of documents, plans, manuals, war diaries, journals and books as well as a collection of over 250,000 images.

The Tank Museum is an independent Museum and registered Charity. See www.tankmuseum.org.

SELECTED READING

Campbell, Christie *Band of Brigands* (2008)
Cathart, Tom *Iron Soldiers: How America's 1st Armored Division Crushed Iran's Elite Republican Guard* (1994)
Cross, Robin *Citadel: The Battle of Kursk* (1993)
Doherty, Richard *Hobart's 79th Armoured Division at War* (2011)
Essame, H. *Patton the Commander* (1974)
Fletcher, David (ed.) *Tanks and Trenches* (1994)
Guderian, Heinz *Panzer Leader* (1952), *Achtung Panzer!* (1937)
Horne, Alistair *To Lose a Battle: France 1940* (1969)
Kershaw, Robert *Tank Men* (2009)
Liddell Hart, Basil *The Other Side of the Hill* (1948)
Macksey, Kenneth *Tank versus Tank* (1999)
Mellenthin, F.W. von *Panzer Battles* (1955)
Ogorkiewicz, Richard *Tanks 100 Years of Evolution* (2015)
Rotmistrov, Pavel *Tank against Tank* (in Main Front, 1987)
Zaloga, Steven and Forczyk, Robert *Battleground: The Greatest Tank Duels in History* (2011)

PICTURE CREDITS

The publishers would like to thank the following sources for their kind permission to reproduce the pictures in this book.

Original Photography: Matt Sampson
Archive Photographs: The Tank Museum Archive, except p60 (bottom left) Mary Evans/J. Bedmar/Iberfoto, p64 (top) Photo © Paris - Musée de l'Armée, Dist. RMN-Grand Palais, p186 Uri Kadobnov/AFP/Getty Images, p147 (bottom right) AKG-Images

PUBLISHING CREDITS

THIS IS AN ANDRE DEUTSCH BOOK
This edition first published in 2018 by André Deutsch
First published in 2016 by André Deutsch
A division of the Carlton Publishing Group
20 Mortimer Street
London W1T 3JW

10 9 8 7 6 5 4 3 2 1

Text, photographs and memorabilia © The Tank Museum 2016

Design © Carlton Books Ltd 2016, 2018

A catalogue record for this book is available from the British Library

Editor: Victoria Marshallsay
Design: Russell Knowles, James Pople
Picture Research: Steve Behan
Production: Emily Noto

ISBN: 978 0 233 00534 8

Printed in Dubai